Between Mecca and Beijing

MODERNIZATION AND CONSUMPTION AMONG URBAN CHINESE MUSLIMS

MARIS BOYD GILLETTE

STANFORD UNIVERSITY PRESS

STANFORD, CALIFORNIA

Stanford University Press
Stanford, California

∞ Printed in the United States of America on
acid-free, archival-quality paper.

Library of Congress Cataloging-in-Publication Data

Gillette, Maris Boyd.
Between Mecca and Beijing : modernization and consumption among urban Chinese Muslims / Maris Boyd Gillette.
p. cm.
Includes bibliographical references and index.
ISBN 0-8047-3694-4 (alk. paper) ISBN 0-8047-4685-0 (pbk., alk. paper)
1. Consumption (Economics)—China—Xi'an (Shaanxi Sheng) 2. Xi'an (Shaanxi Sheng, China)—Social conditions. 3. Muslims—China—Xi'an (Shaanxi Sheng) I. Title.
HC430.C6 G56 2000
306.3'0951'43—dc21 00-027259

Original printing 2000
Last figure below indicates year of this printing:
09 08 07

Designed by Eleanor Mennick
Typeset by Robert C. Ehle in 10/13 Sabon

ACKNOWLEDGMENTS

Many people and institutions helped me write this book, and I am deeply grateful for their support. My first and largest debt is to the residents of the Muslim district, whose contribution to this work is manifest on every page. These few words can only begin to represent the gratitude and appreciation that I feel for the many friends who gave me so much. Among them, I would especially like to acknowledge the generosity and friendship of the Ma, Sheng, and Wa families. In addition, Feng Zenglie of the Shaanxi Education Institute freely shared his knowledge, thoughts, and hospitality with me until his death in 1996. Ma Jishu, *ahong* at the Small Mosque, also gave me much detailed information and many wise words during the five years that we were friends before his death in 1999. I miss both these men very much. Ma Liangxun, vice-director of the Nationalities and Religious Affairs Commission of Shaanxi Province, has been a wonderful intellectual sparring partner and source of information. Wang Yarong, Lian Zengxiu, and Li Li'an of the Shaanxi Academy of Social Sciences took the (not inconsiderable) trouble to host me as a foreign scholar and greatly facilitated my work. I would also like to thank Yunxiang Yan of the University of California at Los Angeles and Tian Changshan of the Shaanxi Daily for their help in setting up my field site in Xi'an.

My research was first written as a dissertation under the guidance of James L. (Woody) Watson, Rubie S. Watson, and Mary M. Steedly, all of Harvard University, and Jonathan N. Lipman of Mount Holyoke College. I have benefited greatly from their knowledge, critiques, and friendship. Woody and Jonathan in particular have been among my most enthusiastic supporters, going far beyond the line of duty in giving me detailed comments, ideas, and moral support. Pam Summa read, edited, and made suggestions about multiple drafts of this work, helping me to express my ideas more clearly and to see the humor in this process. Jun Jing of City College New York and Eriberto P. (Fuji) Lozada of Butler University gave close readings to portions of this book and helped me refine my ideas. At Haverford, I have received helpful intellectual prodding from my departmental colleagues Wyatt MacGaffey and Laurie Kain Hart, both of whom read and commented upon parts of this work and gave me stimulating work of their own to read. Mark Gould of Haverford's Department of Sociology read and critiqued the entire book, in some cases offering comments on multiple drafts. I have benefited enormously from his unerring ability to find the hole in the argument. James A. Millward of Georgetown University as one of the reviewers for Stanford University Press offered detailed suggestions and helpful criticisms that I found very useful indeed. I am also grateful for the comments of one anonymous reviewer.

Funding for research and writing came from the Committee on Scholarly Communication with China, Haverford College, the Luce Foundation through a grant administered by the Fairbank Center for East Asian Research, the Cora Du Bois Charitable Trust, Foreign Language Area Scholarship, the Mellon Foundation, Sigma Xi, NCR, and the Harvard Anthropology Department. Portions of Chapter 7 were first published in *The Consumer Revolution in Urban China*, edited by Deborah Davis (Berkeley: University of California Press, 1999), and parts of Chapters 4 and 5 appear in *Feeding China's Little Emperors*, edited by Jun Jung (Stanford: Stanford University Press, 2000). I would like to acknowledge the logistical and technical assistance of Kathy McGee and Lisa Gavioli (Haverford '99). Finally, I am also grateful for the capable editing of Julie DuSablon for Stanford University Press.

M.B.G.

Men make their own history, but they do not make it just as they please; they do not make it under circumstances chosen by themselves, but under circumstances directly encountered, given and transmitted from the past.

—Karl Marx, *The 18th Brumaire of Louis Bonaparte*

CONTENTS

ILLUSTRATIONS

BETWEEN *Mecca* AND *Beijing*

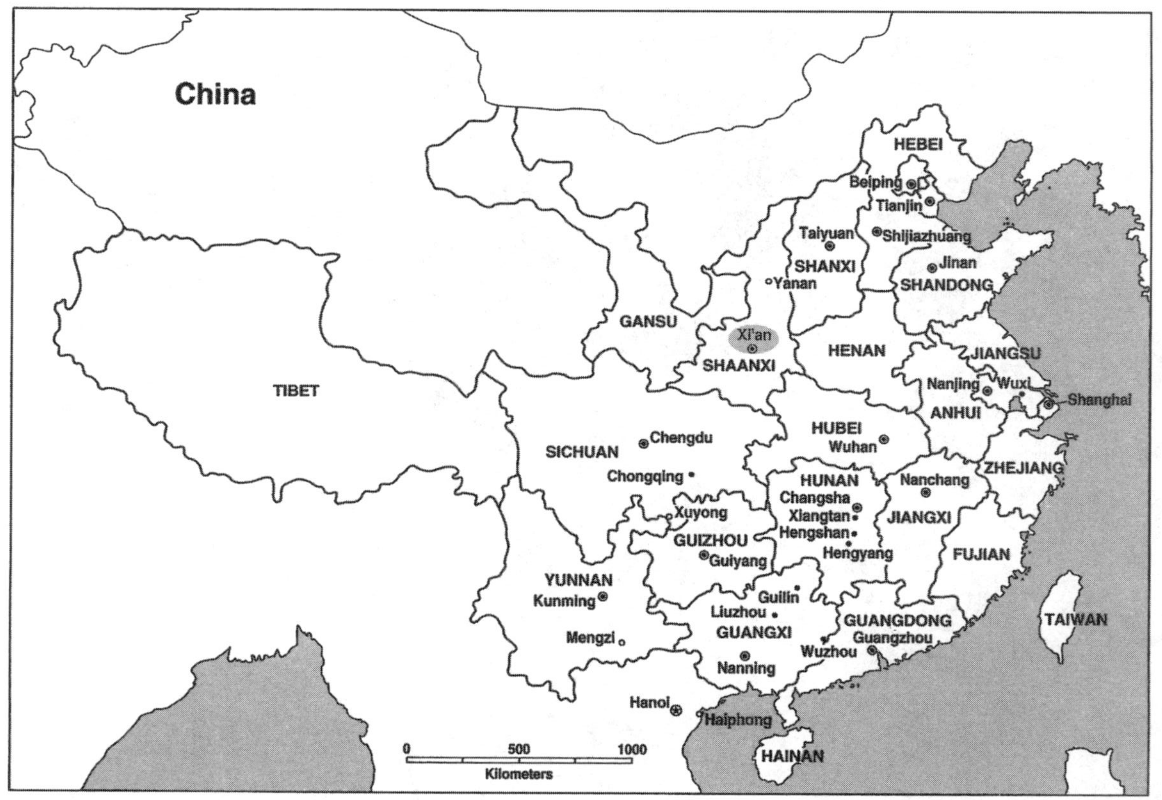
China
TIBET
GANSU
SICHUAN
Chengdu
Chongqing
YUNNAN
Kunming
Mengzi
Xuyong
GUIZHOU
Guiyang
Xi'an
SHAANXI
Yanan
SHANXI
Taiyuan
HEBEI
Beiping
Tianjin
Shijiazhuang
Jinan
SHANDONG
HENAN
JIANGSU
Nanjing
Wuxi
Shanghai
ANHUI
HUBEI
Wuhan
HUNAN
Changsha
Xiangtan
Hengshan
Hengyang
Nanchang
JIANGXI
ZHEJIANG
FUJIAN
TAIWAN
Guilin
Liuzhou
GUANGXI
Nanning
GUANGDONG
Guangzhou
Wuzhou
Hanoi
Haiphong
HAINAN
0
500
1000
Kilometers

Chapter One

MODERNIZATION AND CONSUMPTION

On a hot day in June 1996, I sat with Xue and Yan at a large table near the wide-open storefront of their family's restaurant. It was midafternoon, and the temperature had soared well above 100 degrees Fahrenheit. Barley Market Street was nearly deserted, and there were few signs of activity in the neighboring restaurants and food stalls. Since the restaurant was nearly empty, most of the half-dozen employees were taking their afternoon naps, and we were free to talk. It was a familiar pattern for the three of us, reminiscent of many afternoons we had spent together during the eighteen months I had lived in Xi'an, the largest city in northwest China, in 1994 and 1995 (see Map 1).

That day we were talking about fashion. Of the three of us, Xue was the one with the most expertise; when I first met her she had been working at one of the city's largest and most popular department stores. Xue's interest in fashion was reflected in her clothing. She tended to dress up more than most of the Chinese Muslims who lived in her neighborhood. That afternoon, rather than wearing the flowered, rayon pajama set of matching long-sleeved shirt and trousers that was typical summer garb in the Muslim district, Xue wore a dressy teal blouse with lace and pearl decorations over her loose trousers. She commented that skirts, particularly short skirts, had recently become popular in Xi'an. More and more young women were wearing miniskirts—but not in her neighborhood. Thinking about this, Xue explained, "We Hui people are more feudal" (*Women Huimin bijiao fengjian*). Her sister Yan listened in tacit agreement.

This was not the first time that I had heard Xue describe herself and the other residents of the Muslim district as "feudal." At the time I did not question her choice of words. During fieldwork in Xi'an, my experience was that people frequently spoke in terms of what and who was "feudal" or "traditional" (*chuantong*) and what was "modern" (*xiandaihua*), what was "backward" (*luohou*) and what was "progressive" (*xianjin*), what was "parochial" (*tu*) and what was "cultured" (*you wenhua*) or "civilized" (*wenming*). Ordinary Chinese used these words to describe people's dress styles; the food they ate; the houses, neighborhoods, and cities they lived in; and their occupations. They also described different social groups in this way. Many times I heard Xue and her neighbors characterize themselves as "feudal," or claim that other Chinese thought that the Hui people were "feudal."

Later I wondered what it meant that Xue called herself "feudal," and what wearing miniskirts had to do with being less "feudal," or, as the residents of this Chinese Muslim neighborhood were more likely to say, more "modern." Xue's comments indicated that she made a connection between consumption practices, such as wearing miniskirts, and a process that she and other locals referred to as "modernization" (*xiandaihua*). The terms that Xue and her Muslim neighbors used to describe their own and others' consumption choices (as well as other aspects of social life) had connotations that transcended their local setting. The ideas that these words conveyed were part of an ongoing Chinese dialogue about development and the conditions under which "modernization" or material and spiritual "progress" could occur.

Over the course of the twentieth century, successive Chinese governments had affixed the concepts, of which "feudal" is one example, through which "modernization" was understood. This discourse had emerged under the influence of Western theories of social evolution and the linkages between race, culture, and nation. During the mid-1990s, the developmental ideas expressed by words such as "feudal" affected how people like Xue understood themselves as individuals and as members of groups and influenced how they interpreted their experiences and how they behaved. In this book, I argue that the residents of the oldest and largest Muslim district in Xi'an used consumption to manipulate ideas about social development and position themselves more favorably within a state-sponsored evolutionary ideology. Through their consumption practices, Xue and her neighbors appropriated "modernization" for themselves, and in the process they challenged the state's official role as purveyor of and guide to "modernization."

"Feudal" and Other Ideas

"Feudal" is the common English translation of the Chinese term *fengjian*, a word that comes from the Chinese classic the *Zuo Chuan* (Li 1971:78). Originally, *fengjian* described a decentralized system of political organization in ancient China. Toward the end of the nineteenth century, Chinese intellectuals and officials resuscitated fengjian as a model for reforming the imperial government and limiting its powers (Duara 1995:153). Their efforts were stimulated by the Qing dynasty's inability to maintain sovereignty and control over its imperial territory and internal affairs. After China lost the Opium Wars and ceded the island of Hong Kong to Britain in 1842, the imperial government was forced repeatedly to acquiesce to the territorial and commercial demands of several Western nations and Japan. These concessions made an enormous impact on Chinese elites because they demonstrated China's weakness and vulnerability to foreign nations. Reform of the Chinese political system along the lines of a federated or fengjian state was one strategy that some scholar-officials devised to restore China to what most Chinese considered to be her proper international preeminence (Duara 1995:153–7).

Less than twenty years later, however, the use of fengjian as a positive political model had disappeared. By 1910, "feudal" had become the cause of China's crisis rather than the solution to her international defeats. Fengjian's shift in meaning coincided with the rising popularity of socialist ideas among the many Chinese intellectuals who had studied abroad, particularly those who had studied in Japan (Li 1971; Duara 1995:201). At this time, fengjian, intimately associated with the Chinese past and the classical Chinese canon, became the term used to translate the Marxist concept of "feudal." Marx viewed feudalism as a backward form of economic organization associated with medieval Europe and the precursor to capitalism (see Marx [1858] 1989; [1848] 1988). Following Marxist usage, fengjian moved from being a progressive political alternative designed to make China a modern state to become the antithesis of progress and a mark of stagnation. A negative understanding of "feudal" as a failure to develop and as the characteristic feature of Chinese tradition persisted in China up through the 1990s (see Cohen 1994a; Link 1992:155, 193, 200, 286). The political success of the Chinese Communist Party (CCP) is in part responsible for this perspective, though the attack on Chinese tradition began well before the CCP took power (see Cohen 1994a; Schwarcz 1995; Spence 1981).

Marx's model of social development (historical materialism) was a sequence of evolutionary stages. Like most nineteenth-century developmental theorists, including Lewis Henry Morgan and Herbert Spencer, Marx contended that societies progressed, when they did progress, through a series of developmental stages from primitive to modern social orders. Many late nineteenth-century social thinkers posited that human societies evolved along a unilinear developmental trajectory until they reached the culminating point: the "modern," urbanized, industrial nation-state. Western Europe and the United States exemplified the outcome of evolutionary progress. The result of these ideas was a new, teleological reading of human history as a universal progression from barbarism to civilization.[1]

In the late nineteenth and early twentieth centuries, theories of social evolution in both Marxist and non-Marxist forms provided Chinese elites with a framework for interpreting their country's political and military inadequacies. This was because social evolution could be used both to interpret the particular past of a particular society and as a universal model for ranking contemporaneously existing societies. Each society was measured for its level of civilization, with stages of advancement primarily determined by technology. Fengjian or "feudal" was one of many new words that were used to express this radical new model that could characterize the reasons for China's defeats and humiliation. Like "feudal," other developmental concepts were also created by appropriating words from ancient Chinese classics. These included "machine," "progress," "economy," "class," "revolution," "democracy," and "production." Other social evolutionary ideas required neologisms, most of which Chinese intellectuals borrowed from modern Japanese; these included such terms as "modernization," "science," "industry," "nation," "race," "culture," and "tradition."[2] All were necessary to locate China within a hierarchically ordered model of social development and to understand how "traditional Chinese culture" had affected "modernization."

"Race," "Culture," and "Nation"

"Race," "culture," and "nation" were three of the primary subjects of social evolution. In the social evolutionist framework, "race" does not refer to skin color or depend primarily on physiology, though many groups that were characterized as races were said to share physical traits. Race refers to a group that putatively possesses a shared descent or genealogy that is made manifest in a supposedly unique culture or "genius." According to much late nineteenth-century thinking, the proper destiny for such a collective unit was nationhood. This idea has continued to influence twentieth-century politics throughout the world (see, e.g., Hart 1999; Bringa 1995; Brubaker 1996). Racial identity was thus the political rationale for the nation-state, and it was often asserted that the nation's development depended on the quality of the race upon which it was founded (see Dikötter 1992:97–125; Duara 1995:17–50). A familiar Western term that may help clarify this relationship is the German idea of *das Volk*, the German "people" or "race" that justified the *Anschluss*, the movement to unify all Germans into one nation-state. The founding of the German Reich in 1870 and the unification of East and West Germany after the Soviet Union collapsed in 1989 were both predicated on the idea of the German "people" (see Brubaker 1996:2, 112–4). The Chinese term that I am rendering as "race," *minzu*, was borrowed from Japanese at the turn of the twentieth century and is most likely a translation of *das Volk* (Lipman 1997:xx). Minzu means both "nation" and "race." It is often translated as "nationality" in late twentieth-century English writing.

In the 1860s, the concept of "survival of the fittest"—a synonym for natural selection—emerged as a characterization of international politics (Dikötter 1992:99). In the political struggle for survival, the states that possessed the most "modern" traits were destined to succeed, whereas those that had not developed such characteristics would decline and fail. China, frequently referred to as "the sick man of Asia," was an example of a maladapted state. The crucial determinant of a nation's successful evolution was the civilizability of its race. Races that were technologically inferior or "primitive" at the time when these theories became popular (which coincided with a period of Western colonial expansion) would not develop into modern nation-states, at least not of their own accord. Those states, namely the Western European nations, the United States, and (slightly later) Japan, whose "superior" racial populations had enabled them to modernize, embarked on a "civilizing mission" to assist those societies that had not reached such heights (see Macauley [1835] 1971 for a British example of this rhetoric; see Robertson 1995 for examples from Japan). Thus, theories of social evolution legitimated Western and Japanese imperialism.

Because the fate of the nation was predicated upon race, the question for Chinese elites faced with China's political and military weakness was the civilizing potential of the Chinese "race." The "genius" of the Chinese people, their culture and tradition, was evidence for the Chinese race's capacity to develop. As my discussion of fengjian may suggest, intellectuals took different stances on the value of Chinese culture. Some elites, convinced of its superiority, advocated the adoption of Western science and technology while maintaining Chinese tradition. The belief that

Chinese society was the highest manifestation of civilization had a long history in China, although this notion had been undermined by the late nineteenth-century foreign incursions (Elvin 1994:44; see also Duara 1995:56–61, Harrell 1995b:18–20, Schwartz 1994:246–7). For this type of elite, the central problem was, in the 1917 words of the scholar-official Hu Shi, "How can we best assimilate modern civilization in a manner as to make it congenial and congruous and continuous with the civilization of our own making?" (cited in Schwartz 1994:73; compare Chatterjee 1993:116–34).

Other Chinese intellectuals, however, perceived modernization and Chineseness as fundamentally at odds (see Cohen 1994a; Schwarcz 1995; Watson 1995). Many members of the Chinese intelligentsia during the early twentieth century disparaged and rejected Chinese tradition, blaming Chinese culture for China's supposed stagnation at a "feudal" stage of development. Their "ferociously iconoclastic antitraditionalism" was powerfully articulated during the May Fourth Movement of 1919 and expressed repeatedly throughout the twentieth century by the Nationalist and Communist governments of China, Chinese elites, and urbanites (Cohen 1994a; see also Link 1992; Schwartz 1995; Watson 1991b; Watson 1995). The solution that many elites proposed was to reform Chinese culture along "modern" lines: the members of the Chinese race should prove their capacity for nationhood by demonstrating that they were "civilized" according to the standards of Western culture (see Fitzgerald 1996). These intellectuals and officials faulted Chinese culture but did not accept that the Chinese had a racial impediment to modernization. The Chinese government (rather than foreign imperialists) would teach the Chinese "race(s)" to become civilized and modern (Anagnost 1997a; see also Dikötter 1992).

One preoccupation of the intelligentsia and the successive governments between the 1890s and the 1990s was how many races there were in China. The state needed to affix the number of races in China in order to evaluate their levels of social development. Although both the Nationalist and Communist governments believed that all China's races required official guidance to progress, the amount, nature, and duration of governmental assistance would vary depending on where a particular race ranked on the developmental trajectory. The evolutionary stages of the peoples of China in turn affected where and how the national process of modernization would be implemented. They also showed which "race" was most qualified to lead the others to develop.

Racial discourse and racism had been present in China since at least the thirteenth century (Lipman 1997:35–7; see also Duara 1995:51–82; Crossley 1987), coexisting with the notion that anyone who behaved in a culturally Chinese fashion was or could become Chinese (see Harrell 1996a, 1995b; Cohen 1994a; Watson 1991b). During the twentieth century, officials and intellectuals combined indigenous Chinese racism with Western ideas about social evolution to determine the nation's racial makeup. The long-standing faith in the supremacy of Chinese culture and Chinese folk notions about non-Chinese "barbarians" were manifest in what groups counted as "races" and how their level of development was assessed. Not surprisingly, the race that the CCP identified as the most civilized and modern was the Han race, that group of Chinese citizens who the party took to epitomize traditional Chinese culture.

In some respects, the CCP took the Soviet Union as a guide when determining the racial composition of the Chinese nation and establishing a political order. In the USSR, the new Communist government had applied the term "nationality" to various "races" that it hypothesized existed within the former Czarist empire. Many of these "races" were endowed with corresponding political entities, such as the Central Asian "republics." The Soviet officials adopted these policies to control and channel the political expression of collective identities, draining them of their content while nominally legitimating them (Brubaker 1996:25, 31–2; see also Dreyer 1976:43–60). Ultimately, the state aimed for the disappearance of nationality identities as they became modern under official tutelage. The CCP designed its nationality policies to emulate the Soviet Union's, with similar goals in mind. However, in the USSR and in China, Communist nationality policies had the opposite effect. Rather than promoting the disappearance of racial identities, the two governments created new categories of collective solidarity and the institutions to reinforce them (see Brubaker 1996:23–54; Gladney 1990, 1991, 1998b).

In the People's Republic of China (PRC), the CCP dispatched a series of ethnological missions, led by prominent Chinese anthropologists, historians, and sociologists, throughout China between 1950 and 1956. The goal of these missions was to amass sufficient information on the Chinese people so that the minzu could be identified and classified according to Marx's model as either primitive, slave, feudal, bourgeois-capitalist, socialist, or communist societies, in ascending order of modernization (Dreyer 1976:142; Harrell 1995c:80, 88 n. 17). Shortly after the 1956 series of missions were sent, two scholars (one of whom, Fei Xiaotong, was a student of Malinowski) published preliminary results in the *People's Daily*, an official channel of communication in the PRC. In the article, they indicated that local ascriptive criteria for collective identity did not constitute real minzu status. The article states:

> A self-reported name of a nationality [minzu] cannot be used definitely for the establishment of the existence of such a nationality. For individuals may feel that they belong to a common community and this may not necessarily conform to the facts. This situation still exists in modern nations. And since many of the minority nationalities in our country are still in the precapitalist stage of development, the possibility for the conclusion above mentioned is all the greater. (Cited in Eberhard 1982:152; see also Dreyer 1976:142–4)

Officially, the policy for establishing minzu identification was to use the four criteria developed by Stalin: each race had to possess a common territory, language, form of economic livelihood, and psychology. Formal allegiance to Stalin's definition of "nationality" persisted through the first 50 years of the PRC's history (see, e.g., Jin 1984). Despite the government's pretensions to "scientific" method, however, pre-nineteenth-century Chinese racial categories strongly influenced the identification of minzu (see Gladney 1990, 1991; Harrell 1995c).

Although few Chinese (and too few scholars) ever question the label "Han," lack of adherence to Stalin's nationality criteria is nowhere more apparent than in the case of the Han minzu. The vast majority of Chinese citizens were classified as Han; in the late 1990s, the Han "race" constituted 91 percent of the total population (Gladney 1998b:108). In the 1950s, as in the 1990s, members of the Han minzu lived dispersed over the entire Chinese landmass. They spoke a wide range of Chinese dialects, including several mutually unintelligible languages. Han Chinese engaged in various forms of economic activity, including rice agriculture, wheat agriculture, aquaculture, numerous types of commerce, industrial labor, and clerical and academic work. As for their "common psychology," the multiplicity of belief systems to which members of the Han nationality adhered, which included atheism, Buddhism, Catholicism, Confucianism, Daoism, Protestantism, and several different syncretisms, indicated that they had none. The only way to make sense of the racial label "Han" is to view it as roughly analogous to the group most would call "Chinese," which basically meant those who were regarded as Chinese by Qing dynastic officials. Because late-imperial folk categories were the de facto determinant of racial classification, not all the people who considered themselves Chinese were included in the Han minzu, and some who regarded themselves as non-Han were placed in this group (see, e.g., Harrell 1990; Gladney 1991: 261–91).

Although from the perspective of international politics and modernization the Chinese race was backward, the PRC government viewed the Han as the most advanced of all the races within China (Dreyer 1976; Eberhard 1982:156–8; Harrell 1995b). Sinocentric ideas about the superior achievements of Chinese civilization affected the party's position on the Han "race." Although the CCP took the primary role in creating a new socialist civilization and modernizing China, officials regarded the Han minzu as the "older brother" who should guide, direct, and assist China's other, less advanced races. The government classified a few non-Han minzu as having achieved an equal level of development to the Han. The rest, including the Hui minzu to which the residents of the Xi'an Muslim district were assigned, were placed at more primitive stages on the evolutionary paradigm (Dreyer 1976: 147–50; compare McKhann 1995:41 n. 4). Because I want to emphasize the fallacies upon which the idea of minzu are based, the prejudices behind minzu classification, and the extent to which minzu are accepted as natural, I generally have translated minzu as "race."

The Hui Minzu

Through the first 50 years of the twentieth century, "Hui" was primarily a religious category. All Muslims in China were called Hui. The term for Islam was "the religion of the Hui" (*Huijiao*), and to call oneself a "Hui person" (*Huimin*) was to state a religious affiliation. Yet while "Hui" meant "Muslim" for several centuries after Islam's entry into China, the concept also contained a racial component. This derived from three sources. First, the early Muslims in China were from "the West" (*xi yu*), places usually identified as Arabia (*Dashi*) and Persia (*Bosi*), and were strikingly different from the Chinese in culture, language, and physiognomy. Like other foreigners in China during the seventh through ninth centuries, these Muslim traders were known as "foreign sojourners" (*fan ke*). Second, although the Hui people of the late-imperial period spoke, looked, and acted Chinese in most respects, their practice of Islam produced some striking cultural differences between them and non-Muslim Chinese. Third, between the seventeenth and the nineteenth centuries, the Hui people of northwest China were involved in numerous bloody conflicts that caused many Chinese (including a number of government officials) to believe that they possessed a racial predisposition to violence and were inherently uncivilized.

By the late-imperial period, the perception of Hui as non-Chinese had more to do with Islamic practice than any discernible Arab or Persian physiological traits or cultural practices. If, as James L. Watson has proposed, being Chinese before the mid-twentieth century was based on knowledge of a shared oral tradition and adherence to a set of standardized ritual practices (see Watson 1993, 1991b, 1988; see also Cohen 1994a), then Islam was the factor that caused the Hui to be excluded. Those known as Hui at the turn of the twentieth century were well versed in the oral lore that Watson describes, and historic and contemporary evidence suggests that the Hui followed Chinese ritual in most respects (see, e.g., Ting 1958; Warren [1920–1921] 1940; Broomhall [1910] 1966; Gillette 1998). Where the Hui deviated from Chinese patterns it was due to Islamic observance (see Lipman 1987; Gladney 1991:21–6; Aubin 1991).

The first record of Chinese racial slurs against Hui people dates from the thirteenth century. Not coincidentally, this period was a time when "barbarians," namely Mongols, ruled China; during this dynasty (the Yuan) substantial numbers of Muslims were given government offices because of Mongol anti-Chinese bias (Lipman 1997:31–8).[3] By the early twentieth century, a perception of Hui as violent and irremediably savage was common in China. This derived from the three centuries of violent armed conflicts that had occurred in northwest China between different Muslim communities and between Muslims and non-Muslims. Many of these outbreaks were couched in terms of religious differences, primarily differences among different Muslim factions, but economic and political concerns were always also at stake (see Lipman 1997:89–166).

The case of a group of Fujian Hui studied by Dru Gladney illuminates how the Chinese government divorced the term "Hui" from religion and enhanced its racial content during the PRC's first 50 years of existence (Gladney 1991:261–91). When the government conducted its ethnological missions during the 1950s, a group of Fujianese who were descended from foreign Muslims were assigned to the Han nationality. Although these people possessed written genealogies that demonstrated their Muslim ancestry, they were not included in the Hui minzu because they were not practicing Muslims. In 1979, however, this group was awarded Hui status on the basis of its genealogical claims. The

Fujian Hui story demonstrates that in the first half of the twentieth century, the government, like most Chinese, equated being Hui with being Muslim. Those who did not "act Hui" but, like the Fujian Hui, fit Chinese cultural norms, were given Han nationality status. By the end of the twentieth century, however, the category "Hui" was no longer dependent on Islamic observance. The "Hui nationality" were a "people," a "race" whose membership was determined by descent, not by religious practice.

When the CCP was evaluating the evolutionary stage of the Hui "race," the Hui were designated as backward relative to the Han; religion was the primary reason (Dreyer 1976:149). When, during the Maoist era, the Hui were "accused of maintaining feudalist, anti-socialist and exploitative practices" (Gladney 1998b: 108), practices related to Islam and to religious institutions provoked these criticisms. However, because the CCP had determined that the Hui were a race and not a religious group, Hui feudalism was attributed to their race's arrested evolutionary development. The government, which tended to equate "civilization" with Chineseness (see Dreyer 1976:264; Harrell 1995:15–6, 23), saw the Hui race's lack of cultural achievements as indicative of their need for tutelage from the Han race and the (largely Han) party.

To promote and disseminate its classification of the Hui (and the other non-Chinese "races"), the PRC government (inspired by the USSR) funded scholars to write "concise histories" (*jianshi*) and other texts that established the "facts" about the Hui race. These texts discuss racial "origins," characterize the Hui nationality's essential traits, and illustrate where the Hui fall in the universal progression of history and the nation's developmental hierarchy (see, e.g., HZJS 1978; see also Lipman 1997:xxiii–xxiv; Litzinger 1995). For the Hui, such work has established that the Hui race "originated" (*xingcheng*) in the Ming dynasty from a mixture of Arab, Persian, and Central Asian roots (traced patrilineally); that the Hui possess an inherited predisposition for commerce; and that, although "culturally backward" (*wenhua luohou*), illiterate, and poor at the time of the PRC's founding, the

Hui have made great progress under the CCP's guidance and assistance (Bai 1951; Lai 1992; Xiang 1983:103; see also Gladney 1998b).

Modernization

The PRC government (and the Nationalist government) engaged in social classification in order to determine what was required for China to modernize. Modernization was measured primarily in material terms, with technology serving as the main index; "civilization" was its ideological and ethical counterpart. After the CCP gained power in 1949, increasing industrial and agricultural production was defined as a critical task. To do so, Mao's government implemented new forms of economic organization, creating a Soviet-style planned economy and placing production and distribution under central control. The state collectivized property and put land under government ownership. Agricultural labor and production were reordered to more closely resemble the organizational modes of industry, and the party created a national work unit system to rationalize labor and the distribution of health care and other benefits. The CCP paid special attention to developing heavy industry and improving the military, and with the technological assistance and aid of the Soviet Union (until the Sino-Soviet split in 1960), undertook numerous construction projects. The results of some Sino-Soviet joint projects, including a number of buildings, still stood in Xi'an during the late 1990s.[4] These changes were not solely material, organizational, or economic, of course; they were also integral aspects of the party's program for (re)socialization.

Although a great deal of "modernization" occurred during the first 30 years of the PRC's existence, the CCP failed to achieve its goal of "surpassing Great Britain and catching up with the United States" (*chaoying ganmei*) by the time of Mao's death. One problem that kept the state from meeting its goals was the lack of work incentives that resulted when benefits were disassociated from performance under the socialist system. Even more damaging were the repeated, violent political campaigns that the party conducted to root out "counter-revolutionaries" (variously defined). When Deng Xiaoping assumed power in 1978, he promised to speed up modernization and end ideologically inspired social turmoil. Deng proclaimed as his goal the "four modernizations" in agriculture, industry, military affairs, and science and technology (science and technology being considered one category). Although it would be erroneous to characterize Deng as having had a tightly formulated plan to modernize China, he regarded creating an economically efficient society as the necessary first step (Lieberthal 1995:126). The economic reforms that Deng implemented centered on privatizing state and collective enterprises, creating a free market, and soliciting foreign investment. During the nineteen years of Deng's reign, the number and kinds of institutions that the CCP turned over to the private sector and the size and scope of the free market expanded almost continuously, except for a short period following the 1989 student protests and government crackdown.

Like the Maoist regime, the Deng government stressed material development and technology to demonstrate China's successful progress toward and achievement of modernization. In his first ten-year plan, Deng proposed that China complete 120 major projects, including the construction of steel and iron plants, power stations, oil fields, and rail lines (Spence 1981:357–8). During the 1980s and 1990s, CCP leaders continued to single out technological feats such as the Three Gorges Dam hydroelectric project and the building of a proton accelerator as indications of China's progress (Link 1992:67). However, under the Deng regime the CCP's emphasis on major technological accomplishments and infrastructural development was coupled with increased investment in consumer goods and state promotion of personal consumption (Lieberthal 1995:146–9; see also Davis 1999a; Gold 1993).

Most ordinary Chinese citizens shared the government leaders' material standard of modernization. For example, many residents of the Xi'an Muslim district pointed to such infrastructural improvements as electricity, paved roads, and running water as evidence of China's modernization since the 1940s. Where these urbanites may have differed from national leaders was in their tendency to be most concerned with the material changes that had led to visible improvements in their own lives. For example, some local residents referred to the new street lights that the Xi'an municipal government installed and the new underground shopping mall it completed in 1997 as "modernization"; this kind of development received little attention as a symbol of modernization at a national level. Commodities such as washing machines, motor scooters, televisions, VCRs, and a host of clothing and other personal fashions also served as powerful and personally relevant indices of modernization (see also Gladney 1998a; Upton 1996).

Consumption

Some scholars have suggested that consumption is the most common form of expressive activity that exists in industrialized, urban societies (Willis 1991; Miller 1987). Historically, social theorists (including most thinkers concerned with modernization) have tended to privilege production as the most significant and creative social act. Consumption has often been portrayed with a negative cast, as, for example, Marx's description of insatiable consumer desires driving a relentlessly expanding and horrifyingly destructive market (Marx [1848] 1988) and Veblen's contrast between productive "efficiency" and wasteful "conspicuous consumption" (Veblen [1899] 1953). More recently, however, consumption has attracted a good deal of scholarly attention as a domain in which individuals and groups engage in the work of the imagination, producing social and cultural identities (see, e.g., Agnew 1993; Appadurai 1986, 1996; de Certeau 1984; Douglas and Isherwood 1980; McCracken 1988; Miller 1987, 1992, 1995a, 1995b; Orlove and Rutz 1989; Wilk 1994; Willis 1991). Consumption is a venue in which consumers can assert or affirm values, enunciate and sometimes realize wishes, and create and maintain public, semipublic, and private images.

In some respects, consumption is an arena in which urbanites and industrial workers exercise considerable control. When buying, renting, and using commodities, consumers make choices and put products to uses as they see fit (see de Certeau 1984; Miller 1995b; Mintz 1996; McCracken 1988; Friedman 1990; Belk 1995). As Willis points out, even window-shopping can be seen as an assertion of control in an imaginative realm: window-shopping enables individuals to appropriate the images and goods they have seen for creative reuse (Willis 1991:31).

The potential for consumption to provide individuals with opportunities to exert control over and exhibit creativity in their lives must nevertheless be reconciled with the presence of constraints on consumer agency. Consumption practices are affected by a number of variables, the most obvious being budget constraints. The kinds of services and goods that producers make available also limit the opportunities and options of buyers, renters, and viewers (Appadurai 1996; Miller 1995b), as do the social networks within which they function (Orlove and Rutz 1989). Advertising too plays a role in shaping consumption; corporations and marketing personnel strive to create demand and manipulate desires and needs.

This study investigates the relationship between an ideology of modernization and a set of consumption activities that I witnessed in the Xi'an Muslim district during the mid-1990s. In a broader sense, it is a study of how ideology affects consumption and how consumption can be used to manipulate ideology. The group of Chinese Muslims that I studied were influenced by a set of conceptual categories about race and development. They used a state-sponsored evolutionary framework to make sense of themselves and the world around them. However, although the residents of the Xi'an Muslim district worked within this conceptual apparatus, they used their consumption practices to actively pursue modernization for themselves (rather than wait for the government to provide it) and to reposition themselves within an ideology of social development. Through the goods they bought, rented, and used; the styles they adopted; and the commodities they rejected, these Chinese Muslims combated the racial stereotype that the Hui people were "feudal" and poorly equipped for modernization. They showed themselves to be more "civilized" than their Han neighbors or the local government. They turned "tradition" into an economic asset, and challenged the CCP's monopoly on "progress" by appealing to an alternative set of criteria for evaluating society.

The next six chapters focus on related sets of goods and fashions and how they were (or were not) consumed. In Chapter 2, I examine consumption practices that relate to the Xi'an Muslim district as a physical space. Residents characterized their neighborhood according to racial traits they believed the Hui minzu possessed and to architectural and spatial standards they saw as representing developmental stages of modernization. In Chapter 3, I look at two other elements that define the Muslim district as a place: the mosques and mosque schools. Consumer practices related to these institutions showed local residents' efforts to locate themselves within an international Muslim discourse of authenticity and to grasp an Islamic locus of progress. In Chapter 4, I investigate the production and consumption of foods that locals defined as "pure and true" (*qingzhen*) and as "traditional" (*chuantong*). Here I explore the positive significance of "traditional," despite its place in the government's evolutionary history. In Chapter 5, I discuss the consumption of food that residents saw as quintessentially "modern" and "scientific." Locals used such foods to present themselves as progressive and to prepare their children to succeed in a "modern" world. In Chapter 6, I follow the rise of an antialcohol movement in the Muslim district. This movement called into question the state's developmental paradigm and modernization trajectory by locating the source of "civilization" in Islam. In Chapter 7, I look at trends in bridal appearance and wedding consumption. Through selectively appropriating goods and images associated with modernization, Xi'an Muslims resituated themselves within national evolutionary hierarchies and universal history. In the final chapter (Chapter 8), I discuss how residents of the Muslim district worked within an evolutionary paradigm while rejecting certain aspects of the state's model of progress. I reflect on the role that Islam played in enabling residents to reconceive "modernization," and I evaluate how the government's own policies created opportunities for this group of Chinese Muslims to reframe the state's evolutionary paradigm.

Fieldwork and Writing

This book is based on eighteen months of field research that I conducted in Xi'an between January 1994 and August 1995 and during four short visits in the summers of 1992, 1996, 1997, and 1998. Conducting ethnographic research in China was much less difficult during the mid-1990s than it had been even ten years previously, but as a foreign researcher I was still subject to certain constraints. Visiting scholars required an institutional sponsor to conduct research in China, so I became affiliated with the history department of the Shaanxi Academy of Social Sciences. I was fortunate that they were willing to host me: the Hui were considered a "sensitive" (*mingan*) topic to study. This was in part because of racial relations and in part because of Muslim protests over books regarded as offensive to Islam (see Gladney 1991 for a description of Hui protests during 1989). During 1993, residents of the Muslim district organized public marches over a book that Hui throughout the northwest found offensive; this "social unrest" delayed my fieldwork for several months while officials stewed about granting permissions. As my colleagues at the academy told me, everyone wanted assurance that "nothing would happen" while I was there. After arriving, I was gently warned against disrupting the local community or espousing views that did not depict the Xi'an Hui in a favorable light. All survey and questionnaire work was prohibited. I was also refused permission to live in the Muslim district and ultimately lived in the foreign students' dormitory at Northwest University (*Xibei Daxue*), a fifteen-minute bicycle ride from the area.

That being said, I was subject to no other restrictions. I came and went freely in the Muslim district, as frequently as I wished. I was not required to be accompanied by a member of the Academy, but could visit the area's mosques, businesses, and households alone. Published materials on the Hui were available at local Muslim bookstores, and the district's Religion and Nationality Office, the branch of the district government that dealt specifically with Islam and "minority nationalities," occasionally provided me with official documents to peruse. Officials who worked there and the vice-director of the provincial Religion and Nationality Affairs Commission agreed to unlimited interviews. I rode my bicycle into the Muslim district almost every day and spent most of my time in the homes and businesses of local families, the ten mosques, and the Hui Middle School.

Most of my insights into the Muslim district come from intensive contacts with six extended families. Aside from these informants, whose friendship, generosity, and tolerance for stupid questions was remarkable, I interviewed and spoke casually with an estimated 200 adults and had contacts at each of the ten mosques. Despite the large size of the Muslim district (30,000 in 1994, according to official sources), I never ceased to be amazed by the intimate and detailed knowledge that residents possessed of one another. It was never the case that I could speak of a particular religious specialist or family without others knowing who they were or being able to link them to someone they knew, even if the people being discussed lived on the opposite side of the district. A number of factors contributed to this intimacy: the smallness of the physical area that comprised the district, high levels of intermarriage between the families living there, the schooling system that was based upon residence, and residents' preference for operating private enterprises in or near their homes.

My extended presence in the Muslim district was somewhat puzzling to most people, because I am neither Chinese nor a Muslim. Almost three months into my fieldwork, I wondered if any Hui were ever going to talk to me for more than five minutes; unlike the Han people I had met in Xi'an, residents of the Muslim district were guarded and seemed uninterested in speaking to a foreigner. My first break came through Yan, one of the young women with whose story I began this chapter. I visited Yan's family's restaurant frequently during my first few weeks in Xi'an, and one day a woman approached me about giving English lessons to her daughter. A few days later I was teaching Yan English at her family's home. Yan's desire to study English faded after about two months and disappeared entirely as she prepared for her wedding in October 1994, but she and her family became some of my closest friends and most valuable informants. Other contacts came from volunteer teaching at the Hui Middle School and persistent visits to the local mosques, which tended to be places for socializing as well as worship.

This is not the book that I imagined writing when I first began visiting Xi'an in 1992. At that time I had not thought about investigating consumption behaviors, and although I knew that the PRC government promoted modernization and an evolutionary ideology of progress, I never imagined that the people I was interested in paid much attention to such things. However, as anyone who has conducted ethnographic research will know, the researcher is led by the interests of his or her informants. During the weeks and months of fieldwork, I was struck by the importance that residents placed on consumption and commodities and by the way they interpreted consumer acts. Residents of the Muslim district used consumption to evaluate their own and others' status, not merely in terms of wealth, but in terms of social development. Their words and acts forced me to think about "tradition" and "modernization" in a new light, causing me to recognize even more clearly the real sociological consequences of the ideas and concepts that we use to make sense of the world.

Chapter Two

HOUSING, EDUCATION, AND RACE

Xi'an's Muslim District or Hui Quarter

Just west of the Ming-dynasty Bell Tower in the city center and directly adjacent to the Drum Tower lies the residential district known locally as "the Hui quarter" (*Huiminfang*), or, more simply, "the quarter" (*fangshang*). This area, which occupies about one square mile, housed approximately 30,000 Hui or Chinese Muslims in 1994 (Wu 1992:99). Like most parts of Xi'an within the city wall, the Hui quarter was densely packed with residences. Unlike elsewhere in the city, however, it also housed ten mosques, several historic monuments, and a hundred or more small shops, food stalls, and eateries.

The quarter's mosques and historic monuments, particularly the Great Mosque (*Qingzhen Dasi*), drew large groups of Chinese and foreign tourists. In the mosque's vicinity were a multitude of shops with an array of goods and foods calculated to entice visitors into the nearby streets to look for a curio, a bargain, or some tasty cuisine. Many Xi'an natives who lived or worked near the quarter also foraged there for food: the area was renowned for the "little eats" (*xiaochi*) that residents sold. Lamb stew (*yangrou paomo*) and round, pan-baked flatbreads (*tuotuomo*) were two of the most popular Hui specialties.

Most of the quarter's shops and eateries were small-scale family enterprises. They contrasted sharply with the major department stores, imported designer-label specialty shops, and huge restaurants on the main city streets encircling the district. Local

Hui called their commercial endeavors *xiao shengyi* or "petty business," as opposed to *shangye* or *qiye*, terms for business or commerce that connoted larger, more formal enterprises and industry. Most of the quarter's streets were lined with small restaurants, dry goods stores, bakeries, butchers, and sweets shops and were patrolled by a plethora of bicycle-drawn carts laden with prepared foods for sale (see Figure 1). Near a few of the area's mosques clustered some knickknack shops, antique stores, art galleries, and a couple of "Muslim products" (*Musilin shangpin*) stores that sold religious objects ranging from Qur'ans to veils. The vast majority of these private enterprises were run out of family homes. Most families dedicated one or more rooms on the ground floor of their house to running a business. Most Hui entrepreneurs who did not run shops or eateries out of their homes rented or purchased space on the main commercial streets of the quarter. Regardless of where the business was located, for the Hui of my acquaintance the family enterprise was an extension of the family living quarters. The space for gainful employment was not segregated from the space for domestic tasks and relaxation: for example, Mingjie's family used the kitchen at their business to prepare food for guests when hosting company and the courtyard of their family's residence as an extra storage space for the store. Similarly, the family enterprise was frequently a site for socializing, and the family home was often used to conduct business.

Most businesses also spilled beyond their architectural confines onto the public sidewalk. Hui entrepreneurs used the sidewalk for food preparation, storage, and seating for customers. Patrons used whatever space remained to park their bicycles while they ate or shopped. Often they were forced to leave their bicycles in the street. Proprietors' usurpation of the sidewalk for commercial purposes also forced pedestrians to walk in the crowded streets, dodging bicycle and car traffic as best they could. The biggest streets in the quarter were only wide enough to allow a single car to drive through, and much of the area consisted of small alleyways so narrow that a bicycle could barely squeeze by (see Figure

FIGURE 1. A bicycle cart vendor sells food on one of the quarter's street markets.

2). Traffic jams were frequent. Making the streets of the quarter even more difficult to navigate were deep potholes and the habit that most people engaged in construction had of storing materials such as sand, bricks, and concrete in the street in lieu of any other place to put them. This chaotic appearance was accentuated by the absence of trees and grass. The Muslim district had no lawns or gardens, unlike some other parts of Xi'an. Although some families had trees or potted house plants in their courtyards, these were rarely visible from the street.

Day and night the quarter was filled with the din of petty commercial activity. In the morning and early afternoon, sellers of meatball soup (*hulatang*), fried dough (*youtiao*), and steamed stuffed buns (*baozi*) hawked their wares, giving way to meat skewer sellers and noodle stalls at night. The shouts of street peddlers, the ringing of school bells, and the loud honking of frustrated taxi drivers trying to pass through the crowded streets filled the air.[1] The sounds of the call to prayer also permeated the Muslim district five times each day, but in syncopation, as each mosque independently determined the proper time for worship to begin. The sounds of Arabic chanting, which were broadcast by loudspeakers, defined the boundaries of the Hui quarter: residents formed an aural community whose members heard the sounds of worship throughout the day.

Most Xi'an Muslims (including many who did not live in the Muslim district) engaged in Islamic ritual practices in the quarter. Observances ranged from ordinary worship to life cycle and feast day celebrations. Most religious activities took place in either the mosque, the family home, or both. Ten of Xi'an's eighteen mosques were located in the quarter, and it contained the city's largest single concentration of Muslim residences. During the major Islamic holidays, such as the Feast of the Breaking of the Fast at the end of Ramadan, the Feast of Sacrifice that marks the culmination of the annual pilgrimage to Mecca, and the Prophet's Birthday, the area's religious character became even more visible than usual. At those times, residents bedecked their houses and the mosques with lights, banners, colored flags, and pictures of,

FIGURE 2. An alleyway in the quarter, decorated for the Feast of the Breaking of the Fast.

for example, religious architecture in Mecca (see Figure 2). The provincial and municipal Islamic Associations, organizations created by the Chinese Communist Party (CCP) to mediate between the government and the nation's Muslims, often hosted public martial arts demonstrations, film showings, and guest lectures on the Feast of the Breaking of the Fast and the Feast of Sacrifice.

The state had selected these two feasts as "nationality holidays" (*minzu jieri*) for the Hui, one part of a package of "customs and habits" (*fengsu xiguan*) that the government formally recognized as characteristic of the Hui race. Because the Hui were guaranteed the right to celebrate these holidays, all state organs that dealt with the Hui nationality formally marked these religious festivals in some way. As in most official references, "nationality" in the phrase "nationality holiday" meant "minority nationality." Only China's minorities had "nationality holidays"; the Han had none. Institutionalizing racial "customs and habits" such as "nationality holidays" was one way that the CCP supported its classification of China's non-Han races as more "backward" and less modern than the Han, who, under the party's guidance, had moved beyond such "feudal superstitions" during the 1950s.[2] This type of state policy guaranteed that the (minority) "nationalities" were marred with "customs and habits" (we might say "culture") that evidenced their low levels of social development, justified the state's evolutionary hierarchy, and demonstrated the need for state intervention to modernize these groups.

Three middle schools and five primary schools, all accredited by the Ministry of Education, existed in the quarter.[3] All were "nationality schools" because they exceeded the official requirement for "nationality" designation, which was to have 30 percent non-Han students. Very few of the teachers at the quarter's schools were Hui; at least 80 percent belonged to the Han nationality. Because the quarter's schools were "nationality" institutions, they celebrated the Feast of the Breaking of the Fast and the Feast of Sacrifice, even though the schools were entirely secular. None held classes and some hosted formal celebrations on these days. For example, during the Feast of the Breaking of the Fast in 1995, the Hui Middle School celebrated with an all-school rally where students and teachers performed and special guests attended.

In accordance with government policy, most students in Xi'an attended school based on where they lived. This was common practice throughout the PRC (see, e.g., Ikels 1996:155). However, parents with sufficient money and connections could pay for their children to attend schools outside of their neighborhood. Several of Xi'an's public schools, in the interest of generating extra income, accepted a limited number of fee-paying pupils in addition to their students who attended based on residence. The exceptions to this system were the high schools that the government had selected to fuel its modernization program, called "key point" (*zhongdian*) schools (Ikels 1996:148). These schools accepted students on the basis of test scores rather than residence. They received a disproportionate amount of government resources and were known for academic excellence. However, as with the ordinary schools, sufficiently wealthy and well-connected students could purchase the opportunity to enroll in key point high schools.

The Muslim district had one district-level key point high school. It was considered far inferior to the city-level key point schools located in other districts. Very few residents of the quarter attended the municipal key point schools or attended high school at all. Of the Hui Middle School's 1994 graduating class of 70 students, only 16 percent (11 students) tested into high school: 3 percent (2 students) went to city-level key point schools, 6 percent (4 students) attended the district's key point school, and 7 percent (5 students) went to ordinary high schools. A total of 9 other students paid to go to high school: 4 attended the district's key point high school, and 5 attended ordinary high schools. These figures, which were typical for the quarter during the mid-1990s, were drastically lower than the Xi'an city-wide figures; for example, in 1994, 67 percent of middle school students continued their education (42,600 students out of a total of 63,100 middle school graduates); the figure rose to 72 percent (46,000 students out of a total of 63,500 middle school graduates) in 1995 (Xi'an Statistical Bureau 1996:381).[4]

Municipal residential designations determined school composition, but the government's districting did not correspond to urbanites' mental maps. The Hui quarter was not an official zone, but was part of the larger Lianhu District. This lack of formal state recognition did not affect its existence as a place in Xi'an. Xi'an urbanites all knew where the quarter was, including officials. Official documents referred to the Lianhu District (e.g., Wu 1992), but this did not affect government policy, which was to give the quarter special treatment. Officials tacitly recognized the quarter as an entity when they neglected to enforce municipal policies about sidewalk usage, taxes, or urban renewal there.

City officials told me that Xi'an Hui had been established in this part of Xi'an since the tenth century. Other sources indicated that Muslims had lived in this spot even longer: a stone stele in the Great Mosque records that the mosque was first built in the eighth century (it has been rebuilt several times; most of the current structure dates from the Ming dynasty). The quarter's streets also evidenced a long-standing Muslim presence. Names such as Western Sheep Market Street (*Xiyangshi*), Big Leatheryard Street (*Dapiyuan*), Small Leatheryard Street (*Xiaopiyuan*), and Barley Market Street (*Damaishi jie*) testified to the historical tradition of Hui commerce in the area; occupations such as butchery (lamb and beef only), leather working, and food selling were Hui specializations (or were regarded as such).

In 1998, the quarter was the only part of the city that retained a number of houses that were more than 100 years old. Its private homes and narrow, convoluted alleyways contrasted sharply with the wide streets and high-rise apartment complexes that characterized most other places in Xi'an. Large state-run and collective work units (which were divided into spaces for administration, labor, dining, and residence) dominated Xi'an, and the majority of retail and food sector businesses found outside the quarter were large-scale enterprises. The quarter stood out as a dense conglomeration of small private businesses and homes.

Locals frequently quoted two proverbs about Hui residence patterns. The first was that the Hui were "widely scattered but locally concentrated" (*dafensan xiaojizhong*). This proverb meant that while members of the Hui nationality lived in every province of China (unlike, for example, the Tibetans, most of whom live in Tibet and Western China), in each area where there were Hui, they tended to live clustered together. The city of Xi'an had several examples of this phenomenon: in addition to the quarter, other smaller and more recently formed Hui neighborhoods existed in the eastern part of the city near the railroad station, and in the southern and northern parts outside the city wall.[5] Perhaps because they were more recent historical entities (for example, the Hui community near the railroad station had been in existence a mere 50 years), these Hui residential districts lacked the linguistic demarcation that the Hui quarter possessed. In the eyes of Xi'an urbanites, the city had only one *Huiminfang*.

Another phrase that Hui frequently applied to themselves was that they liked to live "around the mosque" (*zai qingzhensi de zhouwei nei*). Local Muslims often identified themselves as "belonging" to one of the quarter's ten mosques. When explaining where they lived, or who they were, families would say "we are the Middle Mosque's" (*women shi Zhongsi de*) or "we are the Great Mosque's" (*women shi Dasi de*). People generally lived near the mosque to which they claimed allegiance, but in some cases, their loyalty outlasted the residence pattern. This was most often true of Hui who moved outside of the quarter for work-related reasons; they continued to identify themselves as belonging to the mosque near their former home. The men of such families usually attended that mosque on holy days and for the occasional Friday collective worship (*zhuma*, Arabic *juma*). I knew several Hui families who had moved out of the quarter in order to set up a restaurant in a part of Xi'an where little Hui food was available (there were a large number of food-selling establishments in the quarter, so competition was stiff), or because their work unit provided housing in a different section of the city. Many of these Hui would speak about their "old home" (*laojia*) on, for example, Barley Market Street. They often still possessed rights of usufruct and ownership to part of a house in which parents or siblings lived.[6] Most Hui returned to their "old home" to host circumcisions, engagements, weddings, funerals, and mourning rituals as well as to visit.

The Quarter as a Living Space

The Muslim district's physical boundaries were indeterminate, and its population fluctuated. Many Hui who never lived in the quarter interacted regularly with those who did: for example, several young men who resided near the railroad station studied the Qur'an at the Great Mosque. Han frequently visited the district, and a few Han families lived there; most of the quarter's businesses depended on Han patronage to survive. Yet despite this permeability and unboundedness, residents of the quarter and their kin felt a strong sense of belonging to a defined unit. They clearly distinguished between those who were "people of the quarter" (*fangshang de ren*) and those who were not. In this study, I use the term "Xi'an Hui" to refer to those Hui who had close and frequent contact with the Hui residents of the Muslim district and possessed rights to property there, whether or not they actually chose to make the quarter their home.

A rapidly diminishing number of the quarter's residents lived in old buildings called "level houses" (*ping fang*). Most of these houses were more than 100 years old and had been passed down in families for generations. Hui who lived in such homes owned the building but did not own the land underneath it, since all land in China belonged to the government. Level houses were built of white-washed mud and straw, with a few timber beams for supports (see Figure 3). Their floors were gray flagstones or pounded dirt. Window openings were covered with rice paper and decorated or protected by wooden lattices, making these houses dark and cool.

Level houses lacked most modern conveniences. They were heated by small mobile cooking stoves (which to my eyes looked like diminutive oil drums) and by ovens located under raised sleeping platforms (*kang*). Some of these homes had private wells—wells being the sole source of water in this area before the

FIGURE 3. A "level house" (*ping fang*).

1960s—but few were in use. Most people who lived in level houses drew water from public faucets. These were spaced a few blocks apart on most streets and were also found inside the primary and middle schools that dotted the area. The level houses lacked toilet facilities, but this was true of most of the quarter's residences. The government did not provide private homes with running water, and residents preferred not to have "dry toilets" (pits or buckets) in their homes because of the dirt and odors. Instead, they used the walled and roofed cement-covered pits dug in the ground, usually without running water, that the government provided. When residents wanted to bathe they visited the shower facilities provided by the local mosques (Map 2 shows the layout of the quarter, including the placement of mosques and government sanitation facilities).

Level houses were built in a courtyard style: four adjoining buildings, each one room deep, formed a square or rectangle, leaving open a space in the middle for a courtyard. Off to one side was a narrow entranceway that could be shut by a large wooden gate.[7] Usually each building surrounding the courtyard contained one family, and the families who shared a courtyard were related agnatically, by blood on the father's side. For example, in one fairly typical case, three brothers and a male patrilineal first cousin (father's brother's son), along with their respective families, lived together in a level house.[8] Houses were built in close proximity and either shared external walls or were separated by narrow walkways. Adjacent level houses were sometimes but not always owned by relatives. The blocks of the wider streets in the quarter were the width of two back-to-back level houses.

Most of the quarter's inhabitants did not live in level houses. Since the mid-1980s, many had constructed two- or three-story houses on the site where their family's level house formerly stood. This trend of replacing level houses with multistory ones was continuing when I did my fieldwork. During the six years that I visited Xi'an between 1992 and 1998, some street in the quarter always had house construction ongoing, and usually many did. If

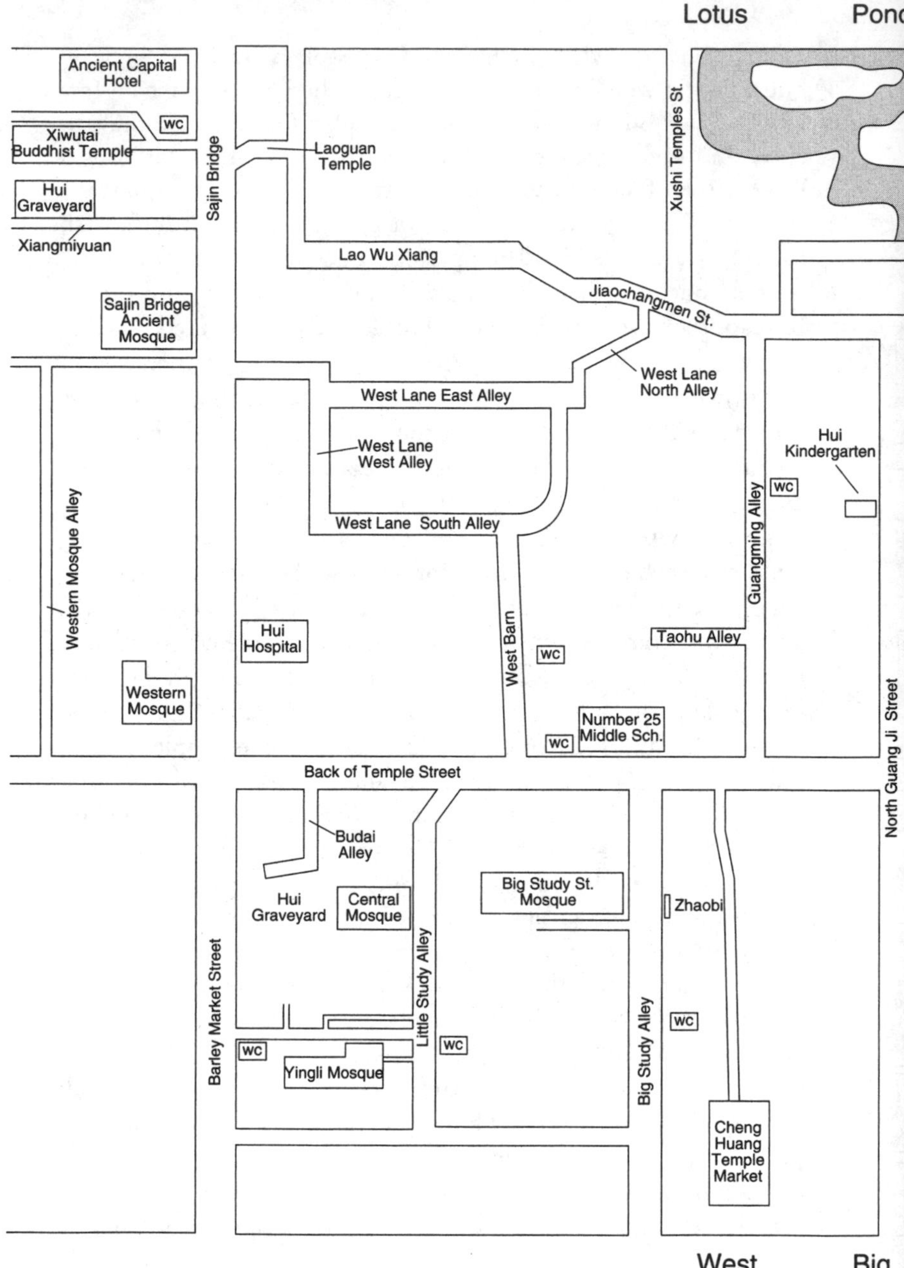

Lotus
Ponc
Ancient Capital Hotel
WC
Xiwutai Buddhist Temple
Hui Graveyard
Xiangmiyuan
Sajin Bridge
Laoguan Temple
Xushi Temples St.
Lao Wu Xiang
Jiaochangmen St.
Sajin Bridge Ancient Mosque
West Lane North Alley
West Lane East Alley
West Lane West Alley
Hui Kindergarten
WC
West Lane South Alley
Guangming Alley
Western Mosque Alley
West Barn
Hui Hospital
WC
Taohu Alley
Western Mosque
Number 25 Middle Sch.
WC
North Guang Ji Street
Back of Temple Street
Budai Alley
Hui Graveyard
Central Mosque
Big Study St. Mosque
Zhaobi
Little Study Alley
Barley Market Street
Big Study Alley
WC
WC
WC
Yingli Mosque
Cheng Huang Temple Market
West
Big

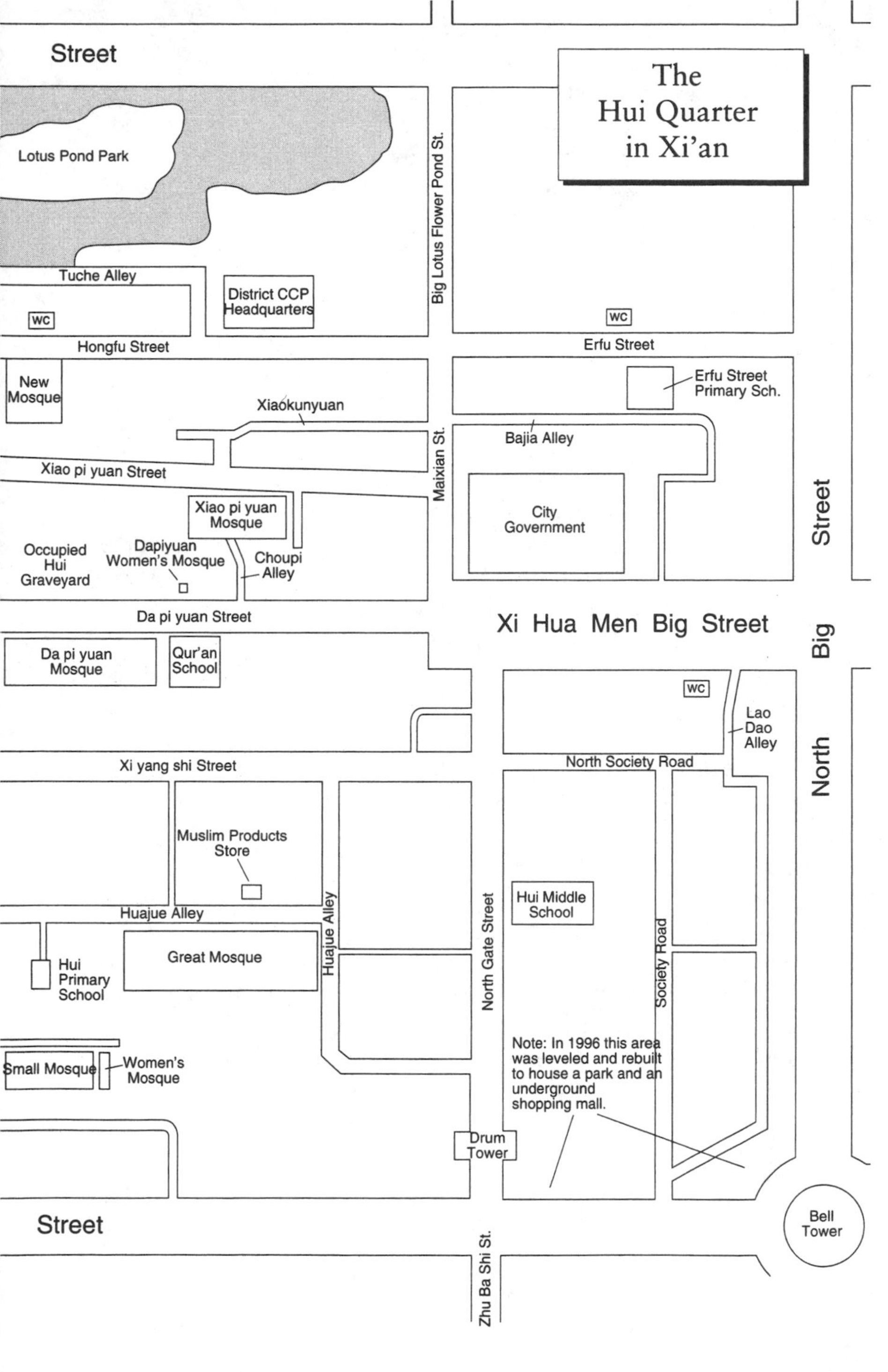

The Hui Quarter in Xi'an
Street
Lotus Pond Park
Tuche Alley
District CCP Headquarters
WC
Hongfu Street
Big Lotus Flower Pond St.
WC
Erfu Street
Erfu Street Primary Sch.
New Mosque
Xiaokunyuan
Bajia Alley
Xiao pi yuan Street
Maixian St.
Xiao pi yuan Mosque
City Government
Occupied Hui Graveyard
Dapiyuan Women's Mosque
Choupi Alley
Street
Da pi yuan Street
Xi Hua Men Big Street
Da pi yuan Mosque
Qur'an School
WC
Lao Dao Alley
Big
Xi yang shi Street
North Society Road
North
Muslim Products Store
Huajue Alley
Huajue Alley
North Gate Street
Hui Middle School
Society Road
Hui Primary School
Great Mosque
Small Mosque
Women's Mosque
Note: In 1996 this area was leveled and rebuilt to house a park and an underground shopping mall.
Drum Tower
Street
Bell Tower
Zhu Ba Shi St.

a family was not building a new home, then they were making additions on an older house that no longer filled its owner's needs (or desires). These houses were known as "multistory houses" (*lou fang*), the same word used to refer to apartment buildings or any multistory building. Apartment buildings were in fact the inspiration for multistory houses, which mimicked their construction in materials and appearance (see Figure 2).

The multistory houses demonstrated residents' desire to modernize and their ingenuity in maximizing available space in the face of government building and land restrictions and families' budget constraints. City and provincial officials informed me that the municipal government restricted the height of buildings within the Xi'an city wall. Buildings near the wall could not surpass it in height, and those located in the city's center had to be lower than the Bell and Drum Towers. For this reason, most buildings in the old city were no more than five stories high. There were a few exceptions to this rule, most notably the sky-high Grand New World Hotel on the edge of the quarter and the Hyatt Hotel; both of these inns were joint foreign-Chinese enterprises built during the reform period. Before 1979, Xi'an had only three or four multistory buildings, all of which had been built by the Soviets. As one resident explained it, "We [Chinese] didn't have the technology to construct tall buildings."

In the quarter, most multistory houses were no higher than three stories. When residents first began reconstructing their houses, most built two-story homes; adding a third story became more common during the 1990s. One man, described by his neighbors as someone who had more money than he knew what to do with, built a private home that towered five stories into the sky. This occasioned some griping, in part because of the ostentation, in part because the taller the homes rose, the less light fell into neighbors' courtyards. A religious student (*mullah*) in his mid-twenties who lived near this man commented sarcastically, "What is he going to do, install an elevator?"

Multistory houses recapitulated the courtyard arrangement of level houses, with four buildings surrounding an open, paved courtyard. They resembled level homes (and differed from apartments) in terms of residential arrangements: multistory homes were filled with relatives rather than unrelated individuals and families. Specific families, usually agnatically related, owned either separate floors of the level houses or separate structures. For example, in one case I knew in 1994, Mingxin, his wife, Xiulan, and their two school-aged sons lived in a two-story house in a courtyard complex shared by two other buildings. These three structures formed a small courtyard that was actually one half of the courtyard of the preexisting level house. On the half where Mingxin and his family lived, the other two multistory houses included Mingxin's brother, his wife, their unmarried daughter, adult son, his wife, their newborn son, Mingxin's patrilineal cousin, his wife, and their two children.

The amount of space that a family possessed related to its stage in a developmental cycle (see Harrell 1982:150–81 for examples of the developmental cycle in Taiwan). When an adult son married, he and his wife were given a separate space to live in, often the upstairs floor of a multistory house. After this couple had children, their per capita living space decreased. During the 1980s and 1990s, the typical response to such pressures was to expand the parents' house. Only in a few cases that I knew of did the adult son and his wife find a separate apartment to live in.

Multistory houses were constructed of steel poles, bricks, and cement, like the apartment buildings that they imitated. They had ample windows, which were plated with glass. Most were heated by mobile or stationary coal stoves or electric space heaters. As with the old level houses, in the new multistory homes the cooking area was often outside in the courtyard.

The courtyards of the quarter were multipurpose sites. In addition to using them for preparing food, families frequently ate there. They also used courtyards for chatting with relatives, neighbors, and business associates; watching children; washing and drying clothing; storing belongings; and hosting ritual events. Courtyards provided an intermediate space between private and public arenas in the quarter, being less private than rooms inside the house and less public than the streets or food stalls. Courtyards could be shut off from the street by closing the tall wooden doors at the entranceway, but few families chose to do so. Leaving the courtyard gates open gave family members greater access to what was happening on the street, be it a gathering of neighbors, the arrival of an itinerant salesperson, or the solicitations of beggars. It likewise made the family more accessible. Visitors to a particular home made their presence known by walking into the courtyard, where some member of the household was likely to be at any given time.

The local wedding ceremony provides an example of how courtyards served as an intermediary space. When a family who lived in either a level house or a multistory house hosted a marriage or some other life cycle commemoration, most of the activities took place in their courtyard. These rites of passage included relatives and a few specifically invited guests, but neighbors, persons who attended the same mosque as the host family, and itinerant beggars freely wandered in as well. Beggars usually ate and departed quickly, but neighbors and fellow worshippers would stay for the festivities. Close relatives and friends also felt free to bring their friends without notifying the hosts.

During a wedding, the host borrowed tables from the local mosque to set up in the family's courtyard. These were used to feed guests and as a setting for Qur'anic recitation by local "men of religion" (*laorenjia*).[9] The *ahong* or religious specialist would later seat himself at one of these tables when he acted as witness to the marriage, a ceremony known as *fan yizabu*.[10] The courtyard was also where ritual teasing of the groom, and later the groom and bride, took place. It was the space where people sat, relaxed, and chatted during the six to twelve hours that most guests stayed at a wedding.

Multistory houses differed significantly from level houses with respect to modern conveniences. Facilities in the multistory houses were as modern as the family wished and could afford. Some multistory houses possessed running water, showers, and toilets. The families I knew who had showers in their homes rarely used them;

they preferred, like the residents of the level houses, to bathe at the mosque. This pattern suggests that families installed bathing facilities less for their functional convenience than for the opportunity to purchase consumer goods that demonstrated their wealth and their awareness of first world standards for sanitary facilities. Families who possessed a shower met an internally defined standard of what a modern house should include—whether they used it or not.

Having even an inadequate shower in the house conveyed a message about the family's economic level and determination to modernize because families had to pay to get running water in their homes. The municipal government had not put together a water system to service the city's private homes. Because the Muslim district contained few state institutions or enterprises, water was less available there than in other parts of Xi'an. In addition, city officials did not adequately maintain the existing water facilities, including faucets, drains, and toilets. Residents constantly complained about poor sanitation. The public toilets were filthy and stank. Ill-designed sewers meant that during rainstorms the streets and alleys of the quarter flooded. The limited number of public water spigots forced some families to haul buckets of water for long distances in order to cook and wash. Even for those who lived close to a faucet, supplying the family with water was a tedious and repetitive chore that was also time consuming, because people frequently needed to wait in line to use the faucets.

Faced with such inadequate provisions, some residents acted privately to improve their water and sanitation facilities. I knew of a few streets in the quarter whose inhabitants had pooled their money to install water pipes for the neighborhood. If the residents of a single block or alley could elicit the agreement of all their neighbors, garner their monetary contribution, and pay the government a substantial fee, they could have pipes installed and part of the city's water supply diverted into their area. The city government refused to service or repair these pipes, however, and in the event of a drought they were the first to have their supply of water cut off—as happened during the summers of 1994 and 1995.

The deteriorating quality of the roads was another sore spot in the quarter. All the roads in the Muslim district were paved with asphalt, because the government did not consider any of its streets important enough to warrant concrete. In June 1996, the poor condition of Dapiyuan Street stimulated a religious specialist at the Dapiyuan Mosque to broker an agreement among the street's businesses to fund repaving. The precedent set by families who banded together to improve water supplies most likely made such a cooperative effort conceivable. However, when I returned to the quarter in 1997 and 1998, the road's condition looked as poor as it had ever been.

In the vast majority of Xi'an's municipal districts, residents lived in high-rise apartments provided by their work units. Work units had been part of the government's efforts to industrialize and modernize China in the years following the communist victory, so they were equipped with employee housing that contained heat, running water, toilet facilities, and cheap cafeterias for employee meals. Although most Xi'an Hui had joined state work units during the 1950s, very few had applied for work unit housing. Residents cited "problems with eating" (*chifan de wenti*) as the key difficulty: as Muslims, they could not eat in the work unit canteens without violating their religious principles, and private cooking was strongly discouraged during the initial push for collectivization (see Watson 1991a for a discussion of collectivized eating in the PRC). Because the newly founded state enterprises had difficulty housing large numbers of employees in a short period, the local government allowed Hui to remain in their private residences. Some Han residents who lived within the city walls had also remained in their own homes.

The government exacerbated the gap between the quarter and other parts of the city during the economic reform period. In the 1980s, the city government began a massive demolition (*chaiqian*) and urban renewal (*jiucheng gaizao*) project that entailed replacing all the old housing and most of the old storefronts with new ones. One local official told me that this project was financed in cooperation with private businesses. Investors had provided the money in exchange for the right to sell or rent space in the edifices they constructed. The new buildings were modernist high rises made of steel, glass, and concrete. They were equipped with running water, central heating, and private toilets and showers. Their upper floors were designated as apartments, and the ground floors were used for business and retail space. At the time of my fieldwork in 1994 and 1995, the Hui quarter was the only part of Xi'an within the city wall that had not been included in the urban renewal project.

A few Hui, only a small percentage of the community, lived in housing provided by their work units. These homes, on the peripheries of the quarter, consisted of apartments in five- or six-story residential complexes. Like the quarter's private multistory houses, they were constructed of steel poles, bricks, and cement. The number of rooms provided for employees in work unit apartments depended on the size of the family being housed, the seniority of the employee, and the relative affluence of the unit in question. Each apartment was equipped with a kitchen, bathroom, running water (at least part of the time, but often not hot running water), central heating, bedrooms, and a common area. The few Hui that I knew who lived in work unit housing shared their flats with the members of their nuclear families.

Some work units, such as the Hui Middle School on the eastern side of the quarter, had only a tiny amount of housing for employees. Instead of providing all the staff with places to live, employers like the Hui Middle School gave most of their employees a small monthly stipend to help defray the cost of renting an apartment elsewhere. Hui Middle School teachers described this stipend as woefully inadequate. However, because most were Han and not native to the quarter, having housing within the Muslim district was not a priority.

As a residential, commercial, and tourist district, the quarter was a uniquely Hui space. It had a long historical association with Chinese Muslims and a lengthy tradition of small-scale enterprise. The CCP had altered the quarter, particularly when the government shut down private commercial activities and restricted religious observance under Mao, but since the 1979 reforms Hui businesses had flourished, religious activities had resumed, and the quarter was recognizably a "nationality district" (*minzu diqu*). The Maoist government had done much to modernize the district by paving roads, building sanitation facilities, and constructing some schools (others had been built by the Nationalist government). Under Deng, the government had promoted modernization by encouraging private enterprise and otherwise seemed to have left the quarter alone. Since the 1980s, residents appeared to be in charge of their own living area. They had opened businesses, rebuilt their homes, and installed running water. They decorated the streets with banners and broadcast religious services into the air. However, even though residents looked like they exercised considerable control over the Muslim district, the state's ideology of progress and modernization had profoundly shaped their perceptions of the quarter and their activities there.

Perceptions of the Quarter

Inhabitants' opinions of the quarter were overwhelmingly unfavorable. Most women and men characterized it as unpleasant, and many blamed the local businesses for what they perceived as its degeneration. For example, on one occasion Lanying, a woman in her mid-40s who had been an accountant but now helped her father sell noodles, was walking with me the few blocks between her marital and natal homes. Suddenly she burst into complaints about how the local stores and restaurants had taken over all the sidewalks and were endangering pedestrians by forcing them to walk in the street amid the car and bicycle traffic. Using the public sidewalk for one's business was illegal, she stated, but one could pay a fee for occupying this space to the government (*zhan ling fei*) and then operate as one pleased. She explained that nowadays, Hui were making so much money from their businesses that they could afford such expenses.[11]

Lanying's comments were echoed on another occasion by a Hui man in his 40s sitting by the curb of the same street that she and I had walked down. "Look at how dirty (*zang*) this place is," he said. He wistfully remembered how, before the reform era, the streets in the Hui quarter were "so clean" (*ke ganjing*). Now that everyone was running a store from the front of their house, he said, the streets were a mess. Gesturing up and down the street with his arm and shaking his head, he sighed about how the quarter had deteriorated during the past ten years.

The first time that I met Chao, a 26-year-old Hui man who was a university graduate, he asked whether I thought the quarter was a good place or a bad one. When I explained that I was there to study the area rather than to evaluate it and that I had never thought about the quarter in those terms, he told me that he thought it was a bad place. Chao explained that the problem was that Hui were only interested in business, and not even large-scale business, but merely small-scale ones that families could set up easily. The petty enterprises of the quarter earned a good deal of money, he said, but instead of investing it in expansion, Hui just used it to buy things and "play" (*wanr*). People in the quarter had low expectations and were easily satisfied if they had a little money, Chao stated. He thought that residents were rough and boorish (*cu*) and had a bad influence upon one another. This was especially true at the schools. Chao said that Hui students were bright (*congming*), but they learned bad habits from one another and had no positive reinforcement at home. He criticized Hui parents for not understanding what studying was (*meiyou xuexi gainian*). Chao summarized his views by stating that all Hui had were "economic demands" (*jingji shang de yaoqiu*); they lacked entirely "cultural demands" (*wenhua shang de yaoqiu*). To prove his point, he remarked that when he was accepted into university in 1987, he was one of only three students from the entire quarter. By contrast, 39 percent of the total number of high school students in Xi'an entered university in 1987 (Xi'an Statistical Bureau 1988:527).

Many residents stated that the family enterprises of the quarter meant that children lacked "a studious environment" (*xuexi huanjing*) at home. A common complaint I heard was that Hui parents were too busy operating businesses to oversee their children's homework. Residents believed that without proper parental guidance, students paid little attention in school, and many parents complained that children who started out highly motivated were quickly led astray by their classmates' bad examples. Upon completing middle school, most students went into private enterprise, thus continuing the cycle.

Even those parents who wanted to help their children felt unable to do so because they had received so little education themselves. The parents of the 1990s school-age children had attended school during the 1960s and 1970s—or more precisely, had not attended school then. During the Cultural Revolution's initial political campaigns (1966–1969), the schools closed and the students were told to go home. When the schools reopened, remembered Mingxin, all the students automatically advanced to higher grades. "We didn't even take a test" (*lian kaoshi dou meiyou kao*), he protested. At this point, the national education system shifted from teaching theoretical and empirical knowledge to experiential wisdom. Students were told to study the workers, farmers, and soldiers (*gong*, *nong*, *bing*) and many were strongly encouraged to go to the countryside to work. Those who went remembered this with bitterness. Conditions were difficult, and the young people could provide little practical assistance and were a drain on rural resources. Speaking of her three years in the countryside (1968–1970), Lanying said, "They [the government] said that the farmers would welcome us. In fact, they didn't want us! And the city didn't want us either." Lanying was allowed to return to Xi'an earlier than most because of illness; others stayed for eight to ten years.

A young Hui man in his twenties whom I met at the Western Mosque also blamed the occupational and educational characteristics of residents for the dirty, chaotic, and crowded condition of the Muslim district. He said the quarter's poor physical condition resulted from its "low-class" residents (*cengci di*). If more Hui were educated, he said, then the quarter would be clean and orderly, "like America." The problem with the quarter, he and most other residents agreed, was that it was a place of "low cultural quality" (*wenhua suzhi di*). On the whole, both Hui and Han residents of Xi'an believed that the Hui "do not care about culture" (*bu zhongshi wenhua*) and that "Hui are good at business, not at culture" (*Huimin shanyu shengyi, bushanyu wenhua*).

The government promoted the stereotype that the Hui *minzu* excelled at business. In texts produced in state-funded research institutions and universities, scholars characterized the Hui race as having inherited a predisposition for commerce from the Arab and Persian merchants who came to China between the seventh and ninth centuries (see, e.g., Lai 1992; Hu 1993). Members of the Hui nationality and the government agreed that Hui had an innate facility for business. Since 1979, Hui have benefited from this supposed racial predisposition by receiving official support and encouragement to take advantage of the state's economic reforms (Gladney 1998a).

Residents' use of the phrase "low cultural quality" and their references to their lack of "culture" were also ideas that they took from government rhetoric. I frequently heard officials in Xi'an utter such remarks. "Culture" and the concept of "cultural quality" came from government propaganda. "Improve [our] cultural quality" (*tigao wenhua suzhi*) was an official slogan frequently written on signs and painted on walls. "Culture" or *wenhua* in this phrase refers to a body of knowledge defined by the government; it is not culture in the sense of "customs and habits" (*fengsu xiguan*). The most basic aspect of *wenhua* was literacy in Chinese (see Harrell 1995b:89). Beyond that, "culture" was what the state produced in its national educational system. The longer a person attended school, the higher his or her "cultural level" (*wenhua shuiping*), and the better equipped he or she was to assist in China's development. Given official emphasis on the four modernizations, students and their parents privileged scientific and technical knowledge (*like*) over "literary" knowledge (*wenke*) (see also Ikels 1996:163–6).

Although "education" was roughly synonymous with "culture" in the slogan, the term *suzhi* ("quality") implied an innate capacity to become educated as well as educational achievement. *Suzhi* was one concept in a national eugenicist discourse concerned with (re)producing citizens of the highest mental and physical quality. "Improving the people's quality" (*tigao renmin suzhi*) was integrally related to the CCP's racial and evolutionary ideas. China's success at modernization depended on the CCP's correctly engineering the "cultural quality" of the PRC's citizens (see Anagnost 1997a). When residents used the state's concept of "low cultural quality" to disparage the quarter, their words implied that its residents possessed inferior intellectual capacities as well as lacked education.

Many elements of the residents' understanding of themselves derived from state ideology. The government was responsible for dividing up China's populace in terms of race, for affixing racial characteristics, and for rating Chinese citizens' "cultural quality." The concept of "culture" that residents used to measure themselves was defined, promoted, and dispensed by the state. However, although residents of the Muslim district accepted that they possessed an innate proclivity for commerce, they did not entirely accept that their "low cultural quality" was an expression of their intrinsic racial inferiority. Rather, they held the government responsible for their lack of "culture," blaming officials for the quarter's poor educational facilities and their own lack of educational opportunities and accusing state officials of neglecting the quarter.

Parents criticized the quarter's schools for providing their children with a poor education. Without exception, every single parent I spoke with told me that the district's schools were inferior. After learning that I taught English at the Hui Middle School, one woman who ran a small noodle restaurant in front of her house and was the mother of two middle-school-aged boys, said that "those who had the means" (*you yidianr banfa de ren*) sent their children outside the quarter to study. "Having the means" meant having the money and personal connections needed to get children into schools located in other parts of the city. Her children both studied at good middle schools in other districts and were doing very well, she was proud to say. In a shop farther down the street, a woman in her 30s explained that the teachers in the quarter's schools were poor (*cha*) and did not care about their students. If she had the money, she said, she would send her son to study outside of the quarter, but the school fees were too high for her to afford it.

Lanying's sister-in-law, the mother of a middle school student, cried to me for an hour one afternoon because she was afraid that her son lacked the grades to get into a high school outside the quarter. Sending him to any of the quarter's schools was useless, she said, for they were "mostly Hui" (*Huimin duo*). It wasn't that the Hui children weren't intelligent, she said, but no one made them work. If her son lacked the challenge of competing with better-educated and more studious Han pupils, he "wouldn't be afraid" and so would not study. Ultimately, she and her husband spent thousands of dollars to send their son to a newly opened private boarding school in the southern part of the city that had computer facilities, high-quality teachers, and strict discipline.

Fathers also censured the district's schools. While I was teaching at the Hui Middle School in 1994, one well-respected local religious specialist withdrew his daughter halfway through the school year. The principal and the girl's teacher were both very unhappy about this because they considered her a good student. When I asked Yingchun about it during a visit to his home, he complained that the teachers at the Hui Middle School were not good, and that the "cultural quality" was low (*wenhua suzhi di*). At his daughter's new school, located in the southern part of the city, she would learn in one year what it took two years to learn at the Hui Middle School, he said.

Perhaps the most direct criticisms of the government came from the Hui Middle School's principal, a Hui from the west side of the Muslim district. Jingxian had an exemplary "cultural quality": she had graduated with a Master's degree in physics from a military academy in Harbin (Manchuria) and would have had a career as a nuclear physicist had not she been faulted for her politically incorrect family background during the Cultural Revolution. Jingxian only agreed to become the Hui Middle School's principal after city officials had gone to extremes to persuade her. When she reached the age of 55, the PRC's mandatory retirement age for women, the local government asked her to continue in her post. She refused. Jingxian told me that since she had passed the official retirement age, she had the power to choose what she would do. She felt that she had received inadequate support and resources from the municipal government while she was principal. Official rhetoric about education had not been backed up by monetary contributions, nor did officials assist her in obtaining and retaining the teaching and administrative staff that she wanted. Jingxian believed that she had had a positive effect on the Hui Middle School (an opinion that many residents of the quarter shared with her), but it was too much of a struggle without the government's assistance.

The parents of 1990s school-age children also blamed the government for their own low levels of education. Many described themselves as "good students" (*hao xuesheng*) who had "loved to study" (*ai xuexi*) but were denied the opportunity to attend school because of the Cultural Revolution. When the political turmoil subsided and the government reinstituted the school entrance examination system, the Hui I knew thought it futile to attempt to re-enter school. Feeling too old and too far behind to compete, they placed their hopes upon their younger siblings and their children.

Education was not the only area in which Xi'an Hui faulted the government for inadequate attention. Residents were eager for the government to improve the quarter's public facilities, particularly water supply, sanitation, and roads. They were also aware that city officials, in order to encourage all forms of commercial activity, chose not to enforce policies about sidewalk use, construction, and peddling merchandise. Although residents knew that their prosperity was the result of Deng's emphasis on marketization and privatization, they also saw the government's drive for economic expansion as drawing attention away from routine city maintenance. Some residents waxed nostalgic about the neat, orderly appearance of the Muslim district under Mao, even as they described themselves as "very poor" before the economic reforms.

Do Actions Speak Louder than Words?

Despite their disparaging remarks, most residents were strongly attached to the quarter. Many informed me proudly that their families had lived there for hundreds of years. Very few chose to leave, including those who were wealthy enough to purchase private apartments in the newly rebuilt parts of Xi'an or those whose work units provided them with relatively inexpensive opportunities to buy housing. Those Hui who did move out generally did not sell their property in the quarter. Rather, when these "expatriate" Hui needed to celebrate a life cycle ritual, they returned to the "old home" to host it. Pragmatic concerns, such as having elderly, immobile relatives who lived in the quarter, motivated these decisions in part, but such actions also suggest that Hui felt they belonged in the quarter and considered it their home.

One of the more striking manifestations of residents' attachment to the quarter could be found at the Hui cemetery. Islamic law dictates that Muslims must be buried and prescribes a set of elaborate mortuary practices. Before 1949, Xi'an Hui buried their dead in the three graveyards located in the quarter. Because the PRC government found the Hui burial practices and cemeteries chaotic, unsanitary, and unsightly, officials took control of the cemeteries during the 1950s (Han and Liu 1987:175). Initially, some Hui ignored the government's efforts to regulate burials and continued to bury their dead in the original cemeteries; during the Cultural Revolution, however, the city leveled two of the quarter's cemeteries and built work units on top of them, thus forcing residents to use the government's graveyards (these two cemeteries had still not been recovered by 1998, although I was told that the mosques and the government were discussing the matter). By the early 1970s, those two cemeteries no longer had space for graves, so the government found a new site, Hongqing. Hongqing was located about an hour outside Xi'an in a Han agrarian community. All Hui from the city, including those not resident in the quarter, buried their dead there.

After a resident of the quarter died and was buried, the bereaved family marked where their deceased relative lay by erecting a tombstone one year after the death. On the front, the tombstone was inscribed with the name of the dead, his or her position in the family (for example, "loving mother"), and his or her descendants. Most were also adorned with a picture of a mosque or some Arabic calligraphy (see Figure 4). When I visited Hongqing, I also noticed that inscribed on the back of the newer stones was the deceased's address (for example, 101 West Sheep Market Street). The practice was clearly a recent one. Older tombstones were blank on the back (this was also true of the tombstones in the old cemeteries in the quarter).

During a visit to Hongqing for a funeral, a friend and I walked down the narrow paths between rows and rows of stones. He pointed out the addresses to me, saying "This Hui was from West Sheep Market Street, and this one was from North Court Gate. But that Hui over there was a Henan Hui, look, he lived over by the railroad station." For anyone familiar with the quarter, each mention of an address revealed a great deal about the deceased. The Hui from West Sheep Market Street most likely belonged to the Great Mosque, as did the Hui from North Court Gate. The former probably lived in a multistory house, and the latter surely lived in a level house: West Sheep Market Street was the home of many affluent petty entrepreneurs, but North Court Gate contained a number of families who were not engaged in private business and were less wealthy, and so had more of the older residences. Both of these people were almost certainly from families that had lived in the quarter for a long time, because their homes were located in its oldest, most densely populated part. In contrast, the Hui who lived near the railroad station was "an outsider" (*wailai de*) and a relatively recent arrival in Xi'an; his address showed that he did not belong to the Xi'an Hui community but rather was a member of a Hui neighborhood established for a mere 50 years. Walking through the cemetery looking at the

FIGURE 4. Tombstones adorned with Arabic calligraphy and mosque images.

addresses on the tombstones, Hui could instantly tell who was from the quarter and who was not, who was from an established Xi'an Hui family and who was not. They gained a sense of who had attended which mosque, engaged in what type of business, and lived in what kind of residence.

The street addresses that Hui carved on their tombstones located them socially and geographically. The emergence of this practice was no doubt linked to the government's removal of the Hui cemetery to a location far outside the city amid Han farmers: Hui began writing the addresses of the dead on the back of their tombstones to link them to their homes and their proper contexts. The act of making public the deceased's address suggests that residents believed that a person's identity was related not only to who their kin were but also to where he or she was from. The inscriptions demonstrate their attachment to the quarter, their home.

Hui also identified strongly with the quarter when they spoke of it. Though they had negative feelings, they also said that it was "easier to be Hui" there, to cite the words of one young female resident. Living in the quarter was intimately associated with being Hui. Many residents pointed out that the Hui who moved outside the quarter quickly assumed Han habits like drinking alcohol and eating pork and stopped coming to the mosques. The Muslim district was a "more convenient" place to live if you were Hui, one middle-aged woman told me. "Other places have fewer Hui." Though Hui criticized the quarter for its chaotic appearance and the low-class nature of its inhabitants, they also regarded it as the best place in Xi'an to live a Hui lifestyle. Only in the quarter could Hui eat without anxiety, attend the mosque with ease, find suitable marriage partners, host proper life cycle rituals, and associate with neighbors who shared their predispositions.

Institutionalization of Hui Inferiority

The ambivalence that residents expressed about living in the quarter was mirrored by the opinions of Chinese officials. Officials treated the quarter as the center of Hui activities, locating a number of government institutions concerning "nationality affairs" and hosting most official events related to Islam there. They also used the phrase "low cultural quality" (*wenhua suzhi di*) in reference to the quarter. In the eyes of many Han officials with whom I spoke, however, the "low cultural quality" was a racial trait, as characteristic of the Hui as their success at business. The state was ideologically committed to viewing the Hui as an evolutionarily backward race; this led officials to erect institutions and create policies that perpetuated a set of variables that were officially viewed as antithetical to modernization.

One of the most important ways that officials institutionalized the Hui race's inferiority was by ensuring that Hui "nationality" practices continued, even while the government castigated them as "feudal," "backward," and "superstitious" (see MacInnis 1989: 7–36 for examples of this rhetoric). The Hui also received a number of affirmative action–style perquisites because of their developmental backwardness. On the national level, the state permitted Hui to have two children, exempted them from practicing cremation, allowed them to enter college with lower exam scores, and gave them disproportionately high political representation (Gladney 1991:161–2, 219–20). In Shaanxi, the provincial government provided Xi'an Hui with graveyards to facilitate Islamic burial practices, allowed Hui to engage in expensive mosque renovation projects (even providing funds in the case of the Great Mosque), and permitted them to construct new religious edifices while refusing analogous requests from Han religious practitioners (namely Buddhists and Christians). The government also defined "nationality holidays" for the Hui during which Hui were entitled to extra days off from work and school, despite the fact that these holidays create bureaucratic hassles because their dates change each year.[12] In Xi'an, the city government did not enforce municipal policies about uses of public space but allowed Hui to use the sidewalks and streets for business and construction materials. Officials did not tax the quarter's private businesses; residents who told me about this said simply, "No one comes to collect." The government made no attempt to license or regulate the many peddlers who worked the district. Officials justified this special treatment by claiming that the Hui were "sensitive" (*mingan*) and "troublesome" (*naoshi*) and required careful handling. The assumption was that residents of the quarter were less capable of modernizing than the Han.

Demolition and Reconstruction

During the 1990s, the Xi'an municipal government took action to change the city's image. In accordance with the national injunction to modernize, officials decided to tear down the old residential and commercial buildings in the city, widen the streets, and construct new, multistory edifices (see Lao, Zhao, and Luo 1993 for an official account). Although the government contracted out most of the work to private companies, officials controlled the project planning and organization, including the decision about which parts of the city would be demolished first. The government also monitored the rebuilding, at least to the extent of prohibiting the construction of buildings taller than five stories in the vicinity of the historic Ming-dynasty city wall. Officials were also in charge of notifying residents of eviction and compensating those who owned private houses or apartments; renters were simply told to leave. All the inhabitants of areas to be rebuilt were moved to temporary housing in the suburbs. The government stated that former residents could move back to the site of their previous homes, but few were able to do so when the construction was completed. The compensation that home owners had received was far less than the cost of the new "modern" apartments. Bluntly put, the project was a de facto gentrification scheme.

When I visited Xi'an during the summer of 1998, the demolition and reconstruction of the area within the city wall was almost completed—except for the quarter. That summer, after more than three years of rumors, officials announced that they would begin demolishing Barley Market Street, a Hui commercial area where officials wanted to build a major traffic artery. Government propaganda blared morning and night over loudspeakers on the street, though the recording was so muddy that residents could not make out what it said. During that summer, "the nation" (*guojia*), as some residents called the government, was trying to arrange meetings with all the property owners on Barley Market Street. The few state-owned buildings had already been evacuated.

Several factors had caused officials to move slowly in reconstructing the Muslim district. Residents said that the predominantly Han government was afraid to begin work on the quarter because it was home to members of a minority nationality. The officials I spoke with made comments that supported this view when they explained the delay by calling the Hui "sensitive" (*mingan*) and the situation "complicated" (*fuza*). According to Liangxun, the vice-director of the provincial Religion and Nationality Affairs Commission, the main reason that the government had been slow to implement urban renewal in the quarter was that officials had had difficulty finding an investor. The quarter was more densely populated than other parts of Xi'an, which made the rebuilding project less profitable. There would be less excess space to rent or sell once residents had been re-housed; the government's own restrictions on building height exacerbated this problem.

Officials had also wanted to find a Hui investor. Barley Market Street, where the government planned to begin, was the quarter's most densely populated commercial district. During the mid-1980s the state had selected this street as the "Hui food and drink street" (*Huimin yinshi jie*) and erected "Islamic decor" to denote this (see Figure 5). The logic behind procuring a Hui investor was twofold: first, a Hui would presumably be interested in improving local conditions, and second, if the reconstruction project was backed by a Hui, it would defuse potential conflicts between the Hui residents and the predominantly Han state.

Though officials failed to find a Hui investor, by 1998 they had located a businessman from the Muslim district who agreed to represent the Beijing company that would fund the renovation. Residents characterized this man as a local boy made good. He had opened a private construction firm as soon as the economic reforms began and made a killing on a hydraulic invention that powered

FIGURE 5. The "Hui food and drink street" gate erected by the local government on Barley Market Street.

water to the upper floors of the many multistory buildings that had sprung up during the 1980s. This invention was obsolete, but the man's social status was firmly established. The government had offered him an official job after he had struck it rich.

Liangxun gave other reasons for the delays. He noted that a large percentage of the quarter's inhabitants engaged in private enterprise. This made it more difficult for the government to move them. Persons employed by work units were more subject to bureaucratic control and had to accept the accommodations that their work units provided. The quarter's residents owned their own homes and businesses and did not depend on the government for income; this made the task of dislodging them more difficult. Residents were unwilling to leave the quarter, but work could not begin until Barley Market Street's inhabitants had been moved out. Other unresolved concerns included the fate of the district's ten mosques, and how the government would ensure the community's religious needs were met during the temporary re-housing and after the reconstruction. Liangxun said that some government leaders had considered creating an alternative "minority nationality district" (*shaoshu minzu diqu*), but the idea had received little support. In 1997, another factor emerged to slow the process: a Hui entrepreneur and resident of the quarter had died during a conflict with some low-level government employees, and the state and local residents disagreed over how the case should be handled. The state's representatives who were at fault were Han. Manslaughter in China merits the death penalty, and the general opinion in the quarter was that the men should be executed. Government officials apparently disagreed: more than a year and a half after the event took place, the men had not been sentenced.

The government's hesitation about renovating the quarter led to some striking visual incongruities. For example, a major four-lane road that passed in front of the provincial and city government complexes stopped abruptly at the edge of the quarter, degenerating into tiny alleyways and crowded houses. In general, the quarter possessed an informal, ragged appearance that contrasted sharply with the orderly, planned look of most other parts of Xi'an.

When I first heard about the reconstruction project in 1994, the Hui with whom I discussed the matter were quite unconcerned. It was only in April 1995, when the city declared it would begin widening Barley Market Street before the end of the year (which did not occur), that people I knew began to talk as if the reconstruction might take place. When I revisited the quarter in 1997 and 1998, feelings had intensified, and not just on Barley Market Street. To the east, the government had leveled all the housing and buildings adjacent to the quarter and built a public garden, roller-skating rink, and underground shopping mall. Residents said that the government had targeted that area, located between the city's Bell and Drum Towers, to make it more attractive to tourists. The Muslim district was abuzz with rumors that the houses near the Great Mosque would be leveled next, so that all three of these national historic sites would be exposed to view. Previously, the two towers, like the Great Mosque, had been surrounded by an unsightly conglomeration of homes, stores, and food stalls.

Residents knew that the proposed reconstruction would bring changes, yet few worried that the new streets and apartments might decrease the quarter's spaces for collective gatherings. Xi'an Hui discussed such topics only in response to my prodding; the two biggest concerns of Barley Market Street residents were the amount of compensation they would receive and what spaces they would be allocated once the street was rebuilt. When I asked the butcher Mingxin and his wife, who lived near the Great Mosque, what they thought of the reconstruction in 1996, they responded by talking about the improvements that the project would bring. When I persisted in my questions about the plan's effects, Mingxin began to speculate on how the reconstruction might affect the area's businesses. He pointed out that now most families ran their enterprises out of their homes and wondered aloud how would it be possible to run an eatery or a butchery from the third floor of an apartment building. It occurred to him that if a family were producing food to sell in their apartment, their neighbors might complain about the heat from the kitchen. Even more important, he felt, was that such businesses needed to be at street level. As he thought about the project, he wondered how the government would accommodate the large number of Hui who depended on private entrepreneurship for their livelihood.

Inhabitants of the area near the Great Mosque were slow to consider the fact that the apartments would provide no place to conduct ritual celebrations. Social births or *manyue* (a ritual that celebrated an infant's having lived to the age of one month), circumcisions, engagements, weddings, funerals, and mourning rituals were all held in the courtyards of private homes. If residents all lived in apartments, there would be no courtyards and therefore no place for preparing food, hosting guests, or engaging in collective Qur'anic recitation. The quarter would lose its collective spaces. During 1996, I heard that some residents had proposed that the quarter's apartment complexes be equipped with large common rooms containing tables and chairs that could be used for Hui rituals. The government had made no definite response, and residents allowed the issue to drop. The apathetic pursuit of this option probably arose from the lack of appeal it had. The only Muslim district apartment complex that I knew that had such a room was a dismal failure. None of the building's residents used it to host ritual events. In 1996, the sister of a woman who lived there tried to rent it for her daughter's wedding. She was prevented from doing so because the room was being used for storage. When I visited this apartment complex in June 1997, the room was still filled with oil drums and large cans.

The government's plans would cause other aspects of local life to change as well, though my acquaintances and friends did not discuss this. After the level and multistory houses had been torn down, extended families would no longer be able to live together. Residents would be assigned apartments by the government and would not control where they, their relatives, or their neighbors lived. The quarter's alleys and doorsteps, and many of the places to sit on the sidewalks (where eateries and shops put stools and tables), would vanish, replaced by rows of institutional apartment buildings. Even if the mosques were left untouched—an unlikely possibility—many important spaces for socializing would disappear.

During a lunch meeting in June 1997, Liangxun pointed out

another potential change that would have profound implications for the quarter. The new high-rise apartment buildings would provide living space for more families than was currently available. This meant that the reconstruction was likely to bring an influx of Han into the quarter. Liangxun did not elaborate on the difficulties that this might cause, but the outcome was clear enough. The presence of large numbers of Han would change the quarter's "racial" composition and affect residents' ability to maintain Islamic purity (see Chapters 4 and 5 for a discussion of Islamic purity with particular reference to dietary practices). An influx of Han might cause conflicts over the celebration of religious rituals and holidays as Han syncretism encountered Islamic monotheism in a close setting. Another question was the effect that a more integrated population would have on Hui marriage patterns: would most Hui continue to marry Hui if their neighbors were Han?

Despite all this, the Hui that I talked to were in favor of urban renewal. Many women and men thought that the new apartments would improve their individual quality of life and that of the community as a whole. No one seemed worried about the fate of the mosques, the possible break-up of the community into temporary housing for a year or longer, or the likelihood that residents would be unable to return to the Muslim district. Instead, Hui pointed to the advantages of living in apartments, which ranged from better facilities to the apartments' potential for raising the "cultural quality" of the quarter's residents.

Reactions to the Reconstruction Project

Residents enthusiastically supported reconstruction. They were convinced that they would continue to live on or near the site of their original homes, even though very few people who had been moved out of other parts of the city had managed to return to their former neighborhoods. Most Hui believed, as the 80-year-old religious specialist Jishu stated, that the government would provide: the state would rebuild the mosques, houses, and shops that it tore down and return such property to its rightful owners.

Guangliang, a man in his 40s who lived in the quarter and was employed by a work unit in the southern part of the city, told me that his entire family was looking forward to the demolition and reconstruction of the quarter. This was in spite of the fact that he had only finished building a two-story home to replace his "level house" in 1994. Guangliang related his eagerness for reconstruction to the appearance of the Muslim district, which he thought looked dreadful. "The entire city has been planned" (*zhengge chengshi dou guihua le*), he said, and the Muslim district could not be left out. Guangliang pointed to the condition of the quarter's roads, which were so poor that he could hardly ride his bike down the street, as evidence of the need for urban renewal. He believed that the many foreign tourists who visited the quarter received a bad impression because of the area's disorderly appearance. Guangliang said that he hoped that ultimately the quarter and all of Xi'an would look like Beijing, the nation's capital and one of the eastern cities that the national government held up as a model for development.

Mingxin, the butcher who speculated about the fate of the quarter's private businesses, also looked favorably on the reconstruction. He indicated the quarter's poor sanitation facilities as a major incentive to rebuild. The street where he lived even lacked a place to deposit garbage (*lajitai*), he said. His house was far away from the public toilet, and the drains on his street flooded every time it rained. Government officials had simply ignored these problems, but when the new apartments were built the city would provide better, more modern facilities.

Huiling was a woman in her late 40s who lived with her husband, two adult daughters, and adolescent son in a small compound that they shared with her husband's brother's family. The first time that I visited her, I noticed that her kitchen roof was constructed of two pieces of thick plastic board and had a large gap in the center. Seeing my gaze, Huiling said, "This old house is falling apart, but soon our family will move to a new apartment." Because she worked for a tiny local branch of the district government, one of the quarter's two "Affairs Offices" (*Banshichu*), she, unlike most residents, knew where her new apartment would be: only a few blocks east of her current home, immediately behind the government office where she worked.

Huiling told me that she liked apartment buildings and was looking forward to moving. "Apartment buildings are much better than level houses," her co-resident sister-in-law agreed (*loufang bi pingfang hao*). This woman's daughter lived in an apartment building, and her visits there had convinced her that apartments were much cleaner. Huiling concurred, remarking that she really hated having to sweep the family's courtyard, which was constantly dirtied by wind-blown dust and trash.

Other women reiterated the favorable comments that Huiling and her sister-in-law made about the projected apartments. For example, 26-year-old Xijuan, whose family sold "little eats," said that when her family was assigned an apartment they would have more space, a separate kitchen, running water, and a bathroom. At that time her mother and sister shared a single room, hauled water from the public faucet down the street, and used the public toilets. Her family wanted their part of the quarter to be torn down first, she said. I asked her whether she too was looking forward to the proposed reconstruction. Xijuan lived with her husband's family in a well-equipped, three-story private home. Xijuan replied matter-of-factly that she thought living in an apartment building would be much the same as living in her marital residence.

Yue, Liangxun's 26-year-old daughter who had graduated from high school and college, also welcomed the proposed reconstruction. She believed that building apartment complexes in the quarter would improve its quality by separating the residents. The Hui of the quarter were "a little too united" (*you yidianr tai tuanjie le*), she said. She believed that residents' closeness circumscribed their educational and occupational horizons, and she thought that dividing the Hui into apartments would cause them to take education more seriously, develop higher ambitions, and explore other careers besides commerce. In other words, if the government modernized the Muslim district's housing, Hui would advance beyond their current state of backwardness.

Yue was not alone in seeing the quarter as too close. Hui women of varying ages and lifestyles spoke to me with embarrassment and frustration about the Muslim district's narrowness. "Our Hui quarter is just these few streets" (*women Huiminfang jiu shi neme ji xiang*), some said. Such comments generally expressed the speaker's sense of confinement and restriction. Some women who uttered this statement felt that the quarter circumscribed their marriage and occupational choices. They thought that living in the Muslim district prevented them from finding husbands with "high cultural quality" and meant that they worked in petty commerce and low-level service jobs. Yan, a young woman in her mid-twenties who sold dumplings at her family's eatery, summed up the situation by saying, "Hui people love to stay at home; they don't like to go out. This prevents us from doing real business" (*Huimin ai shou jia, bu ai chuqu. Bu gan shiye*).

Rebuilding

While the Hui community eagerly anticipated the results of the government's plan, they did not wait passively for the renewal to happen. "Construction in the quarter goes on throughout all four seasons" (*fangshang yinian siji dou you gai fang*), locals remarked. At a time when residents knew that their dwellings would soon be demolished, they continued to start new private rebuilding projects.

One reason that Hui engaged in private reconstruction was to improve their standards of living in the short term. No one knew when the government's project would really take effect; if residents really wanted to modernize then their most certain solution was to take matters into their own hands. Residents who built new multistory houses demonstrated publicly their economic success: they could afford to pay the workers' salaries, the costs of building materials, and the government fees and fines for private construction. The height of the multistory homes, the way that they loosely imitated apartments and sky scrapers, and the "modern" goods with which residents filled them also indicated their owners' successful participation in the modern world. However, immediate modernization was not the only reason that Hui expanded their dwellings. They also rebuilt in response to the government's development program in order to obtain larger apartments when their housing was reassigned.

The government's policy of providing new housing on the basis of the size of a family's previous home was common knowledge all over Xi'an. The policy was known as "take one, give one" (*chen yi huan yi*): one square foot of space in the old house would be exchanged for one square foot of space in the new. When, early in 1995, rumors spread that the city government would soon widen Barley Market Street, Mingjie and his family quickly closed the small restaurant that they owned there. Aifeng (Mingjie's wife) explained to me that if they could finish building a bigger restaurant before the stores and restaurants along Barley Market Street were demolished to make space for the wider street, the city would have to give them a bigger storefront when the project was finished. A few weeks after construction on his new, three-story restaurant began (the upper stories of which later became his son's residence and the sleeping quarters for hired employees), Mingjie took me over to look at the site. Walking down Barley Market Street, he pointed to three neighboring shops whose doors were closed. "Their owners decided to expand too," he told me.

The Barley Market Street storekeepers were not the only residents to begin construction upon hearing of the government's plans. One March afternoon when I visited the Western Mosque, also located on Barley Market Street, I saw a huge pile of fresh lumber lying in the courtyard. Xiye, a woman in her mid-40s who sold tickets for the mosque's showers, told me that the mosque owned some level houses farther up the street that it had been renting to private families and had decided to replace these houses with multistory ones.[13] When I asked why, Xiye said simply that it was related to the government's decision to widen the street. In other words, the mosque, like the other property owners, expanded to increase the amount of space that the government would allocate it after the street-widening was finished.

Urban Renewal, Modernization, and Race

The government presented its urban renewal project as a plan to improve and develop the city. Reconstruction was one tactic the government adopted to modernize. The results it produced were more than cosmetic. The new apartment complexes increased the state's ability to regulate and survey Xi'an's urban neighborhoods, including the Muslim district. Through its rehousing project, the government determined who lived together, whether or not families or extended families were co-resident, and whether neighbors remained neighbors. When the quarter was renovated, officials would also determine the degree to which it remained a primarily Hui area. State control over religious activity would also increase because the reconstruction affected who would reside near the mosque, who lived farther away, and where the mosques were located relative to worshippers. Where officials positioned Hui in the new apartments would strongly influence who engaged in private enterprise. Certain types of businesses and, even more likely, certain entrepreneurs who had cultivated good relations with the government would be rewarded with choice locations. Others would find their ability to run a private business curtailed when they received housing that could not easily be transformed into commercial space. Urban renewal enhanced the government's capacity to shape the quarter and its residents.

In a book about a historic Greek town on the island of Crete, Michael Herzfeld explores the negotiations that occurred between the Greek state, in the guise of the national historical commission that wanted to preserve the European domestic architecture and thus the European history of the town of Rethemnos, and the individual householders in the city, who resented the government's interference in how they used their homes (1991). The Greek state privileged a certain type of identity that contributed to Greece's modern image and furthered its goals of integration in the European community. Officials devalued those architectural forms that did not conform to these desired representations, such as those that recalled the area's Turkish occupation. In his monograph, Herzfeld probes the uneasy relationship between the state, which wanted the householders to assist officials in their efforts to demonstrate that Crete belonged in Europe and Greece in the European Community, and the householders who strategized to control their own living space and meet their own needs.

Rethemnos and the quarter show similar kinds of interactions between state and citizen. In both cases, officials and locals shared the conviction that modernization was a desirable goal. The need for development and progress was not questioned; where citizen and state differed were in their assessment of how to achieve such ends.

From the state's perspective, the Hui race were innately inferior to the Han. The Hui possessed "feudal" customs and habits and had "low cultural quality." Officials used phrases to describe residents of the quarter that were reminiscent of the pre-1949 Chinese image of Muslims as barbarians: the Hui were "sensitive," liable to "make trouble," and required careful treatment. The Hui *minzu*'s level of civilization was so inadequate that officials did not expect residents to behave rationally or to cooperate in the state's plans for modernization. These ideas about the Hui affected government policy.

As we have seen in this chapter, the state institutionalized traits that it interpreted as signs of Hui backwardness. The government created "nationality holidays" and saw that they were commemorated. The schools of the quarter, which residents criticized for being inferior to the schools of other districts, had been designated by officials as "nationality schools," thus linking poor educational outcomes to racial identification. When it came to urban renewal, officials found a Hui to deal with the Hui, which reinforced the notion that residents were not rational and could only deal with one of their "own kind." When officials refrained from enforcing government rules and regulations concerning taxes, use of public space, and construction in the quarter, they encouraged the Hui to behave in ways that confirmed official stereotypes of them as "mercantile" and as intemperate, unreasonable, uneducated, and incapable of modernization without state assistance. The former stereotype aided the government's economic agenda (Gladney 1998a), and the latter confirmed the official evolutionary hierarchy, bolstered a sense of Han superiority, and provided a rationale for government intervention in the quarter.

Residents of the quarter disagreed with the government on several counts. Although they had internalized the discourse of "cultural quality," Xi'an Hui did not accept their "low cultural quality" simply as a racial trait. Residents saw themselves and their children as intelligent but denied the opportunities and environment that they needed to excel. They faulted the state for improperly overseeing the quarter's roads and public works, neglecting the district's school facilities and teachers, and depriving a generation of Hui (the parents of the 1990s schoolchildren) the chance to "raise their cultural quality." Residents were also aware of how officials had encouraged their commercial activities and the state's complicity in the "decline" of the quarter's physical environment.

Xi'an Hui also did not accept that modernization was contingent on the state. They took steps to modernize their own homes, businesses, and mosques when the government failed to act (see Chapter 3 for more on the district's mosques). Residents built their own homes, furnished them with modern goods, and privately made arrangements to have running water and better roads so that they could have first world standards of living. Some tried to give their children higher-quality educations by sending them to better-equipped schools outside of the quarter. They imagined that the quarter could become "like America" and "like Beijing." Through the consumer practices that they undertook to improve their homes and district, residents showed themselves to be better than the government's classification of them stated and capable of modernizing even without the government.

Chapter Three

MOSQUES, QUR'ANIC EDUCATION, AND ARABIZATION

A Tale of Two Mosques

Early in 1994, construction began on a new mosque on the quarter's northern perimeter. Appropriately called the New Mosque, this edifice was being built to house the observances of a group of Muslims who had parted ways with the Yingli Mosque congregation. Disagreements over proper religious practice had created conflict among worshippers at the Yingli Mosque and caused the congregation to divide. A splinter group had hastily established a mosque in a small building on the opposite side of the quarter in 1988. This temporary space was too small and inadequately equipped for long-term use, so the new congregation had petitioned the government for permission to construct a better, more permanent building. The new New Mosque would expand the group's space fourfold and improve their facilities for worship, Islamic education, and other religious activities.

As the months passed and construction proceeded, the New Mosque took shape (see Figure 6). By June 1994, its enormous green dome had risen above many of the surrounding buildings and was visible a block away (the multistory private homes on nearby streets impaired further visibility). Upon entering the mosque courtyard (the New Mosque, like the other mosques in the quarter, consisted of not merely a central worship hall, but also a small courtyard that would eventually be flanked by side buildings), the viewer was confronted by pristine white tiles framing windows in the shape of Moorish arches. Dominating this vision was the massive onion dome in the center of the worship hall's roof, which totally eclipsed the four small white domes that encircled it. Inside, the mosque hall was sparsely decorated: a plain carpet covered the floor, and unadorned wood covered the wall where the *mihrab* (Arabic), the niche that marks the direction of Mecca, was located. The sole ornaments in the room were a large clock on the wall and a *minbar* (Arabic), a raised platform with stairs at its front, made from dark, highly polished wood. Both of these items were functional. The clock marked the times of worship, and religious specialists stood upon the minbar when they gave the exhortation at worship services.[1]

When I left the quarter in August 1995, the New Mosque's congregation had been using their new worship hall for almost a year. Construction on the other mosque buildings had yet to be completed; one reason for the delay was the mosque management committee's failure to convince the family living immediately to the west of the mosque to move. Although the government had designated the land that this family's house was built on for the New Mosque, its use was contingent upon the mosque management committee's ability to persuade the family who lived there to leave, a process that entailed finding the family acceptable housing elsewhere. This family was still living in their original home when I returned to the quarter in June 1998, and the New Mosque's construction plans had not been fully completed. Members of the mosque congregation attributed their difficulty in relocating this family to the fact that the family was Han. "If they were Hui," one man commented to me, "then this business would have been taken care of long ago." Despite this problem, by August 1995 the New Mosque included a worship hall, a two-story ablutions room on its eastern side, and a three-story gatehouse at its entrance. The windows, exterior walls, and rooftops of these subsidiary buildings echoed the white tiles, Moorish arches, and onion domes of the main hall. Although these buildings obstructed the view of the mosque hall from the street, they enabled the New Mosque congregation to hold Qur'anic study classes on the premises, wash at

FIGURE 6. Construction of the New Mosque.

the mosque before worship, and provide their religious specialist or *ahong* with rooms for rest and study in the mosque.[2]

At the Small Mosque located a few blocks away, construction had finished months earlier. The Small Mosque had originally been built during the mid-fourteenth century, but it was severely damaged during China's radical socialist period. After the CCP initiated a campaign for "religious reform" (*zongjiao gaige*) in 1958, the Small Mosque had been used as an entertainment hall (*yuletang*). During 1967 and 1968, Red Guards physically attacked the Small Mosque as a remnant of the "old culture" (*jiu wenhua*) and "feudal superstition" (*fengjian mixin*)—two manifestations of Chinese "backwardness" that Mao had called on all Chinese citizens to eradicate. Si, a man who worked at the Small Mosque, showed me photographs that had been taken there in 1984, before reconstruction began. The mosque was unrecognizable. The roof of the worship hall was caved in on one side, and its supporting pillars were chopped to pieces. Roof tiles had been torn off and brickwork hacked out of the walls. The courtyard was filled with rubble: bits of wood, broken bricks and tiles, and dirt. Nevertheless, Si and the elderly ahong Jishu agreed that compared to some, the Small Mosque had weathered the Cultural Revolution relatively unscathed. Other mosques had been totally demolished, razed to the ground.

By March 1995, the Small Mosque was a pleasure to behold. Its mosque hall had been restored to its original shape, which roughly resembled a rectangle joined to a square, and topped by a steeply slanted tiled roof. Elaborate carvings ornamented the thick blue-green tiles near the roof's edges, and small figurines in the shape of fantastic animals stood on the roof's spine. The large overhanging eaves were supported by ornate brackets, elaborately and colorfully painted with flowers and small landscapes. Inside the hall, attention was focused on the mihrab at the center of the back wall, strikingly painted with golden Arabic calligraphy and a colorful geometric design and lit by an enormous crystal chandelier (see Figure 7). The ceilings were covered with small square

FIGURE 7. Inside the worship hall of the Small Mosque.

paintings of fruits and flowers, reminiscent of Ming-dynasty art motifs.

The Small Mosque complex emulated the courtyard (*siheyuan*) style found in most Chinese architecture from the late-imperial period. Like the worship hall, the side buildings were characterized by colorfully painted woodwork and glazed tile roofs. Gray stone walls and an elaborate roofed gate enclosed the courtyard. On the stone walls, two large friezes, both landscapes, caught the eye. One was clearly an imaginative representation of Mecca, with the Ka'aba at its center surrounded by pagodas and rolling hills.[3]

Construction at the Small and the New mosques, and at seven of the eight other mosques in the quarter, had been funded entirely by local residents. The Great Mosque was the only one that had received government assistance for rebuilding, because it was officially recognized as a national historic site. Reconstruction and restoration at most of the mosques had begun in the mid-1980s, after the government had evicted the factories, schools, and other work units that had occupied them during the Cultural Revolution. When I arrived in Xi'an in January 1994, most of the quarter's ten mosques had already been restored. Six had been rebuilt in a "traditional" (*chuantong*) style similar to that of the Small Mosque (see Figure 8). Two had been constructed in the "Arabic" (*alabo de*) style of the New Mosque. The remaining two mosques contained stylistic elements that resembled both the New Mosque and the Small Mosque architecture (see Figure 9). Both of these stylistically syncretic mosques had originally been built in the first half of the twentieth century, as a result of conflicts that occurred when two Islamic reform movements arrived in the quarter.

The architectural styles of the New Mosque and Small Mosque illustrate a fundamental issue that concerned residents of the quarter: how should one be a Muslim? The Arabic style of the New Mosque, encapsulated by its green onion dome and white-tiled exterior, represented one answer; the traditional Small Mosque, which emulated the monumental architecture of China's late-imperial period, symbolized what residents saw as the opposite

FIGURE 8. Traditional mosque architecture: the minaret of the Big Study Street Mosque.

FIGURE 9. A syncretic mosque: the Middle Mosque. The banner reads "Love your country, love your religion, respect the sayings of the Prophet, and keep the law."

extreme. The architecture of the quarter's mosques made visible a local history of shifting Islamic practices influenced by Islamic reform movements. The Arabic mosques, and the adoption of new forms of Arabic pronunciation and Qur'anic education, exemplified residents' participation in an influential set of ideas and practices that for simplicity's sake I call Arabization. Like modernization, Arabization included a cluster of ideas about development for Muslims. Ideologically, the goal of Arabization was characterized as a return rather than a movement forward, the re-creation of an "authentic" Islam instead of evolution into a higher stage of development. However, although proponents of Arabization used the language of authenticity and the "original" Islam to legitimate the changes that they proposed, Arabization also incorporated elements of modernization as exemplified by the oil-rich countries of the Middle East. Arabization provided residents with an alternative ideological scale on which to evaluate themselves and a model of development that excluded the CCP government and the Han *minzu*.

Arabization as Islamic Reform

The late nineteenth and early twentieth centuries were not only the period during which ideas about evolution and progress took shape and spread; they were also a time of intense debate over Islamic belief and practice. Muslims in the Arabian peninsula initiated a number of Islamic reform movements that affected Muslims around the world. Central to the calls for Islamic reform was a phenomenon sometimes referred to as scripturalist fundamentalism. Scripturalist fundamentalism can be understood as the attempt to reproduce the "one true religion" that Muhammad disseminated through strict conformity to the practices recorded in the Qur'an and Hadith (the sayings of the Prophet) and the rejection of all others. This literal orientation was first espoused during the Wahhabi movement, an organized effort to achieve political and religious reform that began in the Arabian peninsula in the late eighteenth century. An early attempt to rectify Islamic belief and practice, Wahhabism sparked many other calls to return to Islamic orthodoxy and orthopraxy, all of which were (in the eyes of European observers, at least) closely associated with the Muslim violence of the nineteenth century (Esposito 1988:158; Lipman 1997:202–3). By the mid-1990s, proponents of Islamic reform were generally referred to in the Western media as "fundamentalists" and their movement as "fundamentalism" (or in academic circles, "reformism" and "Islamism").

Imitation of Arab dress, architecture, and other practices was an important feature of Islamic reform. From the very beginning, reformers conflated the attempt to conform to the Islam that Muhammad had established with the Arab context in which Islam originally arose (Esposito 1988:120–1). The development of media, communications, and transportation technologies during the twentieth century enhanced the possibilities for Muslims from disparate regions to adopt Arab styles. By the 1980s and 1990s, Arabic dress, architecture, and Qur'anic pronunciation had spread to far-flung Muslim communities as various Muslims strove to recapture the "one true religion" (see, e.g., Bernal 1994; Brenner 1996; Grabar 1983; Horvatich 1994; Macleod 1991; Nagata 1984). Geographical proximity to the sites where Muhammad lived and was active has long given the countries of the Middle East (particularly Saudi Arabia) a special status among Muslims (Eickelman and Piscatori 1990). The reformists' self-proclaimed monopoly on the Islam that Muhammad himself practiced only strengthened the appeal of Arab cultural forms.[4]

One attraction of Islamic reform and emulation of the Arab world was modernization. Bernal (1994) has pointed out that the Middle East proffered a non-Western paradigm of prosperity and modernization for underdeveloped Muslim societies. She and other scholars have noted that calls for reform are also associated with modernization in that they follow upon socioeconomic changes associated with the spread of capitalist markets (e.g., Bernal 1994; Brenner 1996; Watts 1996). The proponents of Islamic reform generally use modern technology, such as videos, cassettes, and the techniques of mass secular education, to promote their agendas (Bernal 1994; Eickelman 1992; Horvatich 1994). Arabization, as the recreation of an "authentic" Islam through reference to the Middle East, was thus a response to modernization even as it provided a model for modernization. In the Xi'an Muslim district (and in other Muslim societies), Arabization was particularly compelling because it was exclusively Muslim.

Processes of Arabization reached China in the late nineteenth century through the efforts of a Gansu Muslim named Ma Wanfu.

Ma made the hajj in 1888 and remained in Mecca to study for four years. After his return to China in 1892, Ma began disseminating the ideas for Islamic reform that he had developed through contact with proponents of Wahhabism. Ma was primarily interested in the religious aspects of Islamic reform rather than the political ones, although he did advocate the separation of Chinese Muslims from non-Muslim Chinese (Lipman 1997:205–6). His reform movement came to be called Ikhwan (Chinese *Yihewani*) after the "Muslim Brotherhood" (Arabic *al-Ikhwan al-Muslimun*) of the Middle East (Lipman 1997:204).

The essence of Ma's teachings was that Chinese Muslims must rely solely upon the Qur'an and Hadith and eradicate those customs and practices that could not be definitively attributed to the Prophet Muhammad. This agenda entailed the rejection of several practices that were common among Chinese Muslims in Xi'an. One was the traditional Chinese form of Qur'anic education known as *jingtang jiaoyu*, originally developed by a religious specialist (*ahong*) from Shaanxi and a great source of local pride. In *jingtang jiaoyu*, Qur'anic students were taught to recite the Qur'an by using Chinese words to produce rough equivalents of Arabic sounds (a kind of transliteration technique for "learning" Arabic). Ma insisted upon direct study of Arabic. He and other Ikhwan proponents also criticized the practice of wearing white mourning garb—which Chinese Muslims shared with non-Muslim Chinese—as a deviant Chinese accretion. In addition, the Ikhwan teachings denounced the custom of paying ahong with food and money for reciting the Qur'an, which posed a significant threat to the livelihood of ahong (see Lipman 1997:200–11 for further information).

Residents dated the first arrival of Ikhwan in the Muslim district to the 1920s. According to some, Ikhwan appeared in Xi'an with the visit of three or four men who had made the pilgrimage to Mecca; others said that a friend of Ma Wanfu's first began to promote reform.[5] Two mosque congregations, the Dapiyuan Mosque and the Western Mosque, claimed to be the site where Ikhwan was first practiced in the quarter. Which mosque originally propounded Islamic reform mattered to many residents because this demonstrated the superiority and moral authority of its congregation, who were the first to follow the "one true path" and recognize the "authentic" Islam (at least according to those who were persuaded by the Ikhwan teachings).

This first wave of reform created profound divisions in the Muslim district. Before this, all Muslims in Xi'an called themselves *Gedimu*, or in local parlance, *Laogaidi*, a name that denotes Gedimu but also carries connotations of intimacy and familiarity. The word *gedimu* is based on the Arabic word for "old" (*qadim*). Gedimu is the oldest form of Islamic practice in China. The arrival of Ikhwan teachings in Xi'an transformed Gedimu into a religious faction because some residents adopted the new practices and rejected the old. Those who espoused the Ikhwan teachings prided themselves on "depending on the Qur'an to establish the religion" (*ping jing li jiao*) and sharply criticized the Gedimu as having been influenced by Chinese customs. They called themselves *Sunnaiti*, "those who followed the path" (Arabic *sunna*) of the Prophet Muhammad.

Numerous conflicts arose among the members of mosque congregations over correct Islamic practice and whether the new ways were better than the old. Some of the disagreements were so bitter that residents had to build new mosques to separate the quarreling factions. For example, one man recalled how at the Ancient Mosque, some Hui accepted the Ikhwan teachings but others loyally adhered to the Gedimu. One day in 1935, the Gedimu followers barred the Ikhwan believers from attending worship there, arming themselves with knives and locking the gates of the mosque to prevent the Ikhwan followers from entering. The reform adherents responded by buying some land a short distance down the street and building the Western Mosque. About ten years later, factional differences also divided the Yingli Mosque congregation. Most Hui who worshipped at the Yingli Mosque followed Ikhwan, but some rejected the new teachings. When the Gedimu adherents found themselves in a minority, they separated from the Yingli Mosque and built a new Gedimu stronghold, the

Middle Mosque, a little way down the road. It was these mosques, the Middle Mosque and the Western Mosque, that possessed syncretic "Arabic" and "traditional" architecture (see Figure 9). Residents also remembered that conflicts between Sunnaiti and Gedimu profoundly affected domestic relations. Adherents of one group refused to marry those from another; households whose members professed different teachings split apart. As Guangliang, a man in his 40s, explained, the two groups were opposed because each side doubted that the members of the other were truly Muslim. "In those days," he said, "people were much more likely to perceive those who weren't exactly the same as themselves as outsiders and enemies."

During the anti-Japanese war (1937–1945), a second tide of Islamic reform reached Xi'an. According to some, these new Ikhwan teachings were not openly disseminated until after 1949. Residents credited pilgrims with initiating this movement. Jiqing, a man in his 70s, explained that Hui pilgrims (*hazhi*, Arabic *hajji*) discovered that Islam in Mecca was practiced very differently than it was in Xi'an and that the Qur'ans printed in the Middle East differed from those in China. They brought back books and, like the advocates of the first wave of Islamic reform, tried to change religious observance to match that of the Middle East. Proponents of this reform movement believed that even the followers of the previous reform movement deviated from the teachings espoused in the Qur'an and Hadith. These new reformers had a reputation for "extremism" (*guoji*) among the Gedimu and Sunnaiti in Xi'an.

Most locals called the followers of the second wave of Ikhwan *Santai*. *Santai* was a Chinese term that meant "lift three times." It referred to adherents' practice of raising the hands to the head three times during daily prayer, whereas the ritual format that most residents practiced was to raise the hands to the head once. The name that the followers of this new teaching adopted for themselves was *Saleyef*, or *Salafiyya*, after the Arabic term for "the first three generations [of Muslims]" (Qiu 1992:819). This name indicated their superior status and greater authenticity compared to both the "old" Gedimu faction and the "followers of the path of the Prophet" Sunnaiti faction.

During the 1990s, factional affiliations still divided the quarter. For example, Mingjie and his son were not on speaking terms in June 1997; according to Mingjie's wife and daughter, this was the result of Mingjie's son's conversion to Santai a few months previously (it should be noted, however, that Mingjie's wife and his son's wife quarreled constantly over household affairs and child-rearing). Si, a man in his early 60s who worked in the Small Mosque, said that he had little to do with his brother because Si was Gedimu and his brother was Santai. As far as Si was concerned, the Santai were "too radical." During 1995, a religious quarrel broke out among the Santai adherents who attended the Yingli Mosque and led to a fist fight. Neighbors informed the local police, and as a result the government closed the mosque for several weeks. The source of the conflict was said to be the Yingli Mosque's religious specialist, who some members of the congregation thought deviated from the Qur'an and the Hadith (he was also suspected of financial wrongdoings). Finally, the government ejected him from the district, but his adherents refused to rejoin the rest of the Yingli Mosque congregation. By June 1997, this splinter group had set up a tent on the northern perimeter of the Muslim district where they conducted their own religious services and Qur'anic education classes; it was still in use when I returned to Xi'an in 1998.

Mosques

Residents of the quarter identified themselves as "belonging to" a particular mosque. Each mosque had its own congregation or as residents said, "neighborhood" (*fang*). As the local term suggests, membership was loosely defined by residence: most families attended the mosque closest to their home. However, historical affiliations and factional differences created exceptions to this rule. For example, one family that I knew lived on Guangji Street. Their home was diagonally across the street from the Dapiyuan

Mosque (Sunnaiti), less than two blocks away from the Xiaopiyuan Mosque (Gedimu), and three blocks from the New Mosque (Santai). Nevertheless, this family patronized the Yingli Mosque, located on the other side of the quarter, a ten-minute bicycle ride from their house. Even though the New Mosque was Santai, this family loyally followed the ahong of the Yingli Mosque and had not transferred their allegiance when the congregation split in 1988. Other families and individuals retained their ties to a particular mosque after moving out of its vicinity because they had grown up near it, because their family had always belonged to that mosque, or because they felt comfortable and at home there. However, if moving brought a family close to a mosque that was of the same faction as the mosque they had previously attended, they were quite likely to patronize that mosque instead.

Xi'an Hui identified themselves with the mosques they attended because mosques played a central role in daily activities. The mosque was easily the single most important institution in the lives of the quarter's residents. The quarter's mosques filled a multiplicity of spiritual and secular functions, a characteristic they shared with mosques in many Muslim communities (see, e.g., Slyomovics 1996:209).

The most basic purpose of the mosques was to provide a space for worship. However, as Jingquan, a 28-year-old mullah (a man studying the Qur'an with the intention of becoming a religious specialist), stressed, this was simply a matter of convenience; Muslims require no sacred space for worship. According to him, the mosque was simply a place where worship could occur without interruption. This comment underplayed the many functions that the mosque performed. For example, the quarter's mosques also notified residents when the time for worship arrived. All ten mosques possessed loudspeakers from which the call to prayer was broadcast five times each day. The chantlike, Arabic calls were clearly audible throughout the district. Their sound created an alternative temporal structure to that denoted by the ringing of school bells and the chimes of the city clock that was located a short distance outside of the quarter, dividing the day into five worship periods rather than 60-minute intervals. The call to prayer reminded residents that their lives were marked by Islamic time, in addition to the work and school schedules they shared with other urbanites (compare Dannin 1996).

Islamic doctrine requires that each of the five daily worship events be preceded by a ritual washing of the hands, feet, face, nose, mouth, ears, and eyes. Unlike most of the district's homes, the mosques contained ablutions rooms with running water for washing. Many also provided small tin pitchers that worshippers used to pour water on the appropriate parts of the body as they washed. Those who worshipped frequently in the mosque left washcloths there, hung on drying racks, clotheslines, or bushes in the mosque courtyard. Most of the mosques also supplied plastic sandals for worshippers to use while washing and for the short walk to the worship hall, inside of which no shoes may be worn.

Collective worship took place in the worship hall. Although Muslim men are only required to worship together once each week (at the Friday *zhuma* service), many older Hui preferred to do so every day.[6] Worshipping together promoted a sense of community, and in addition provided worshippers with a guide to correct ritual observance in the form of the religious specialists who stood at the front of the congregated men. The larger mosques regularly had gatherings of about 50 men for the midday worship during ordinary days, and the smaller mosques had 20 or 30. Retirees, young men studying to become ahong (mullahs), and the men and women who worked in the mosque made up the majority of those who worshipped in the mosque several times each day. When Friday *zhuma* arrived, however, the quarter's mosques were filled. Many men had to worship on rugs in the courtyard because the worship halls were too crowded for them to find a place. For the Feast of the Breaking of the Fast and the Feast of Sacrifice, worshipping men spilled out onto the sidewalks and streets, because every available spot inside the mosque was occupied.

Fewer women worshipped in the mosque than men. At the

Dapiyuan Mosque, for example, the usual ratio was five men to one woman. Middle-aged and older women predominated at most of the mosques I attended, though some mosques, such as the Dapiyuan Mosque, had significant groups of young women as well. Women worshipped in a separate building or room on the mosque compound. They washed in completely separate ablutions rooms. When women worshipped, they were not led by a religious specialist, although some mosques piped in the sounds of the men worshipping via loudspeaker to the room where the women gathered. Lacking a leader to coordinate prayer, women's worship tended to be much more individualistic and idiosyncratic than men's. In general, women treated the time for worship more casually than men and rarely performed their obeisances simultaneously.

In addition to daily worship, *zhuma*, and the collective worship on Islamic holy days, some parts of the Hui funeral sequence also took place in the mosque. Some mosques, such as the Western Mosque, were equipped with special rooms for washing corpses, although corpse washing also took place in the home. At all Hui funerals, the body was brought to the mosque before it was taken to the cemetery. This event was carefully timed to coincide with one of the five times of daily worship, so that when worshippers completed their prayers, they could gather together to perform a final obeisance on behalf of the deceased. At most of the funerals I attended, participants in this rite included the male surviving relatives of the deceased; the deceased's friends, neighbors, and coworkers; regular members of the congregation; and special representatives sent from each of the other nine mosques. Women did not participate (not even when the deceased was a woman), but female relatives were frequently allowed to watch from the sides and back of the mosque.

Mosques were the primary sites for religious education in the quarter. All the mosques conducted daily classes for mullahs that focused on learning to recite the Qur'an in Arabic. Students began by memorizing the Arabic alphabet and learning the sounds that the various combinations of letters and vowel markings produced. Then they progressed to memorizing short passages of the Qur'an until they had completed the entire book. More advanced pupils studied the Hadith (the sayings of the Prophet) and textual exegeses in Arabic. By the time they became ahong they had also learned to write Arabic calligraphy, translate back and forth between Qur'anic Arabic and Chinese, and give exhortations.

The mosques also held after-school study classes for children, which also focused on learning to recite passages from the Qur'an. Although relatively few children studied in the mosque during the regular school year, many parents enrolled their sons and daughters in Qur'anic study classes during the summer. Even the smaller mosques claimed to have 200 and more children attending the summer courses. The Yingli Mosque, in addition to offering Qur'anic Arabic, also held night classes in modern standard Arabic for both children and adults.

All the mosques possessed libraries of materials useful for the study of Islam that they made available to their congregations. Some of these collections were extensive, including old books that Chinese Muslims had used to study the Qur'an for generations, and books from Cairo, Mecca, and other places in the Middle East. Yingchun, a religious specialist at the Dapiyuan Mosque, told me that his mosque frequently purchased scriptures and other Islamic books through a company in India. Several of the mosques also provided religious cassette recordings and videotapes for their members' use. Language tapes from Egypt and Saudi Arabia ensured that students learned "standard" (*biaozhun*) Arabic pronunciation. Videotapes included films of the pilgrimage, mosque scenery, and records of local celebrations, such as the annual visit to the grave of Hu Dengzhou, a famous Ming-dynasty Hui teacher who was buried a short distance outside of Xi'an. A few mosques offered such items for sale. For example, I procured one videotape from the Big Study Street Mosque that instructed male and female viewers how to worship correctly (including washing sequence, body movements during prayer, and Qur'anic recitation) and another from the Great Mosque about its architecture and history.

Local mosques played an important role in "spreading Islam" (*chuan jiao*) to the quarter's residents. Instruction on Islamic beliefs, practices, and history took place during exhortations, but the mosque was also the main site where such tutelage occurred outside of worship times. For example, during Ramadan of 1994, the mosque management committee of the Great Mosque papered the courtyard walls with posters that explained the core religious beliefs of Muslims. The Great Mosque and other mosques during 1994 and 1995 also posted huge photographic reproductions of the Ka'aba and the main mosque in Mecca on their walls. Such efforts were designed to educate local Hui about Islam; they also confirmed the mosque's position as the locus of Islamic authority.

Most of the mosques were also repositories of local history. Large stone steles commemorating events that took place in the quarter during the imperial period studded the courtyards of the Great Mosque, the Big Study Street Mosque, and several others. Though few residents bothered to read these enormous tablets, many pointed to such artifacts as evidence of the quarter's long history. A few mosques also contained old furniture and other objects, such as elaborately carved wooden boxes for storing the Qur'an and ornate clocks, that predated the communist period. Mosques also memorialized more recent history. The Middle Mosque, for example, erected a stele in 1996 to commemorate a religious specialist who had died as a result of the violence that ensued after the CCP's "religious reform" in 1958. Both the Small Mosque and the Ancient Mosque possessed tablets that marked the completion of repairs and reconstruction after the Cultural Revolution.

The quarter's mosques also organized and provided an outlet for local Muslims to meet their Islamic obligations for charity. All Muslims have the duty to tithe (*tianke* or in Arabic, *zakat*). In Xi'an, tithing was defined as donating 2.5 percent of one's annual income for charitable use. Mosques frequently received donations from local residents. For example, one family I knew regularly gave boxes of soap to the mosque, and the owners of small food businesses often contributed food. However, as a result of the rise in local incomes during the 1980s and 1990s, Hui were more likely to donate money to the mosque than goods. Much of this cash had gone toward the reconstruction and repair of mosque facilities. Income from charitable donations was also used to provide religious specialists and mullahs with a monthly salary (see Chart 1 for further information about mosque income and expenditures).

Local mosques also solicited charity on behalf of poor Muslims outside Xi'an. On several occasions in 1994 and 1995, donations of cash, secondhand clothing, and other goods were collected for poorer Hui communities in southern Shaanxi and Gansu. Sometimes such efforts were spearheaded by a single mosque, which announced a fund-raiser and clothing drive to its congregation; on other occasions the local Islamic Association organized all ten mosques to participate jointly in relief efforts.

Because mosques were known as sources of charity, they attracted Muslim beggars. Local residents stated that all the beggars in the quarter were Hui; they pointed to the beggars' dress and their knowledge of Islamic terms such as *nietie* (charity) and *sewabu* ("May God reward you") as proof. Zenglie, a 70-year-old man, stated with conviction that Han would not dare to beg in the quarter. The month of Ramadan, a time when Muslims are especially likely to engage in charitable acts, sparked the arrival of hundreds of beggars (see Figure 2). Xi'an Hui claimed these beggars were "outsiders" from Pingliang in Gansu province, or, with the arrogance typical of Chinese urbanites, "the countryside" (*xiangxia*). Certainly, the beggars dressed less fashionably than the quarter's residents. Many of the young women wore green veils, a Hui custom not practiced in Xi'an but common in other parts of the northwest. For most of these "people away from home" (*lixiangren*), as some residents politely called them, soliciting charity was a part-time, seasonal occupation. During Ramadan many lived in the corners of the mosques and frequently ate there as well. For one month they amassed whatever money and clothing they could—during 1994 and 1995 I saw beggars with huge bundles of clothing wrapped to take home—and then, after the Feast of the Breaking of the Fast, they vanished.

Chart 1. Small Mosque income and expenditures

I. Income The Small Mosque income for February–April 1997 was as follows (note that February was Ramadan, the month when Muslims are especially encouraged to donate):

February	29,656.30 yuan
March	3,461.00 yuan
April	4,151.30 yuan

Income came from the following sources, in descending order:

Charitable donations (*nietie*)
Donations for use of utensils
Rent
Miscellaneous (e.g., one donor paid a month of water fees, another donor gave food, etc.)

II. Expenses Monthly expenses for the Small Mosque were written in two types of charts. The first type of chart was a monthly list of operating expenses, as follows:

Expenditures for February 1997

Date	*Use*	*Cost*
Feb. 1	Bought ahong *China Muslim* magazine [subscription]	28 yuan
Feb. 2	Repaired loudspeakers	312 yuan
Feb. 5	Office supplies	69 yuan
Feb. 6	Microphone	190 yuan
Feb. 9	Three locks	5.8 yuan
Feb. 18	Sieve and solder pot	35 yuan
Feb. 19	Meeting sign (listed rules for meetings)	152 yuan
Feb. 26	Kerosene	17.6 yuan
	TOTAL	809.40 yuan

Total expenditures for March were 231 yuan, total expenditures for April were 2,151.55 yuan (April included money spent for sending off and receiving the hajjis, as well as the electricity bill for the decorative lights the mosque used for the Feast of the Breaking of the Fast).

Chart 1, continued

The second type of chart listed the salaries the Small Mosque paid to its employees, namely ahong, mullahs, and manual laborers. Salaries for February, March, April, and May were listed together, as follows:

Small Mosque February–May Salary Expenses (in yuan)

Name	*February*	*March*	*April*	*May*
Jishu	400	600	600	600
Mingbao	400	600	600	600
Kerong	400	600	600	600
Yeding	200	400	400	400
Jinxi	200	400	400	400
Jian	200	400	400	400
Chenguang	200	400	400	400
Chao	200	400	400	400
Jide	200	200	—	—
Yongxin	200	—	—	—
Zhixiang	200	—	—	—
Lianghai	—	200	200	200
Fuguang	—	200	200	266.60
Qing	200	400	400	400
TOTAL	2,800	4,600	4,400	4,466.60

Posted May 6, 1997 by the purchasing department

Donating money and goods enabled local Hui to express their devotion, but it was also a method for acquiring a good reputation or "name" (*ming*). As elsewhere in China, a good name was a valuable asset, easing business transactions and facilitating access to the state (see Chapter 6 for an example of how "name" functioned in the quarter). Prominently posted on the walls of the mosques were the names of donors and the amount they had given. Some of the mosques posted these signs every week or month, and all the mosques did so during Ramadan and on the other Muslim holy days. Names were recorded in order of the amount given, with the individual or family who had given the largest amount listed first and continuing in decreasing order of generosity. For the most part families gave as a unit, in which case only the name of the male head of the household was recorded. Men whose names appeared frequently on the mosque's donor lists were acknowledged to be "big bucks" (*da kuan*), the term used for those who had struck it rich since the market reforms. Their reputation for wealth, however, did not necessarily translate into a reputation for being devout. As Guangliang observed, "It is easy to be 'religious' when you have money." Only when charitable contributions were accompanied by other acts, such as frequent mosque attendance, did they give the donor a name for being a good (and rich) Muslim.

During the month of Ramadan, a large proportion of the donations was used to hire cooks and buy food for collective meals. The ten mosques provided the evening meal, when Hui broke their fast after sunset each day, for members of their congregation and the gathered beggars. A small percentage of the community took advantage of this Ramadan service. In general, men were more likely to eat in the mosque than women; for example, of the ten tables set up for worshippers at the New Mosque in 1995, only two were reserved for women. Given that women were almost always responsible for cooking in the family, this pattern was not surprising. Residents said that the mosques provided the evening meal so that worshippers would have time to eat before the post-sunset time for worship arrived.

As the Ramadan meals suggest, mosques were an important site for sociability. Meals were served in the Gedimu mosques in celebration of the Prophet's Birthday and for the annual commemoration of the Hui Uprising.[7] More informal gatherings took place on a daily basis. Many older men and women who worshipped in the mosque frequently arrived 30 minutes to an hour early so that they could chat with the other members of the congregation and the people who worked in the mosque. When worship was not in session, children frequently played in the mosque courtyard, usually unsupervised. As the 70-year-old religious specialist Jishu explained, "Some people believe the mosque is a grave place, where they must be serious. In fact this is not so; people are welcome to come to the mosque at any time. Children come and play here; adults chat here. In a sense the mosque is like a second home, a place where people can be comfortable."

The mosques also facilitated socializing in other spaces by providing tables, chairs, dishes, eating utensils, and cooking ware for residents' use. In addition to using them for communal celebrations in the mosque, any member of the congregation could borrow these items at any time. Most families relied on use of the mosque's dishes and tables when hosting life cycle rituals such as social births (*manyue*), circumcisions, engagements, weddings, funerals, and mourning ceremonies. The customary practice was to make a donation for this service, although this was not required.

Providing entertainment was another function that the mosques served. In 1995, several of the mosques organized martial arts (*wushu*) demonstrations in celebration of the Feast of the Breaking of the Fast. Many of the mosques had children's martial arts teams associated with them; the opportunity to see these teams perform drew large crowds. Every Friday, the mosques were decorated for *zhuma* with colorful banners and posters, and on holy days, they were decked with electric lights, large posters and pictures of the Ka'aba in Mecca, flags, banners, and signs. On a few occasions each year, the Great Mosque brought out and lit the hundreds of tiny oil lamps that had been used there before electricity came to the quarter. Such displays attracted locals to visit and enjoy the spectacle, especially at night. Another form of entertainment was watching the men worship on the Feast of the Breaking of the Fast and the Feast of Sacrifice. This tended to be a female pastime, for women were not required to participate in the extra worship periods on these days. Beggars tended to join the women on the sidelines rather than actively participating in worship, positioning themselves by the exits so that the worshippers were forced to pass them when leaving the mosque.

Most of the quarter's mosques engaged in business practices that integrated them even more tightly into the district and provided them with additional sources of income (see Chart 1). Several rented out property on the perimeters of their complexes to small shopkeepers. Others rented parking spaces to local Hui who owned taxicabs, allowing them to park their cars in the courtyard or behind the mosque hall at night. Even more common was the practice of operating shower and bath houses. Most of the mosques' ablutions rooms were equipped with hot water heaters, showers, and bathtubs, items that few of the quarter's residents had in their homes. Persons who wished to shower or bathe were charged between one and three yuan for using the facilities. Except during the month of Ramadan, when a few of the mosques closed their doors to "outsiders" (meaning Han), Hui and Han alike were welcome to shower there. Most mosques also sold soap, shampoo, conditioner, and washcloths for the convenience of their patrons and to generate extra income. A small staff, comprised of both volunteers and paid employees (usually Hui from poorer parts of the northwest) sold tickets and bathing items and cleaned and maintained the facilities. Shower and bathing times were not restricted; customers used the ablutions rooms for bathing even during worship. Most Hui bathed in the mosque at least once a week. Many local residents spent an hour or more bathing, so they could socialize and relax as well as wash.

Mosques also provided a limited amount of housing for religious specialists and their students. Those mosques that hired ahong from outside the community (a not-uncommon practice) set aside living space for them inside the mosque complex. Several mosques in the quarter invited specialists from Gansu and Qinghai to teach and conduct worship in Xi'an for periods ranging from a few months to several years. Some of these men brought mullahs with them, who were also given accommodations inside the mosque. Local ahong and mullahs also received rooms inside the mosques. Although all the religious specialists that I knew had private homes, some would sleep in the mosque on occasion. At the very least, on-site living quarters made it easier for ahong and mullahs to be timely for worship. They also provided spaces for them to study and host visitors and guests.

The quarter's mosques also attracted tourists. The Great Mosque, which was Gedimu, drew the most visitors. Tourists who were not Muslims paid a small fee to enter (in 1994, five mao for Chinese, and ten yuan for foreigners). Some residents claimed that the Great Mosque dated from the Tang dynasty (seventh century) and was the oldest mosque in China. Others believed that the Big Study Street Mosque, an Ikhwan institution, was older, and avowed that this was the site that Muslim tourists preferred to visit. The Big Study Street Mosque and the eight other mosques all received tourist visits, but much less regularly than the Great Mosque, which brought in dozens each day (and many more during the tourist season). Foreigners who wandered through the quarter in search of the exotic or unfamiliar were the most likely to visit the other mosques. Some were Muslims, who came not just to look but to worship and occasionally to donate funds. A man from Oman had provided the Dapiyuan Mosque with enough money to build a religious school (madresseh), fully equipped with dormitories and classrooms, where both male and female students could engage in full-time Islamic studies free of charge. This building, constructed in an "Arabic" style, was completed in 1995 (see Figure 10).

The quarter's mosques influenced residents' economic and social life and helped to address their spiritual concerns. They were central to the neighborhood. It is not surprising, then, that their appearance took on a great deal of importance for residents. How a mosque looked conveyed public messages about residents' beliefs, practices, and allegiances; their status as "authentic" Muslims; and their degree of modernization.

Talking About Mosques

Residents were proud of their mosques. I was frequently told to visit mosques or asked if I had yet seen all ten mosques in the area. Many young couples included shots of the groom's family's mosque in their wedding videotapes, even though Hui weddings did not occur in mosques (see Chapter 7 for more information on

FIGURE 10. The Dapiyuan Mosque and madresseh behind it.

Hui weddings). During the 1980s and 1990s, residents had donated huge sums of money to repair, restore, and in some cases rebuild the mosques. Such contributions were used not simply to make the mosques functional, but also to produce aesthetic monuments to residents' religious commitments and prosperity.

Because they demonstrated the Muslim district's economic success and religious vitality, the mosques were a focus of pride throughout the quarter. The mosques contributed greatly to the reputation for being prosperous and observant that Xi'an Hiu had in Shaanxi and other parts of China. Many "outsiders" from Southern Shaanxi and nearby parts of Gansu visited the quarter to solicit funds for their own mosque building projects. Within Xi'an, the quarter's mosques gave Hui a reputation for wealth among local Han. As one of my colleagues at the Shaanxi Academy of Social Sciences pointed out, the speed with which the quarter's mosques had been rebuilt contrasted sharply with the fate of the Buddhist nunnery on the western perimeter of the quarter, which was still in a state of disrepair in 1998. Residents of the Muslim district had the money to rebuild, but the monastery, largely patronized by Han from the surrounding countryside, could not generate sufficient funds.

Residents were keenly aware of how much money each congregation had invested in mosque construction. I occasionally heard small groups of men comparing the appearance and expense of repairing various mosques and debating which congregation had spent the most. The more elegant and complete a mosque's architecture and facilities were, the more prestige the congregation gained. Also relevant to the status of mosque congregations was the architectural style that they had adopted. The "traditional" and "Arabic" forms were not viewed as equally good in everyone's eyes.

The Small Mosque epitomized what residents called "traditional" (*chuantong jianzhu*) or "traditional Chinese" (*Zhongguo chuantong jianzhu*) architecture. This "traditional" style was problematic for residents of the district, as was made clear to me during a conversation that I witnessed between a Han woman who accompanied me to the Small Mosque and Si, a man who worked there. Upon entering the complex, my Han friend commented that its architecture looked like that of a Chinese temple. "It is not temple architecture (*simiao jianzhu*)," Si responded quickly. "It is *palace* architecture (*gongdian jianzhu*)." This distinction was critical to the patrons of the traditional mosques. To equate their mosque with a temple was to imply that the Islam they practiced was like Buddhism or Daoism—in other words, that it strayed from the one true path.

Some local Hui also criticized the traditional mosques for looking "just like Han temples." To demonstrate the resemblance, Jiqing, the 70-year-old gatekeeper at the New Mosque, pointed out that not only did many of the local mosques look like temples on the outside, but most had images of dogs, cats, phoenixes, and other animals on the inside, which he objected to as violating the Qur'anic prohibition on making images (see Figure 11).[8] In his opinion, the only thing that made these mosques different from temples was the kind of worship that took place inside them. Even so, the architecture rendered the beliefs of patrons suspect. "Since Hui beliefs are different from Han beliefs, Hui mosques should look different from Han temples," Jiqing stated. "For this reason the new mosques are all being built in an Arabic style."

The degree to which the traditional mosques resembled temples was not all that was at stake. Their very association with China and Chineseness was problematic. In the mid-1990s quarter, many residents felt that to be a Chinese Muslim was to be an inauthentic or deviant Muslim. This sensibility came partially from the recognition that Middle Eastern Muslims and Chinese Muslims were different and that the Arab world had an advantage that derived from being the site where Islam was founded. It was also a result of the PRC government's nationality policies, which equated being Chinese with being Han. The government's evolutionary ideology and the benefits package that it gave to the non-Chinese races further increased the Hui investment in not being Chinese (see Chapter 2).

FIGURE 11. A roof tile from the Great Mosque, under repair in 1993.

Jiqing was correct to state that the newer mosques were built in an Arabic style. Both of the mosques that had been built since the 1980s, the New Mosque and the Ancient Mosque, were "Arabic." The Ancient Mosque had been destroyed during the Cultural Revolution, so the congregation had built an entirely new complex after the economic reforms. Of the other Hui congregations in Xi'an (those not in the quarter), seven of the eight mosques (all constructed since 1979) were built in the Arabic style. Photographic evidence and my own observations suggest that Arabic architecture was the preferred style for most (if not all) of the Hui mosques built in northwest China during the Deng era (see Dillon 1996 for photographs). These mosques demonstrated that Hui eagerly consumed the material aspects of Arabization, perhaps even more than the ideological ones.

Members of the New Mosque spoke enthusiastically about their new complex, describing it as having a "truly Arabic" or "truly Islamic" style. Jiqing characterized it as "exactly the same as [the mosques in] foreign countries." On one occasion, he pulled out magazine pictures of Middle Eastern mosques, including the Great Mosque in Mecca, for me to examine. "Look!" he said excitedly. "Just the same as our mosque!" The green onion domes, Moorish arches, and shining white exteriors of the mosques that Jiqing showed me were clearly the model for the New Mosque.[9] Jiqing's pride derived in part from the "authentic" Islam that the Arabic style embodied. The Arabic mosques promoted their congregations' image as Muslims with correct belief and practice.

Some Hui tried to defend the traditional mosque architecture by citing its historical worth. They referred to the Hui heritage and their responsibility to pass on what their forebears had created to future generations. Nevertheless, even those residents who upheld the value of traditional architecture also found it necessary to confirm their authenticity as Muslims through reference to the Middle East. For example, members of the Dapiyuan Mosque laid claim to the authority of the Middle East despite their institution's architecture. The congregation had donated large sums of money to restore the mosque's traditional appearance, striving to rebuild as closely as possible its pre–Cultural Revolution form. Yet at the same time, those who attended the Dapiyuan Mosque emphasized that the Ikhwan teachings they followed were truer to the worship practices found in the Middle East than those of the Gedimu. They also pointed out that the Dapiyuan Mosque's religious specialist had studied for three months at Al-Azhar University in Cairo in 1994, and a young mullah from the congregation had spent two years there. These connections to the Middle East and its "authentic" Islam were a great source of pride for the families who attended the Dapiyuan Mosque, and indeed, although he was still a young man (age 38), the ahong Yingchun was respected in many parts of the quarter.

The Great Mosque was Gedimu and built in the traditional style, but members of its congregation also appealed to a more orthodox, non-Chinese Islam. Although adherents spoke with pride about their establishment's twelve-century history, they were even more concerned to detail its extensive contacts with foreign Muslims. "The Great Mosque is a national mosque," said Xiulan, a member of the congregation. "Muslim delegations from all over the world visit here and meet with its ahong." By stressing the presence of foreign Muslims, Xiulan demonstrated her mosque's participation in the wider Islamic world. Reinforcing such appeals to Islamic authenticity were the artifacts displayed inside the Great Mosque. In the same room where century-old furniture and Islamic objects were kept, photographs of such important Muslim visitors as the Aga Khan and Muhammad Ali were also carefully stored.

Arabic and the Qur'an

Muslims believe that the Qur'an is the literal word of God, and Arabic, as the language of the Qur'an, is sacred. Xi'an Hui treated with reverence any object inscribed with Arabic. Calligraphic quotes from the Qur'an adorned many local homes and mosques, though few residents could read or translate them. Arabic wall hangings were frequently given as gifts to families moving into new homes (usually newlyweds) or starting new businesses. Some women embroidered Arabic inscriptions on the bibs of small children, a sign of religious devotion that also, I suspect, provided a degree of protection for the child.[10]

An event that exemplified some residents' attitude toward Arabic took place during my visit to the Muslim book store across from the Great Mosque in June 1997. After browsing through their collection of Qur'ans, books on Hui culture and history, and Qur'anic study materials, I brought two books on Hui history, a few locally produced pamphlets labeled "Arabic study materials" (*alaboyu jiaocai*), and a small copy of the Qur'an over to the counter where an elderly man and a middle-aged woman were seated. The woman sorted through my selections and asked the man, "Are you going to sell these to her?" He looked at me and inquired if I were Hui, to which I responded that I was not. "Hui" in this context meant "Muslim," a semantic elision common to older residents. When she heard that I was not "Hui," the woman separated out all the materials that contained Arabic and refused to sell them to me. "You don't need these," she said. When I protested, she explained that since I was not Hui, they could not trust me to treat the texts properly. My credentials as a former long-term resident of Xi'an and the friend of several religious specialists in the Great Mosque mattered not at all. "We must take responsibility" (*women dei fu zeren*), she said, indicating that if I mistreated the books, the sin would rest upon her. The man agreed, explaining, "Arabic is sacred (*sheng de*). We can't just sell these books to anyone who wants them" (*bu neng suibian mai*).

The sound of Arabic recitation was as important as its visual representation. At circumcisions, weddings, funerals, mourning ceremonies, and during the month of Ramadan, most residents invited ahong and mullahs to their homes to recite the entire Qur'an. This was especially true of the Gedimu residents, approximately 80 percent of the quarter's population. Members of the reform factions did not recite the Qur'an in its entirety as frequently as did members of the Gedimu, because Ikhwan adherents believed that one should not recite the Qur'an and eat at the same occasion. The local aphorism "if you recite the Qur'an do not eat, if you eat do not recite the Qur'an" (*nianjing bu chi, chifan bu nianjing*) encapsulated this belief. At an Ikhwan wedding, for example, a religious specialist might substitute an exhortation for Qur'anic recitation. However, some Ikhwan followers did ask ahong to recite the Qur'an for them during Ramadan and when mourning a deceased family member at times designated for remembering the dead, such as 40 days after burial.

At rites such as weddings and funerals, the Gedimu host family invited a minimum of 30 men who could recite the Qur'an to attend, one man for each chapter of the Qur'an. The family's mosque provided a set of the Qur'an's 30 chapters, each chapter separately bound. Each man who was able to read Qur'anic Arabic took one chapter to recite, and all 30 chapters were read aloud simultaneously, producing an unintelligible cacophony. This practice was called "reciting a case of the scripture" (*nian yixia jing*), in reference to the container in which the chapters were held. Because few men could translate what they were reading or explain its specific content, the unintelligibility of the recitation was irrelevant. What was important was that the Qur'an was heard in its entirety (a process that took 30 to 40 minutes).

Muslims must worship in Arabic, so some amount of Qur'anic education is required of all believers. As the ahong of the Xiaopiyuan Mosque explained it, all Muslims must recite the Qur'an, otherwise they are not true Muslims. Jishu, the elderly ahong at the Small Mosque, stated that studying the Qur'an was "ordered by heaven" (*tianmingde*). During the eighteen months that I lived in Xi'an in 1994 and 1995, Arabic study was flourishing. In addition to the mullahs, children, and adults who studied the Qur'an in the mosque, I also met several adult women who studied privately at home. High levels of interest in Arabic also stimulated the Yingli Mosque and the Hui Middle School to offer courses in modern standard Arabic, and two new private schools for Arabic and Qur'anic study opened in the quarter in 1995. By the time I left Xi'an in August of that year, the original two stores that sold written pronunciation guides for Qur'anic Arabic and language tapes, along with other items ranging from veils to Qur'ans to books about Islam and Hui history, had been joined by two more stores selling Arabic language books, tapes, and other Muslim paraphernalia.

Arabic classes in the mosques, whether for children, adults, or beginning classes for mullahs, focused on memorizing the sounds of Qur'anic recitation. Few Hui aspired to more than rote memorization of the Qur'an. As Jishu explained, learning to translate, learning grammar, and learning to write were "extremely complicated" (*mada de hen*) and unnecessary for any but the most erudite of specialists.

A Brief History of Arabic Study

The high level of interest in Arabic study among Xi'an Hui was a recent phenomenon. Before 1949, mosques did not offer formal Arabic classes other than those for mullahs. Residents stated that the summer classes for children began in 1991 and 1992. Jishu clarified that the custom of sending children to study Arabic in the mosque had long been in existence, especially among families who lived close to the mosque. He stated that before 1949, parents used to send their four- to six-year-old children to the mosque to learn Arabic so their children would be able to recite a few phrases from the Qur'an before they studied "things in books" (*shumianshang de dongxi*)—meaning Chinese books or secular education. Another young man explained that the custom of sending very young children to the mosque to learn a little Qur'anic Arabic, such as the Muslim vow of faith known as the "pure and true words" (*qingzhenyan*), was designed to give children "religious thoughts" (*zongjiao sixiang*). This custom was still common in the quarter during the mid-1990s.

Several men and women who had been children in the 1950s remembered taking Arabic classes in the mosques. Forty-eight-year-old Aifeng could still recognize the Arabic alphabet that she had learned from the religious specialist at the Dapiyuan Mosque.

Ha, a man in his late 50s who taught at the Hui Middle School, said he had forgotten the Arabic he learned as a child at the Great Mosque. Fifty-six-year-old Liangxun, a Hui government official, believed that the practice of holding Arabic classes for groups of children in the mosque originated in response to the government's institution of secular primary education for all children during the 1950s. He thought that the mosques had mimicked the format of secular education in an effort to encourage parents to send their children to study the Qur'an.

By the early 1960s, the collective study of Arabic in the quarter had disappeared in the face of the government's antireligious propaganda and policies. Only a few Hui managed to continue Qur'anic studies secretly during the Cultural Revolution. Most were like Jishu, who did not study the Qur'an for 26 years. After Mao died, the first public Arabic course in Xi'an was offered in 1979 when a local university sponsored night classes in Modern Standard Arabic at one of the quarter's primary schools. Qur'anic education in the mosques began in 1985 under the auspices of the provincial Islamic Association. Interest in Arabic had grown rapidly since then. As Li, a 50-ish woman who sold bread for a living, put it, "Then [meaning during the Maoist era] the Qur'an was far away, but now it is close. From the fifties to the seventies, we believed in Islam in our hearts, but didn't dare to worship. Now lots of people study the Qur'an and Arabic."

Talking About Qur'anic Education

Although most Hui approved of Arabic studies, not all agreed about how Qur'anic Arabic should be pronounced or what the best strategies for learning Arabic were. Like mosque architecture, Arabic pronunciation and Qur'anic study methods were issues over which Hui debated the worth of indigenous and Middle Eastern practices.

Differences over Qur'anic study centered around the merits and failings of *jingtang jiaoyu*, literally "scripture-hall education." *Jingtang* education methods relied on written Chinese transliterations of Arabic to teach students how to pronounce and recite the Qur'an (see Figure 12). The spoken sound of the Chinese characters created a rough approximation of the Arabic sounds but did not convey the meaning. Jishu, whose knowledge of the Qur'an was highly respected in the quarter by members of all factions, was a proponent of *jingtang* education. As one of the few local ahong who had received extensive Qur'anic education before 1949, Jishu was proud of his ability to teach the authentic form of *jingtang* education. According to him, the core of *jingtang* education was a kind of pronunciation and a way of speaking (the terms he used were *fayin*, *kouqi*, and *yuqi*) that was based on Hui tradition. Although he believed that the content of *jingtang* education was the same as what he called the "new" kind of religious education, he noted that people who had received *jingtang* education tended to put things differently than those who had not. As an example, Jishu called God "Allah," pronounced "An-la-hu," whereas those who were taught in the new ways called God "the true God," pronounced "zhen-zhu." Jishu's word for God was based on a Chinese transliteration of the sound of the Arabic word, whereas the new term for God translated the meaning of the Arabic word. When I pointed out that the *jingtang* pronunciation sounded more like the Arabic, Jishu agreed. "*Jingtang* language is closer to the original language" (*yuanwen*), he said.

Zenglie, a professor of Hui culture and long-time resident of the quarter, described *jingtang* language as a mixture of Arabic, Persian, classical Chinese, and the local dialect. Zenglie pointed to the religious exhortations given at the Friday collective worship and on special occasions as examples of *jingtang* education. During exhortations, religious specialists used words of foreign origin, mostly Arabic and Persian, according to Chinese grammatical rules. They also included words from classical Chinese and the local dialect, sometimes reversing the usual Chinese word order. A common reversal that Zenglie pointed out was the verb "forgive": Xi'an Hui said *shurao* rather than the standard Mandarin *raoshu*. The eclectic linguistic mixture that resulted from *jingtang* educa-

开端章

بِسْمِ اللّٰهِ الرَّحْمٰنِ الرَّحِيْمِ ۝

米嘿勒宁马哈然嘿俩命思比

奉大仁大慈的安拉之名。

اَلْحَمْدُ لِلّٰهِ رَبِّ الْعٰلَمِيْنَ ۝١ اَلرَّحْمٰنِ

宁马哈然乃米来而立比然嘿俩林杜木哈立艾

〔一〕赞颂归于安拉，众世界的主，〔二〕大仁

الرَّحِيْمِ ۝٢ مٰلِكِ يَوْمِ الدِّيْنِ ۝٣ اِيَّاكَ نَعْبُدُ

杜布而乃开牙引。泥地命要克利马米嘿然

大慈的主，〔三〕报应日的掌握者。〔四〕我们只

وَاِيَّاكَ نَسْتَعِيْنُ ۝٤ اِهْدِنَا الصِّـ ... اط

外托拉水南地嘿以奴而太思乃开牙引我

崇拜你，我们只向你求助。〔五〕求你指引

FIGURE 12. Photograph of *jingtang jiaoyu* text.

tion, with its high percentage of foreign terms, was difficult even for residents of the quarter to understand in its entirety.

Jingtang education was criticized on a number of fronts. Liu, a Sunnaiti, described *jingtang* education as "outdated" (*lao banfa*) and "parochial" (*tu*). He proudly stated that the children who attended the Dapiyuan Mosque (to which he belonged) learned "standard Arabic pronunciation." Liu disapproved of *jingtang* education because it taught incorrect terms and wrong usage. For example, Liu said that in the past, all Xi'an Hui used to say "Salaam Aleiku*n*," ending this common greeting (from Arabic, meaning "peace to you") with an *n* sound. When Hui went to Saudi Arabia on the pilgrimage, however, they learned that Muslims there pronounced the word "Aleiku*m*" ("to you") with an *m* sound at the end. Despite this incontrovertible evidence of incorrect pronunciation, adherents of *jingtang* education persisted in saying "Aleikun" with an *n* sound. Liu attributed this to the "boorish" (*tu*) and "uncultured" (*meiyou wenhua*) religious specialists in the quarter.

Yingchun, the 38-year-old ahong of the Dapiyuan Mosque, voiced similar criticisms. The Gedimu, he said roundly, "blindly followed the traditions of their ancestors." The Arabic pronunciation they taught was "Buddhist" (*fojiao diao*) and strongly influenced by Han customs. Xiulan, a Gedimu who sent her son to Arabic lessons year-round, also criticized *jingtang* education as teaching "Chinese Arabic" (*Hanyu de awen*), rather than the correctly pronounced Arabic that her Sunnaiti nephew studied. A more cautious middle-aged Santai adherent explained that the problem with *jingtang* education was related to the history of Islam in China. Over the course of many years, Chinese Islam had been affected by "local culture" (*dangdi wenhua*)—his careful euphemism for "Han culture"—and practices like *jingtang* education that deviated from the Qur'an and the Hadith had arisen.

Jingtang education was used in the Gedimu mosques, but Gedimu were not its only practitioners. The adults I met who studied the Qur'an on their own all used *jingtang* methods, buying pamphlets that contained a line of Arabic followed by a written Chinese transliteration and then a Chinese translation (see Figure 12). Some elderly men I knew had recopied the entire Qur'an into a Chinese transliteration, which they used when called upon to recite. When one 50-ish woman, a member of the more radical Santai faction, described her Qur'anic studies, she said that she used the methods of "Grandfather Great Teacher Hu" (*Hu taishi baba*). "Grandfather Great Teacher Hu" was the name many locals gave to Hu Dengzhou, the Ming-dynasty teacher who had created *jingtang* education.[11] Aware of the Ikhwan critique of this form of Qur'anic education, she carefully refrained from calling her study methods "*jingtang* education." Instead she referred to them by invoking the name of a prestigious historical figure, Hu Dengzhou.

Aware that some residents criticized *jingtang* education for being Chinese, inaccurate, and deviant, Zenglie tried to legitimate this method of Qur'anic study by claiming it had a historical connection with the Islam of Muhammad's time. He spoke of the isolation of the Hui in China and suggested that being surrounded by Han Chinese had made the Hui community slow to change. Whereas the sizable Muslim population in the Middle East promoted rapid development and transformation, the Hui, far from the center of theological foment, clung to the customs passed down by their ancestors, which had survived relatively intact.

Zenglie argued that the conservative Hui (specifically the Gedimu) had closely preserved the Islamic practices of the Prophet so he could combat the Ikhwan monopoly on the "authentic" Islam. His rebuttal of reformers' critiques resembled Jishu's characterization of *jingtang* language as closer to the "original" Arabic: both men sought to legitimate the Chinese Muslim practices by appeals to history. The woman who studied using the methods of Grandfather Great Teacher Hu validated her practices in a similar manner.

The examples of Qur'anic education and mosque architecture demonstrate that Arabization had affected how the value of local practices was measured. As Muslims, residents of the quarter viewed Saudi Arabia and the Middle East as their point of origin.

At issue was how, and to what degree, Chinese Muslims should imitate the Middle East, and to what extent this entailed rejecting indigenous practices. The growing influence of Arabization forced residents to justify local cultural forms on the basis of age, history, and if possible, closeness to the original Islam. Individuals and congregations developed techniques to garner the cachet of Arabization without completely rejecting practices that were familiar and useful.

Congregations reconciled Arabization and "tradition" through visual, verbal, and practical claims. For example, the Ancient Mosque's Gedimu congregation rebuilt their mosque in an Arabic style, complete with an enormous green onion dome and a white-tiled exterior. Though they rejected the Ikhwan teachings and maintained their "old" forms of Qur'anic education, they adopted the Arabic architectural style in order to demonstrate that they were "authentic" Muslims. At the Dapiyuan Mosque, the Ikhwan congregation reconstructed their "traditional" mosque complex, but also bragged about their specialists who had studied at al-Azhar, their newly built Arabic-style Qur'an school funded by an Omani visitor, and the "standard" Arabic pronunciation their students learned (see Figure 10).

Arabization and Modernization

The intense concern that residents had with replicating Middle Eastern models was relatively recent. Arabization intensified during the 1980s and 1990s. This process can be explained in part by the increased contacts that Chinese Muslims had had with the Middle East since the early 1980s; close imitation of the Muslim heartland only became a possibility after sizable numbers of Hui had had opportunities to visit the Middle East; learn about it through television, videos, and cassettes; and receive visitors from Arabic countries. Between 1980 and 1987, China's national Islamic Association organized 25 delegations to Islamic countries, hosted 36 Islamic groups from more than twenty countries and regions, sponsored more than 2,000 hajjis, and sent students to study in Pakistan and Egypt (Gladney 1992:327). During the 1980s and 1990s, Muslim visitors, Islamic organizations, and Middle Eastern countries donated and loaned money for the construction of mosques and schools all over China. For example, Ningxia Muslims received an interest-free loan of $189 million from the World Islamic Bank (Yu 1992); in the Xi'an Hui quarter, the generous tourist from Oman who funded Dapiyuan's new Qur'an school was one example of residents' contacts with the Middle East. Another was the dozen or so local men who had gone to Cairo, Yemen, Saudi Arabia, Malaysia, and other countries to study Islam since the late 1980s. In addition, rising numbers of Xi'an Hui made the hajj during the mid-1990s: 59 in 1994, 62 in 1995, 74 in 1996, and 88 in 1997.

Although much of the force of Arabization came from the Middle East's position as the sacred center of the Muslim world, Arabization also allowed residents to assume some of the Middle East's affluence and modernization. To Arabize meant to become more like the wealthy, technologically advanced societies of the Middle East. For example, the videotapes and language cassettes for Qur'anic study, which had become widely available only during the 1980s, relied on technologies that residents associated with modernization. Arabization entailed "modernization" as well as a return to the "authentic" Islam.

An important way in which Arabization represented and produced modernization was through language study. During the mid-1990s, residents became more concerned with speaking "standard" Arabic, not just for Qur'anic pronunciation but for business. Jingxian, a college graduate in her 40s who was the principal of the Hui Middle School, was one of the first to see the benefits of learning Arabic through the methods of secular education. Jingxian said she disapproved of *jingtang* education because it did not teach students how to speak Arabic or even instruct them in grammar. Its uses were wholly religious. In the fall of 1994, she hired an Arabic teacher for the Hui Middle School to teach Modern Standard Arabic as an extracurricular class that focused on acquiring conversational fluency and used the methods of secular mass education. Other institutions soon joined the Hui Middle School in offering Modern Standard Arabic, including the Yingli Mosque and the religious school associated with the Dapiyuan Mosque. According to the signs that the Yingli Mosque posted advertising their Arabic classes, they promoted a "scientific" (*kexue*) understanding of Arabic as well as "standard" (*biaozhun*) and "correct" (*zhengque*) pronunciation.

Some Hui studied Arabic to maximize possible business opportunities with the Middle East and create a niche for themselves as brokers between China and the Arab world. For example, Yu, the young woman who taught Modern Standard Arabic at the Hui Middle School, was a graduate of the Arabic Languages and Literature Department of Beijing University, which she had attended as a paying student.[12] She (and her parents, who had paid for her education) believed that learning Arabic was a good investment for young people. Like other residents, Yu saw Modern Standard Arabic as a language of opportunity for business and for tourism: it "had a lot of future" (*hen you qiantu*). Although most Chinese viewed English as essential knowledge for those who wished to engage in international business or tourism, a number of residents voiced concerns that knowledge of English had become too common to ensure a person a good job. As Muslims, Hui believed that there was a natural affinity between themselves and other Muslims. By learning Arabic, Hui could maximize what they saw as their "natural" advantage to bring foreign investment, trade, and tourism to the quarter (and money to their pockets).

When residents linked Arabic study to technology, science, and economic development, they spoke the language of modernization. What is more, they did so in a way that excluded non-Muslim Chinese. Because the Han *minzu* was not Muslim, the Middle East was not open to them as a paradigm for modernization. By contrast, the consumption of Arabic architecture, Arabic language, and "Arabic" education allowed Hui to maximize their kinship with Middle Eastern Muslims. Arabization gave residents an Islamic model for development and enhanced an Islamic scale of value. It also opened up opportunities for business, travel, study, and tourism.

Arabization and the State

Government reactions to Arabization were mixed. Officials said that the factional squabbles were a "headache." Even when there were no open conflicts, the lack of coordination between the different factions was a regular source of annoyance for officials. In addition, the increasing numbers of pilgrims caused the government anxiety and engendered discussions about imposing a cap on the number of residents who could make the pilgrimage each year. The state did not fund the rebuilding of any Arabic style mosques, but local officials did support the visual imitation of Arabic architecture when they built a formal entrance to Barley Market Street (see Figures 1 and 5). After officials labeled Barley Market Street Xi'an's "Hui food and drink street," they erected an archway to advertise the area's new designation.

The local government did not impede the study of Arabic, but neither did officials act to promote it. According to Liangxun, the vice-director of the provincial Religion and Nationality Affairs Commission, the Chinese government did not advocate study abroad for Hui, nor did it help set up educational exchange programs between the Middle East and China. The Hui who had gone abroad to study Islam had done so entirely through their own initiative. Each had received complete financial support from the foreign government in question. To some extent, the vigorous interest in Arabic study provoked official uneasiness. In 1995, the district government initiated a survey of "sites of religious activity" that would clarify the extent of Qur'anic study in the quarter. The knowledge that this survey generated would give officials a better understanding of the residents' interest in Arabic and provide the information needed to regulate Arabic study. During the mid-1990s, Qur'anic and Modern Standard Arabic classes had not received explicit state permission. In other parts of China, government officials closed down Qur'anic study classes (see, e.g., Gilley 1995; FBIS 1990).

Arabization threatened the government in that its power and direction were not under state control. A major official concern was that the study of Arabic or the Qur'an should not lead to subversive thoughts or actions; the government wanted Hui to be patriotic and adhere to national goals. A common slogan posted on signs in the quarter and heard repeatedly at state-sponsored Islamic events, such as the tea party (*chahuahui*) officials held for the Feast of the Breaking of the Fast in 1994, was "Love your country, love your religion" (*aiguo aijiao*) (see also Figure 9). The state actively promoted attendance at government-established schools for ahong in Beijing and Ningxia. In 1994 and 1995, local officials selected ahong from the Great Mosque to attend these institutions free of charge. Residents said that patriotism and loyalty were a theme at these schools and that the curriculum included political study (a euphemism for Marxist-Maoist theory and nationalist indoctrination). Officials knew that ahong wielded a great deal of influence over the Hui community. Those who stressed the importance of loyalty to the government and espoused cooperation and obedience to official policies helped the state maintain control over modernization and the Hui nationality.

When the provincial government sought to restrict the number of Hui who traveled to the Middle East in 1995, the Hui official Liangxun (a member of the Great Mosque congregation) protested. He argued that pilgrims and students studying abroad demonstrated a "consciousness of opening" (*kaifang yishi*) in the quarter. Liangxun told the other officials that the connections made through such foreign travel were potential sources of investment, trade, and joint business opportunities. By appealing to the national imperative to modernize, Liangxun was able to defuse some of the officials' anxiety and persuade the government to abandon the proposed restrictions on Hui travel in the Muslim world, at least for 1995. Yet the discussion also gets at the crux of the state's relationship to Arabization (and Islam): the state wanted modernization and the Hui to be firmly under official direction. Arabization threatened the CCP's monopoly on modernization and stimulated the Hui to act in ways that officials neither understood nor controlled.

Mosque Styles, Qur'anic Education, and Modernization

The preferences of some Hui for mosques built in the Arabic style and for Arabic pronunciation that adhered closely to Middle Eastern norms were part of an ongoing redefinition of "authentic" Islamic observance in the quarter. Arabization presented the Middle East as the authoritative model of legitimate Islamic practice for Muslims. It also gave Muslims access to a distinctly Islamic form of modernization. Although Arabization's roots in Xi'an date from the early twentieth century, the process of reconsidering and recasting local Islamic observance accelerated sharply in the wake of the Deng reforms. Beginning in the early 1980s, Middle Eastern models became more available than ever before in the quarter's history, through travel abroad, tourism, mass-produced goods, and the media.

Arabization's appeal was largely predicated on the Arab world's position as the sacred center, but emulating Middle Eastern models in architecture and Qur'anic education also enabled Xi'an Hui to tie themselves to a modernization that was exclusively theirs. Arabization showed residents how to be good (orthodox) Muslims while drawing them nearer to prosperity, development, technology, and even "science." The strong commitment that residents expressed to Arabization though their consumption practices gave officials cause for alarm. Arabization's index of development did not correlate fully with the state's vision of modernization, and its authority was located beyond the government's control.

Chapter Four

TRADITIONAL FOOD AND RACE

Food was a major preoccupation for residents of the quarter. Its importance stretched far beyond nutrition; among other things, food also provided many Hui families with a livelihood. In 1996, officials estimated that 50 percent of the Muslim district engaged in the production and sale of food. According to Liangxun, a 56-year-old Hui official, before 1949 as much as 80 percent of the community made their living this way (see also Xiang 1983:103). In addition to nutritional and economic functions, food and eating practices were key vehicles through which residents expressed values and traits that they regarded as fundamentally Hui. Food and eating were the most frequently used tools in residents' lexicon for establishing and maintaining difference from the Han and affirming Hui superiority.

Most Chinese Muslim ideas about food revolved around the concept of *qingzhen* or "pure and true." The centrality of qingzhen to Hui food was readily apparent: residents emblazoned the characters for this word on restaurant and eatery signs throughout the quarter and imprinted it on the foods they packaged for sale. A qingzhen label on food for sale or a qingzhen sign in a restaurant instantly conveyed to customers that they were getting a Hui product, not a Han one. Because qingzhen was so basic to Hui entrepreneurship, the city and provincial governments promoted its use as a marker of Hui "nationality tradition." According to one official document, "fostering the excellence and traditions of the Hui nationality in the food and meat business" was a goal for the district government (Wu 1992:104). In 1992, officials gave licenses for private food businesses to 5,000 residents. They also hung one of the largest qingzhen signs that existed in the quarter over the entrance to Barley Market Street, newly designated as a market district "with nationality flavor" (Wu 1992:104). The state also devised policies to adjudicate which foods, restaurants, and even factories were qingzhen and which were not.

Official involvement with qingzhen was one means by which the state disseminated its racial definition of the Hui people and institutionalized its official vision of the Hui race's position in the national hierarchy of social development and process of modernization. By contrast, local understandings of qingzhen evidenced an alternative vision of the Hui, one that derived its force from Islam. Residents turned the government's promotion of qingzhen food as "nationality custom" to their economic advantage while maintaining their own, autonomous evaluation of the Hui people and their worth relative to the Han.

The Islamic Dietary Restrictions

The Islamic food prohibitions as stated in the Qur'an undergirded Xi'an Hui understandings of qingzhen. However, "pure and true" transcended simple dietary restrictions. Qingzhen influenced how Hui prepared their food, what they ate, who they ate with, who they socialized with, how they expressed their religious commitments, and how they did business. This was often manifested in ways that had little to do with the Qur'an or Islamic doctrine.

The Islamic dietary restrictions derive from God's revelations to Muhammad in chapters two, five, six, and sixteen of the Qur'an.[1] Passages in these chapters and the conclusive statement in chapter 80, verses 25–32, make clear that the vast majority of plant and animal life are available for Muslims to eat:

> We poured down rain abundantly,
> Then We cracked the earth open under
> pressure (of germination)
> And We made corn grow,

> And grapes and herbage,
> Olives and dates,
> Orchards thick with trees,
> And fruits and fodder:
> A provision for you and your cattle.

God prohibited only four types of food to Muslims: (1) animals that have not been consecrated to God and properly slaughtered (including those that die of disease and old age, are killed by another animal, or have been improperly killed by humans, for example, strangled or beaten to death); (2) blood; (3) pork; and (4) alcohol. With regard to the fourth prohibition, Muslims disagree as to whether God meant to forbid any intoxicating substance or merely certain kinds of alcohol (see Campo 1995:396). All four kinds of food are defined as impure and therefore unlawful (Arabic *haram*) and not permitted for consumption.[2] Muslims may eat all other foods, including foods made by non-Muslims who believe in the unity of God (meaning Jews and Christians). All foods that do not fall into one of the four forbidden categories are pure and lawful to consume.

The Arabic word *halal* is the term most commonly used in Muslim legal discourse and in everyday speech and writing to refer to the food that Muslims may eat. Though *halal* is usually translated in English as "lawful" or "permitted," most Muslims relate the definitions of lawful and unlawful to notions of purity and pollution. As Tapper and Tapper note, these concepts are "more or less coincident" (1986:65; see also Murphy 1986:86–7). Ideas about lawfulness and purity and unlawfulness and pollution regulate Muslim marriage practices, ritual behavior, sacred spaces and times, and the human body and its functions as well as food consumption and preparation.

Three of the four Qur'anic injunctions that determine which foods are *halal* and which are *haram* apply to meat and its byproducts. This is significant because meat is usually the central component of a "proper meal" (Caplan 1992:17; see also Douglas 1971). Ethnographic examples from many societies, both Muslim and non-Muslim, support the idea that meat often carries a symbolic weight that other foods lack (e.g., Ahern 1981; Murphy 1986; Tapper and Tapper 1986; Thompson 1988). This was the case among residents of the Muslim district and, scholars argue, is true of the Hui nationality in general.

Scholarly Treatment of the Hui Diet

Although few Western anthropologists (or other scholars) study Chinese Muslims, most of those who do discuss Hui dietary habits and the idea of "pure and true." Many more Chinese scholars study the Hui than do Western scholars, but a much lower proportion of their work has been devoted to the subject of food. Since 1949, Chinese scholarship on the Hui, which is funded by the state, has generally restated official ideas about the Hui race's origins and characteristics through historical, economic, sociological, and cultural studies (see, e.g., Hu 1993; Lai 1992; Li 1988; Ma 1993). By contrast, few Western scholars have accepted the PRC's evolutionary paradigm or *minzu* classification as an accurate representation of empirical reality (see Harrell 1995b, Lipman 1997:xx–xxv). The Western social scientists who have studied the Hui have been influenced by Barth's model of ethnicity as a collective representation hinged upon the construction and maintenance of boundaries (Barth 1969). They have attended closely to food as a boundary maintenance mechanism, in part because the Hui themselves see food as separating them from other groups.

Gladney bases his 1991 book *Muslim Chinese* on the concept of qingzhen and the different meanings and practices associated with it in four geographically distinct Hui communities in the PRC. He argues that qingzhen stands for ritual cleanliness, moral conduct, authenticity, and legitimacy (1991:13). How this constellation of ideas and practices was played out varied greatly in the four communities he studied. Gladney argues that the Hui of the northwest expressed qingzhen by "Islamic ritual purity," whereas Hui of the southeast limited their concern with qingzhen to the authenticity of their genealogical claims to descent from foreign Muslim ancestors (1991:322). By contrast, the urban Hui whom Gladney studied in Beijing lived out qingzhen by maintaining the pork taboo and engaging in certain specialized occupations, whereas in a rural Hui community outside of the capital, Hui focused on keeping their community pure through endogamy, only marrying other Hui (1991:322–3).

Pillsbury's studies of the Hui are based on research she conducted in Taiwan. Although her work is not as extensive as Gladney's, her 1975 article "Pig and Policy" focuses on what many Hui regard as the single most salient aspect of qingzhen: the pork taboo. Both Gladney and Pillsbury stress that Hui abstinence from pork creates a boundary that makes the Hui separate and distinct from the majority Han Chinese population (Pillsbury 1975, 1978; Gladney 1991, 1992). Government policies in Taiwan and in the PRC (including some that deal with food; see section entitled "Qingzhen and the State") have heightened this sense of separateness, contributing in the case of the PRC to the belief that the Hui are a distinct "race" and fostering strong "nationality" sentiments (see Pillsbury 1975; Gladney 1991). Xi'an Hui beliefs and practices relating to food indicate that they regard the difference between pure and impure as analogous to the differences between Hui and Han. They see food and eating practices as expressing the innate traits that both groups possessed; if anything, such a conviction is bolstered by the government's racial policies. However, residents' understandings of qingzhen differ from those of the state. For Xi'an Hui, qingzhen is centered on Islam, and Islam provides an index for evaluating Hui and Han that differs from the "modernization" paradigm that the government espouses. By this local measure, the Hui are far superior.

What Is Qingzhen?

When I asked residents to explain what qingzhen meant, most people responded by talking about food. Many Hui described the most salient aspect of qingzhen food as cleanliness (*ganjing*, *ganjing weisheng*). Food can be clean in several respects, and one of the most fundamental is in its content. As Jishu, *ahong* of the Small Mosque, put it, qingzhen means "Hui must eat clean things." He said that proscribed foods such as pork, alcohol, and blood as well as animals that had not been slaughtered in the Islamic fashion were "dirty" and Hui could not eat them.

Residents stressed that pork was especially dirty. They believed that the pig was a disease-carrying animal with filthy habits, living in dirt and eating trash. Jiqing, the New Mosque gatekeeper, exemplified the dirtiness of pigs by the speed at which pork rots. According to him, if a person took a piece of pork and a piece of lamb and left them out for a week, when that person returned to examine the two meats the pork would be maggoty and disgusting, whereas the lamb would be "good," that is, it would have dried and still been edible. This explanation of pork's dirtiness also appears in a pamphlet sold by one of the quarter's Muslim products stores (Ma 1971).

The remarks that Jishu and Jiqing made suggest that when Hui talked about foods being "dirty" and "clean," they were concerned with more than simple sanitation, though many residents also applied the term "sanitary" (*weisheng*) to qingzhen foods. Several Hui men, ranging from a historian at a local college, an ahong, the janitor at the Hui Middle School, and Jiqing, explained that pigs were dirty not only because they were unsanitary but also because of their nature. These men divided all animals into two sorts: those that were morally good (*shanliang*) and those that were fierce, ugly, and frightening (*xiong'e* and *kepa*). A book on qingzhen foods written by a man who attended the Western Mosque makes a similar dichotomy, substituting *youmei*, "good, beautiful," for *shanliang* (Bai 1992). Of note is that the terms for moral goodness (*shanliang*) and beauty (*youmei*) were interchangeable, as were the words for fearful (*kepa*) and ferocious (*xiong'e*). Many Hui I knew believed that appearances and intrinsic qualities were closely related, an idea they shared with most Han Chinese.

According to the men, sheep and cattle possessed particularly "good" natures. The "goodness" of sheep and cattle was manifested by their gentleness, harmlessness, and the fact that they digested their food twice. Pigs, on the other hand, were "the opposite" of sheep and cows and the opposite of morally good. One reason this is so, writes the author of the *Guide to Qingzhen Foods*, is that pigs "do nothing": they provide no milk or fleece and are not beasts of burden (Bai 1992:3). The janitor and the ahong also explained the bad nature of pigs by stating that God had changed the evil spirits of the world into pigs, thus the souls of pigs were fierce and evil. Still another young man, overhearing my conversation with Jiqing at the New Mosque, told me that pigs were unfilial (*bu xiaojing*). Filial piety (*xiao*, *xiaojing*) is, of course, the quintessential Confucian virtue and the foundation of the traditional Chinese family system (see, e.g., Harrell 1982; Baker 1979); the young man was rejecting pork because pigs did not meet Chinese standards for proper behavior, standards that Hui and Han shared despite the supposition that the Hui were "non-Chinese." This man said that pigs' lack of filiality was demonstrated by the way piglets climb all over their mothers when they suckle; lambs and calves, by contrast, kneel when they drink their mothers' milk. He and a few other men also claimed that pigs mate indiscriminately with their parents, but cows and sheep never do. These differences in behavior demonstrated conclusively that the animals whose meat the Hui ate, namely sheep and cattle, were highly moral, and that the animal whose meat was eaten and prized by the Han, the pig, was highly immoral.

Although none of the women I spoke to ever elaborated such systematic explanations of the pig's uncleanliness, they too were convinced of its filth. Women were especially concerned with keeping pork away from food, cooking utensils, and the house. They talked about how important it was for Hui not to eat anything that had touched pork or come into contact with lard. Chen, who worked in the public showers owned by the Western Mosque, spoke at length about Hui fears that pork products would "pollute" (*ran*) their food. Because pork was so contaminating, Hui could not use cooking or eating utensils that had ever touched it. Therefore, she said, "we are not willing to eat one mouthful of your food, nor drink one mouthful of your tea" (*women bu yuanyi chi ni de yikou fan, he ni de yikou cha*). Fears about coming into contact with pork products or utensils or dishes that had once contained pork caused residents, male and female, to avoid food that was not prepared by Hui, to refrain from patronizing non-Hui restaurants or food stalls, and to avoid eating or drinking at the homes of non-Hui. In the past, it was said, residents had also refused to use wells that were not owned by other Hui, restricting themselves to those in the quarter.

These avoidance practices mostly affected Hui interactions with Han. The vast majority of Xi'an residents were Han, with the Hui being the city's only significant minority population (Muslim or non-Muslim). Avoidance of non-Hui restaurants did keep residents away from foreign franchises like Kentucky Fried Chicken, of which there were two in Xi'an. More serious were the effects of the pork taboo on Han food businesses. Perhaps unsurprisingly, the Han who lived in or near the quarter did not operate restaurants or produce food for the market. The few Han residents of the Muslim district also said that they avoided bringing pork products into their homes.

More deeply felt than residents' refusal to patronize Han restaurants or food stalls were Hui behaviors in social situations that involved Hui and Han. Xi'an Hui refused to eat or drink in Han homes and in all other institutions, including government offices, that were not owned and run by Hui. Their rejection of non-Hui food and drink was a striking violation of hospitality in the Chinese setting, where all visits that were not strictly business (and many that were) included both the offer and the receipt of at least a small quantity of food or drink. Even a cup of hot tea, the most common form of hospitality offered to guests in China, was unacceptable to a Hui if it were given by a Han. The very cup in which the tea was served, if it belonged to a Han, would cause most residents to refuse it, because they believed that simple washing could not cleanse Han dishes of the residue of pork. Residents' rejection of Han hospitality was all the more striking because it was unidirectional. Although Hui refused Han hospitality, Han accepted Hui food and drink, freely consuming Hui foods and using Hui crockery (see Pillsbury 1975 for a discussion of this issue with reference to the Hui on Taiwan).

The residents' belief in the impurity of pigs also affected many other aspects of their lifestyle. Aside from shunning pork, pork products, and utensils that had been in contact with such foods, residents also avoided uttering the words "pig" or "pork." Hui born in the astrological year of the pig, for example, said they were born in the year of the *hai*. Hai is the twelfth of the twelve branches in the Chinese "heavenly stems and earthly branches" calendrical system (*tiangan dizhi*); it makes a good substitute for the word "pig" because the pig is the twelfth of the twelve signs of the Chinese zodiac (*shuxiang*).[3] Residents also avoided the common term for pork, which is literally "pig's meat" (*zhu rou*). They referred to pork as "meat" (*rou*) or "big meat" (*da rou*) instead. Use of the word for pig (*zhu*) was limited to curses. For example, 24-year-old Yan, lowering her voice so that no one else would hear, told me about being so angry at her fiancé that she called him a "fat pig" (*fei zhu*). On another occasion, when the two of us were practicing English alone in her room with the door shut, she became so annoyed with herself for forgetting her English vocabulary that she berated herself under her breath for having a "pig's brain" (*zhu nao*).

In addition to what was eaten, how food was prepared also determined which foods were qingzhen and which were not. Yan, who worked in her family's restaurant, stressed the care that Hui took with food preparation when explaining qingzhen. She pointed out that Hui washed vegetables, dishes, and hands in separate basins and kept different types of food "segregated and in order" (*fenjie*). Other Hui, both men and women, also explained that Hui sanitary practices were integral to making their food *qingzhen*: a number of residents indicated that Hui, unlike Han, washed frequently and paid close attention when they cooked. One man noted that the character for *qing* ("pure") has the ideographic representation of water in it, which, he said, showed that Hui "rely on water" (*yi shui wei zhu*) and were particularly clean.

Hui made a point of using only running water for washing, a practice advocated in the Qur'an (see Tapper 1994:220). It is not clear how many residents were aware of this proscription; college-educated Liangxun could explain the Hui custom of using pitchers to ensure their water was moving only by saying that water in a basin was simply less clean. Most residents of the quarter would not wash with water that was sitting in a basin. If running water from a faucet were not available, Hui would produce running water by pouring it from a pitcher. In Xi'an, water pitchers were a symbol that Hui and Han alike associated with qingzhen and the Hui people.[4] Many of the signs and advertisements for Hui restaurants and food products included a picture of a pitcher; the district government also used this symbol on the plaques that they distributed to Hui owners of restaurants and food stalls. The repugnance that residents of the quarter felt toward using water in a basin derived in part from their familiarity with the Han use of standing water. Many Han I knew shared a basin full of water between several people when they washed. They would also use and reuse the water contained in a basin over the course of an entire day. I never saw any residents of the quarter engaged in such practices, even though for many families procuring fresh water meant that they had to haul large quantities from the public faucet.

Residents' claims to better sanitation practices than the Han spoke to national goals for improving personal hygiene. During the first half of the twentieth century, Sun Yat-sen and other leaders of the Nationalist party believed that the Chinese race must improve its sanitary habits if the Chinese were to successfully shake off foreign imperialism (see Fitzgerald 1996:9–12, 104–5). Sanitation and personal hygiene were seen as important indices of the Chinese race's degree of civilization, which in turn determined their capacity to create a modern nation-state. The PRC government has continued to devote attention to modifying (or modernizing) the sanitary habits of Chinese citizens through propaganda and urban reconstruction. Although the state had varying degrees of success in persuading Chinese citizens to cease spitting or to wash dishes more carefully (see, e.g., Ikels 1996:28–9), cleanliness retained an association with modernization. The success of McDonald's in Beijing has been partially dependent on its high standards for hygiene, which contribute to its modern image (see Yan 1997; Watson 1997b:33–4). By claiming they had superior standards of cleanliness and hygiene, residents demonstrated to their own satisfaction, and in the terms of at least one aspect of official ideology, that they were more civilized and better equipped to modernize than Han Chinese.

Although the concept of "pure and true" addressed food, consumption, and food production, residents did not stop at food when talking about qingzhen. A banner that hung over one of the main food-selling streets in the Muslim quarter proclaimed qingzhen to be "that which is not polluting . . . that which is not false" (*qingzhen: bu ran yue qing, bu wei yue zhen*) (see Figure 1). Several Hui entrepreneurs told me that "pure and true" meant earning money honestly and being frank in all one's dealings. Mingjie, who operated an eatery on Barley Market Street, stated that qingzhen meant that Hui should not deceive others, gamble, take interest on loans, curse, or hit people—sentiments that were shared by many other residents. During a discussion about the meaning of qingzhen that I had with Mingjie and two other Hui businessmen, the three men described qingzhen as keeping honest business practices through being clear about the price and value of goods, selling clean things, and always giving customers the full value of the goods for which they had paid. To do anything else, one of the men said, is *haram* (unlawful).[5]

Residents took qingzhen to signify belief in Islam, religious observance, and being Hui. For example, Jiqing stated that the qingzhen signs hung above restaurants showed that the cook was a "believer" (*mumin*). A Hui middle school teacher told me that in the larger sense "pure and true" was about "carrying out Islam in practice as well as in theory" and "keeping the rules of the Qur'an." When I asked Yan what qingzhen meant, she replied that "qingzhen means the Hui people" (*qingzhen shi Huimin de yisi*).

A quick look at local linguistic usage demonstrates how these three categories—belief, observance, and being Hui—overlapped in the eyes of local residents. "Islam" was once known as "the pure and true religion" (*qingzhenjiao*), and mosques were still called "pure and true temples" (*qingzhensi*). A more common term for Islam than the "pure and true religion" was the "Hui religion" (*Huijiao*). I often heard older residents use this term during my fieldwork, though sometimes their younger colleagues would correct them, telling them that the name of their religion was "Islam" (*Yisilanjiao*) and that "Hui" was the name of their *minzu* (race or "nationality"). *Huili*, "Hui calendar," was often used as a synonym for the Islamic calendar (*Yili*). Many residents used the term *Huimin*, literally "Hui person," as a synonym for "Muslim" (*Musilin*). Most preferred to refer to themselves as "Hui people" (*Huimin*) rather than the official "Hui nationality [members]" (*Huizu [ren]*). In short, just as among the Central Asian Muslim Durrani Pashtuns "things Durrani and things Muslim are held to be identical" (Tapper and Tapper 1986:65), residents of the Muslim district did not separate Hui from Muslim. This conflation served them well in the "modernizing" PRC, because Islamic doctrines of purity and rules for religious observance enabled the Hui to see themselves as ideologically and socially superior to Han and all other non-Muslims.

Dirt and Contagion

Residents of the quarter believed it was difficult, if not impossible, for things that were considered defiled to be either cleansed or contained. They shared their belief in the polluting and infectious nature of impure substances with other Muslims, and such ideas can be found in manuals of Islamic law (see Reinhart 1990). The fundamental contagiousness of impurity was made clear by the extremes to which Xi'an Hui carried out their avoidance of pork and pigs. For example, it was not sufficient that the quarter's Hui residents did not eat pork; they also insisted that the Han people living there abstain.[6] Residents did not only refuse to raise pigs themselves, but they also prevented anyone from bringing pigs into the quarter, even temporarily or in transit. Cows and sheep, on the other hand, occasioned no comment. The residents' refusal to use any utensils and dishware that belonged to pork-eaters, their abstinence from all cuisine not prepared by Hui, and their reluctance to utter the word "pig" all indicate that they regarded pork as an actively contaminating substance. Alcohol, another prohibited and impure substance, was similarly regarded as contagious (see Chapter 6).

During a public speech at a neighborhood rally (described in Chapter 6), Yingchun, the Dapiyuan Mosque's ahong, explained the polluting nature of impure substances by using the metaphor of putting lamb stew into a dirty bowl. Regardless of how good the stew was, he said, once you put it into a dirty bowl you could not eat it, because the stew had become dirty. His point was that things pure and things polluted could not co-exist together; indeed, Yingchun stated, getting rid of prohibited things was one of the two basic requirements for Muslims (the other being to have belief). The message was clear: Hui could not be pure in the presence of polluted things—or people.

You Are What You Eat

The residents' descriptions and characterizations of animals illustrated a system in which animals, like people, were categorized as either moral and good or fierce and evil. Terms such as *shanliang*, "good," and *xiong*, "fierce," were commonly used by Hui and Han alike to describe individuals or groups of people. I heard Xi'an Han describe Hui as "fierce" on a number of occasions. Residents characterized animals as belonging to one or the other category based on the environment in which they lived (clean vs. dirty); what they ate (grass vs. trash); how they behaved to others (gentle vs. fierce, filial vs. unfilial); and how they looked (beautiful vs. frightening). In this formal system, pigs did not behave as "proper" animals (compare Douglas [1966] 1994). Pigs fell on the negative side of animal behavior; they wallowed in dirt rather than lived in grassy pastures, and they ate human rubbish rather than plants. They lacked the human traits that residents considered desirable that could be manifest by animals: they treated their parents without respect and were ugly. At the opposite extreme of the spectrum were sheep: animals that ate suitable food, were beautiful in appearance, and lived a lifestyle considered appropriate according to local standards for animals and humans.

Residents stated explicitly that they ate in such a way as to avoid impurity. Their eating practices and their beliefs about the nature of animals also suggest that they ate to maximize purity. Although residents did not articulate this idea, it was the logical corollary to their beliefs about impure substances, which polluted those who consumed them, and the binary oppositions that Hui men used to classify animals and meat. If pure substances possessed the power to purify those who ate them, then by eating qingzhen a person became more pure, just as by eating dirty substances she or he became contaminated. Residents' eating practices and notions about food indicated the existence of such a belief, which was founded on the premise that the consumer incorporated the properties of the food she or he consumed.

Xi'an urbanites commonly expressed the notion that people took on the properties of the foods they ate, and many regulated their eating based on the Chinese humoral system. This system divides foods into hot (*rexing*) and cold (*liangxing*) categories. Many Chinese believed (and all those I knew were familiar with the notion) that the consumption of foods with a hot or a cold nature affected the balance of hot and cold within one's body and that an individual could strategically adjust his or her consumption to create a balance when deficiencies existed. For cxample, when a woman had just given birth, she avoided "cold" foods such as fruits and ate a great deal of "hot" foods, such as eggs and chicken. Childbirth exposed a woman to cold through opening her body, and an overabundance of cold caused illness. By overeating "hot" foods after giving birth, a woman decreased her vulnerability to illness and protected both herself and her child.

During a lengthy conversation about food and qingzhen,

Zenglie, a Hui professor of Hui culture, explained that a common principle of Chinese medicine was that one could "eat something to fix something" (*chi shenme bu shenme*). For example, he said, a man with brain damage might eat brains to cure himself, or a person with poor eyesight might increase his or her intake of eyeballs. Zenglie stated that this belief explained the Hui avoidance of "ugly" foods, such as fish with teeth, which were not Qur'anically prohibited. The fear was that eating foods from ugly animals would make a person ugly. Simply put, Chinese medicine hypothesized a direct correlation between what people ate and their state of being. The relationship derived from a theory of resemblance or what Sir James Frazer might have called "sympathetic magic."

Like other Chinese, residents of the quarter believed that foods bestowed their qualities upon their consumers. The internal properties of a food were in turn made apparent by outward manifestations, including appearance and in the case of animals, behavior. Although there is no question that Hui abstained from pork, carrion, and other substances because the Qur'an mandated that they should, the extremes to which they carried out their avoidance of pigs was only intelligible in a Chinese context, where people believed that they assumed the properties of what they ate. Residents rejected pigs because they believed that by eating such animals, or even coming in contact with them, they would become like them.

At the same time, when residents restricted their diet to only those animals that were clean, beautiful, and morally good, they increased their potential for being and becoming pure and good. Sheep and cows were preferred by Hui—who proudly described their cuisine as "based on mutton and beef" (*yi niuyang rou wei zhu*)—not simply because they were not prohibited, but because they were beautiful and moral animals. By eating animals that adhered to Hui moral standards and displayed innate goodness, residents enhanced their own ability to be moral and good. Eating mutton or beef made Hui more pure, more beautiful, more good—more qingzhen.

As "Hui people" (*Huimin*), residents regarded themselves as innately good, or more specifically, "pure and true." Yan encapsulated this belief when she stated "Qingzhen means the Hui people." Residents believed that their behaviors manifested their intrinsic moral qualities: they ate clean food, washed frequently, engaged in honest business practices, and followed the dictates of the Qur'an. By avoiding contaminating substances such as pork and pigs, Hui acted to preserve their "innate predisposition" to be moral. When they consumed foods that displayed qualities they valued, such as beauty, filiality, and propriety, they increased such characteristics within themselves.

They Are What They Eat: Han and Pigs

Just as residents believed that what they ate had the power to improve or detract from their moral nature and revealed their inner qualities, they also thought that what other people ate affected and reflected their characters. As residents' comments and the symbols they used make clear, Hui equated themselves with qingzhen, the purity of water, and the goodness of sheep. They equated the Han people with dirt and with pigs. Residents justified this equation by pointing to Han behaviors they considered immoral, which included eating pork and a number of other activities prohibited or castigated in the Qur'an. These behaviors were external manifestations of the innate inferiority of the Han people compared to Hui, just as the behaviors of pigs demonstrated their basic inferiority to sheep and cattle.

Han Chinese are justly famed for their love of pork, a food that the Chinese government has referred to as a "national treasure" (Pillsbury 1978:659; see also Thompson 1988). Although I never saw any Han residents of Xi'an raising pigs, no doubt because of crowded conditions and municipal regulations, pork was widely available in all parts of the city except the quarter. Pork was sold in butcher shops and restaurants and was commonly eaten as a household dish. The northern Han urbanites I knew did not use pork for elaborate religious rituals of the sort described for rural southern Chinese (see Ahern 1981; Thompson 1988; Watson

1982); in general Xi'an Han limited their ancestral and religious observances to burning paper money and incense. Nevertheless, many served pork as a delicacy at banquets and consumed pork on holidays. In the countryside surrounding Xi'an, which locals reported was entirely Han, pigs were an important feature of rural life. For example, in a village that I visited to the southwest of Xi'an, each household raised at least one pig, a practice one resident said had been encouraged by Mao Zedong.

Hui believed that Han, like pigs, ate trash, had dirty habits, and behaved immorally. Clearly the most condemning aspect of the Han diet was their consumption of pork. However, another frequent criticism of Han that I heard residents make was that Han "ate everything" (*tamen shenme dou chi*). Residents contrasted this practice to what they regarded as the more discerning Hui palate. The "everything" that Han ate included foods that had not been properly washed; prohibited substances like pork, lard, blood, and alcohol; animals that had died of disease, bludgeoning, or in other manners that rendered them prohibited for consumption according to the Qur'an; and animals such as fish with teeth, which Hui avoided because of their ugly appearance and corollary bad nature.

A number of Hui women commented to me that Han treated their food unhygienically. Some stated that Han used the same basin for washing vegetables that they used for washing their bodies or that they placed washed vegetables on the ground before cooking with them—both practices that the women considered dirty. Residents generally accused the Han of being "less clean" than Hui were. Some told me that Han did not wash their hands after using the toilet. Others said that Han bathed infrequently, or at least used to, when "conditions were bad" and few people had ready access to running water. Because Hui directly linked a person's physical condition to his or her moral state, physical cleanliness was an important sign of internal purity and morality. As one elderly Hui man put it, "When your body is clean, your mind is pure." Residents regarded the Han failure to live up to Hui standards of cleanliness as proof of their impurity.

Other practices also evidenced the Han people's lack of morality. Han drank alcohol, gambled, danced, and sang in karaoke bars, all activities that residents avoided for being impure and unlawful. Even more significant, given residents' propensity for commercial enterprise, was that Hui believed Han were dishonest. Many residents told me that Han merchants charged unreasonably high prices. They also complained that Han sellers cheated their customers by giving them less of a product than they paid for: several people claimed that Han merchants would pretend a piece of meat or a handful of vegetables weighed more than it actually did in order to get more money for it (most foods in Xi'an were sold by weight).

The equation Hui made between Han and pigs was demonstrated by the ways Hui behaved toward Han, which was quite similar to the ways they treated pigs. With few exceptions, residents actively tried to minimize their interactions with Han. They avoided Han food, drink, dishes, and eating utensils, making Hui-Han sociability difficult. Residents tended to restrict their dealings with Han to business: they sold prepared food to Han, drove them around in taxis, or worked with them in state-owned work units, but they did not socialize with Han. Many Hui, especially women, children, and older people, avoided Han by rarely if ever leaving the Muslim district (young men were the most likely to leave the quarter because many drove taxis for a living). Residents did not celebrate Han holidays or festivals, which created another barrier between the two groups by obstructing gift exchange. Very few Hui I knew invited Han people to their homes or to important events such as weddings. Fewer still married Han, unless the Han spouse was willing to convert to Islam. I knew of only three cases of Hui-Han intermarriage in the quarter, two of which involved the Han wife's conversion to Islam. The third case, that of a Hui woman marrying a Han man, occasioned a great deal of speculation about the woman's motives; several residents said they suspected she had married the man because he was a Hong Kong resident. Hui used eating as a metaphor and a justification for why Hui did not marry Han: Hui and Han "couldn't eat together" (*chi bu dao yikuar*) and so should not marry.[7] Even Yue and her sister, the two young Hui women I knew who had the most contact with Han, felt strongly that they should and would marry Hui men. Avoidance and separation characterized how most Xi'an Hui interacted with Han and with pigs.

Qingzhen and the State

In his study of Muslims on the Cormoro Islands, Lambek poses the possibility that "food or the incorporative activities of digestion" might "serve most strongly to articulate the nature of identity" (1995:269). An important facet of his argument is that the identities expressed and created through food have political implications. For example, Lambek writes that during the period when Mayotte was debating whether it would join the other Cormoro Islands in independence or remain part of France, the food served by families reflected which of these two political identities families found most appealing.

Eating qingzhen had a political dimension in the quarter too, though it played out somewhat differently than it did on the Cormoro Islands. Government officials involved themselves in the production and marketing of qingzhen foods. District officials promoted the sale of qingzhen foods when they designated Barley Market Street a "Hui nationality food and drink street" in 1992. They tried to foster the sale of qingzhen foods by improving the facilities of Barley Market Street and other marketing areas in the quarter (Wu 1992:104). In addition, the Religion and Nationality Office of the Lianhu District attempted to regulate qingzhen foods by registering and licensing restaurants and food stalls as qingzhen. During the summer of 1996, the provincial government also involved itself in qingzhen regulations when it debated policies for classifying factories as qingzhen. By June 1997, provincial officials had established new regulations for qingzhen and published them in the Shaanxi newspapers, but had taken no other steps to implement the policy.

To regulate the sale of qingzhen foods, Lianhu District officials devised a set of criteria that any food establishment advertised as qingzhen had to meet, or else the government would force the owners to remove such claims. They gave stores that met their requirements a large, shiny official plaque inscribed with the words "pure and true," the name of the Religion and Nationality Office, and a drawing of a traditional water pitcher. Store owners displayed these signs prominently, frequently next to their license for running a private enterprise. Officials from the Religion and Nationality Office made an annual examination of the quarter's restaurants and food stalls to make sure that each establishment billing itself as "pure and true" met the government's criteria. During 1994, one official estimated there were 700 such enterprises in the Muslim district. This number did not include food sellers who peddled their qingzhen products on carts; district officials said there were too many itinerant merchants to regulate.

The state's "pure and true" qualifications had nothing to do with sanitation or Islam. All government-certified "pure and true" food enterprises met three official conditions: (1) the store "representative" (*daibiao*), meaning the person responsible for all dealings with the government, was a member of the Hui nationality; (2) more than half of the business' employees belonged to the Hui nationality; and (3) the cook was a member of the Hui nationality. The official who described the registration procedures to me stressed this last point as especially important. He said that if a restaurant's cook were not Hui, he or she might use any meat available when cooking, especially if pressed for time. By contrast, he said, a Hui cook would always ensure that the meat met with Hui standards.

The local government's criteria for qingzhen differed sharply from the characterizations the quarter's residents gave to me. The official requirements were based entirely on nationality membership. In the state's eyes, if the cooks, store representatives, and most employees were members of the Hui nationality, then the business was qingzhen. Considerations of cleanliness, permitted and pure foods, the moral nature of the animals from which the meat came, and the seller's belief in Islam were not relevant to the official criteria for qingzhen, nor did they influence the government's decision to award its "pure and true" plaques. Government officials defined qingzhen as Hui, but in their usage, Hui was a racial category.

Government officials and local residents agreed that Hui and Han were distinctly different. The state, however, as part of its modernization agenda, promoted a racial understanding of the difference between Hui and Han. From the state's perspective, qingzhen foods were "the genius of a people": a manifestation of Hui cultural achievements and a sign of their racial separateness. As a kind of "nationality tradition," qingzhen foods merited official support. The state was committed to protecting the "nationality customs and habits" of China's minority races, and in turn the presence of such "customs and habits" legitimated the official characterization of China's minorities as backward relative to the Han. In Xi'an, officials acted to promote qingzhen foods because they fit in with the government's plans for economic development. In this respect, the state's goals benefited local residents.

"Traditional Hui Cuisine"

Residents used the terms "qingzhen food" and "Hui people food" (*Huimin shipin*) interchangeably when referring to their cuisine. Many of the foods that residents defined as "Hui" contained lamb or beef. Foods such as cured lamb and beef (*la niuyang rou*), lamb stew (*yangrou paomo*), spicy squash and meatball soup (*hula tang*), lamb soup (*shuipen yangrou*), and breaded mutton and beef (*fenzheng niuyang rou*) topped the list when Hui discussed their cuisine. When residents sold these foods as "little eats" (*xiao chi*), they advertised them in such a way as to capitalize on "tradition" and what might be called the "Hui heritage." The labels of the foods Hui packaged for sale and the signs they hung in their restaurants displayed slogans describing the food as "famous" (*minggui shipin*), "traditionally prepared" (*chuantong caozuo*), a "special product of Xi'an" (*Xi'an techan*), "traditional Hui food" (*chuantong Huimin shipin*), and as having a "long and glorious history" (*lishi youjiu*). Residents also almost always used their immediately identifiable Hui surnames in their food enterprise's name. For example, a family might call their restaurant or food production site "The Old Ma Family Place" (*Lao Ma Jia*), Ma being the most common Hui family name.

In Xi'an, lamb stew (*yangrou paomo*) was the most celebrated Hui food. It consisted of slices of lamb, green bean threads, scallions, and soup broth placed on top of one or two round unleavened breads that the customer had broken into small pieces in his or her bowl. Eaten with chili sauce and pickled garlic, lamb stew was regarded as a specialty of the province and was frequently sought out by Hui and Han alike. Most Xi'an dwellers thought the quarter was the best place to get lamb stew in the city, even though many Hui had opened lamb stew restaurants in other parts of town. The lamb stew restaurants in Xi'an ranged from those that could seat ten customers at a time to some extremely large, elite, and expensive restaurants that specialized in lamb stew but also provided a vast array of other delicacies.

One of the most famous Hui lamb stew restaurants in Xi'an was called The Old Sun Family Place (*Lao Sun Jia*). The owners of the Sun establishment claimed to have special recipes for making lamb stew that had been passed down in the family for generations. Assertions of this sort were commonplace among families in the quarter who sold food (see Bai 1992 for examples). Those who ran The Old Sun Family Place, like many other restaurateurs in the quarter, represented themselves as the preservers of an unbroken culinary tradition, the heirs to the knowledge of past generations who knew how to make lamb stew the good old-fashioned way.

Such claims to historical continuity were easily falsified. During one conversation, Si expressed disgust with the increasing numbers of fakes in China. He told me that no one at the Sun place was even related to the original Sun family who had once owned and run the restaurant. According to him, a great deal of the cuisine marketed as "traditional" in the quarter was inauthentic, because many of the cooking techniques that Hui had once used had been forgotten. Nowadays, most entrepreneurs were "hanging a sheep's head but selling dog meat" (*gua yang tou mai gou rou*): calling themselves traditional but lacking any real knowledge of or connection to the past.

Xi'an Hui knew just as well as other Chinese (if not better) that many of their food preparation techniques and other forms of knowledge ranging from religious to architectural to medicinal had been forgotten or lost during the years of suppression under Mao. After "Liberation" in 1949 and particularly between 1958 and 1978, the PRC government prohibited most expressions of "tradition," castigating it as "old culture" and "feudal," as it sought to build a modern "New China." The majority of the quarter's residents could not remember what life had been like before 1949. Many ahong and elites, who had been the most important repositories of local knowledge in the community, had died during the violence of 1958 and the Cultural Revolution. Yet the vast majority of residents involved in the food business preferred to call their products "traditional" and represented themselves as the practitioners of age-old Hui food preparation techniques.

Why did Hui eat and sell foods that they marketed as traditional, ignoring challenges to the integrity of this claim? The answer to this question has two dimensions, one associated with local ideas about the incorporative power of eating and the other associated with modernization, development, and race.

Eating Hui

Local ideas about eating and the incorporation of a food's essential nature gave residents' consumption of "traditional" foods a significance that went beyond the mundane quest for nutrition or gustatory satisfaction. By eating "traditional Hui foods" Hui incorporated the "Hui" quality of such foods, just as by eating lamb they incorporated the moral qualities of sheep and by eating "hot" foods they incorporated the heat of such foods. Eating served as an important mechanism for residents to affirm that they were Hui and promote their sense of continuity with Hui history.[8] Hui who ate foods associated with their forebears forged a strong connection to the past and defined a past that was uniquely Hui. "Eating Hui" helped residents to constitute and maintain themselves as Hui.

The foods served at Hui rituals demonstrate the integral link between eating traditional food and being Hui. Ritual events such as the celebration of the Prophet's birthday, the annual commemoration of the late 19th-century Hui Uprising, circumcisions, engagements, weddings, and funerals involved both a public recitation of the Qur'an and a communal meal for most residents.[9] Although all these events conveyed messages about who the Hui were and what it meant to be Hui, it was at funerals that the enactment of Hui identity became most critical. Gedimu residents (about 80 percent of the quarter's population) believed that the acts of the living directly affected the fate of the deceased. For example, when residents gathered as a community in the mosque to perform a final public prayer and obeisance on behalf of the departed just before burial, they believed that their prayer would move God to show mercy on the deceased.[10] The bereaved family engaged an ahong to recite the Qur'an daily for a month or longer in an appeal to God to absolve the dead person's sins. Relatives gave donations to the mosque in the name of dead kin on the major Muslim holidays to mitigate the deceased's sufferings and ensure that he or she entered paradise.

Funeral ceremonies were highly conservative events. Whereas Western-style wedding gowns had become popular bridal attire at Hui weddings (see Chapter 7), clothing at funerals was strictly "traditional." Guests at funerals were careful to dress in strict accordance with modesty dictates, covering their bodies from ankle to wrist. All mourners wore white hats, including any non-Muslims who attended the ritual (such as myself). Those persons closely related to the deceased dressed in white robes and specially designed white hats that demarcated their relationship to the dead person in a manner that resembled the Han practices described by Arthur Wolf for Taiwan (Wolf 1970).

Food at funerals conformed to strict notions of what was properly Hui. Two types of food were associated with death in the quarter: a flat, round piece of fried dough called *youxiang* and a kind of lamb or beef soup known as *meirimei*. According to Zenglie, *meirimei* meant "every person receives one bowl" (*meiren yiwan*). *Meirimei* soup resembled the lamb stew that Hui entrepreneurs marketed in Xi'an. The main differences were that consumers did not crumble their bread into their soup bowls for funerals and the soup did not contain green bean threads. *Meirimei* was served by the family of the deceased to all those mourning the death during the funeral sequence (see Figure 13). Eating this soup followed a collective recitation of the Qur'an in the home of the deceased. It was consumed in strict rank order: first the ahong and men known for their devotion, called *laorenjia*, were served, then male relatives and friends, and last the women and children.[11] The other funeral food, *youxiang*, was not served as part of a meal; rather, the bereaved family delivered these cakes to all the relatives and friends of the deceased as a way of notifying them of the death. Residents also sent fried dough to relatives and friends on death-date anniversaries as a way of mourning the dead (see Figure 14). Unlike the lamb soup, *youxiang* were never marketed; fried cakes of this size, shape, and flavor were reserved solely for death.[12]

Because the mourners at Hui funerals knew that their acts helped to determine the fate of the deceased, they chose to observe modesty dictates strictly, regardless of how they ordinarily dressed; to engage in communal worship, regardless of how frequently they did so under normal circumstances; and to eat foods like *meirimei* that were intimately associated with being Hui, regardless of their everyday diet. At the moment of death, who a person was and whether or not he or she was Hui determined whether that person ascended into paradise or descended into hell. When confronted with the death of a Hui, residents were extremely careful to act in ways that ensured God knew the deceased was a Hui. Eating the "traditional" funeral food made certain that the deceased's Hui identity was known to God and to the community and created the opportunity for the living to substantiate and strengthen their own Hui qualities.

FIGURE 13. Making *meirimei* soup.

FIGURE 14. *Youxiang* funeral cakes.

Marketing Hui

When officials protected and promoted qingzhen foods, they served the government in several ways. First, they assisted the economic development of the quarter and so helped it to modernize. Second, they upheld the Chinese constitution, which guaranteed minority nationalities the right to be non-Han. Third, they strengthened the association between the Hui and "tradition," an act that validated the state's characterization of the Hui as backward and less modern than the Han. Residents colluded with the state in marketing their wares as qingzhen and as "traditional Hui cuisine," but for reasons other than those that the government possessed. Hui promoted their foods as traditional because "tradition" made their food sell, because they were invested in maintaining a non-Han identity, and because being "traditional" was a way for them to assert autonomy from state intervention in daily life.

Government officials produced the mid-1990s attachment to "tradition" by their policies between 1949 and 1979. During this era, the state attacked "traditional culture" through propaganda and physical assaults and promoted modernization by bureaucratizing, industrializing, and rationalizing almost every aspect of family life. The use of ration coupons for procuring food and goods, which was theoretically designed to equalize consumption and promote higher standards of living for all Chinese, is one example of how the Maoist state's modernization program affected even the most mundane features of ordinary existence. The most extreme example of the PRC's effort to industrialize and modernize China is the Great Leap Forward. During this period, the government attempted to increase production on a massive scale, turning the whole of Chinese society into one giant factory production team and bringing under state control even so mundane an activity as eating by dismantling private kitchens and creating public canteens (see Watson 1991a).

When Deng Xiaoping ascended to power, the CCP retrenched, lifting its radical policies and backing away from intense intrusion into private life. The combination of these two acts—first suppression and then retrenchment—enabled "tradition" to emerge as a compelling force in the quarter (and elsewhere in China). By interfering so intimately in private life and outlawing "tradition," the state generated an attachment to traditional practices. By withdrawing from its extreme interventionist policies and promoting economic development above all else, the government opened a space in which Chinese citizens could be "traditional," both through the state's withdrawal and through the increasing standards of living caused by economic development. Part of the appeal of "tradition" was its association with the absence of state intrusion. All over China, observers witnessed the (re)appearance of "tradition" in the 1980s and 1990s. This was as true of Han as it was of Hui (Jing 1996, Ruf 1998, and Yan

1996 all provide examples of the emergence of "tradition" in Han communities).

At the same time that the national government encouraged privatization and marketization, officials also reiterated their commitment to the minority nationality policies detailed in the PRC constitution. During the Great Leap Forward and Cultural Revolution periods, the government had used strong-arm techniques to make the non-Han races conform to a Han-based (or Sinocentric) model of the new socialist citizen (see Dreyer 1976:159–235; Brugger and Reglar 1994:320–32). In the reform era, the state renewed its protectionist policies for minority nationalities, providing them with various political, economic, and social benefits because they were not Han. As Gladney has detailed (1991; see also Jankowiak 1993:30–58), these nationality policies gave Hui an added interest in creating and maintaining a distinctly non-Han identity. From the official perspective, the presence of Hui "tradition" legitimated the state's evolutionary ranking of the Hui race. From residents' perspective, the presence of Hui "tradition" strengthened their claims for privileged treatment from the government. Residents benefited from their minority status by receiving tax breaks, permission to have two children, leniency on examination scores for college, and other perquisites (see Chapter 2). These benefits gave them an incentive to depict themselves as "traditional" and to engage in practices seen as distinctively Hui.

The final reason that Hui marketed their food as "traditional Hui cuisine" was because it sold. The commercial viability of "traditional Hui cuisine" was evidenced by the amounts of money Hui restaurateurs and food production enterprises were making in the mid-1990s. To give one example, Yan's family's eatery on Barley Market Street earned 15,000 yuan per month average net income in 1994, a sum that, averaged among the seven members of her family, equals more than 2,100 yuan per month per individual. This monthly salary grossly exceeded the 250 yuan per month that the secretary of the History Department at the Shaanxi Academy of Social Sciences earned.

The marketability of Hui tradition relates to both the emergence of tradition and the reinvigoration of minority policies that had taken place since 1979. "Tradition" in the mid-1990s appealed to a nostalgic sensibility that many Chinese citizens were experiencing, and "nationality tradition" appealed to their desires for exotic culture or, in the CCP's parlance, the "customs and habits" of the more "primitive" races. Probably the most convincing sign of Chinese nostalgia for "tradition" (aside from the money that residents made from selling "traditional Hui cuisine") was the popularity of prime-time soap operas set in the imperial period. Several of these television shows were aired during 1994 and 1995, and almost all the Xi'an urbanites I knew watched them regularly (see also Ikels 1996:235–43). The Chinese appetite for "tradition" also manifested itself in the "traditional" red "dragon and phoenix" gown that some Xi'an brides chose to wear for wedding photographs and as a second outfit during wedding ceremonies. This appetite for "tradition" carried over to "traditional food," particularly those dishes and pastries that Xi'an urbanites did not have the time (or perhaps the inclination) to prepare at home, such as peanut cakes, mung bean cakes, certain types of noodles, and other "little eats."

The counterpart to the nostalgia for a prerevolutionary past that some urbanites felt has been an intense interest in minority cultures. Once again, this interest has been stimulated by the state, both by its ideological framework that defines the minorities as "primitive" and by its economic policies. Since the early 1980s, officials have encouraged the development of tourist industries in minority nationality regions (see, e.g., Swain 1990; Harrell 1990). A great deal of this tourism has been domestic (Schein 1990). Although the Xi'an Hui were less exotic than other minorities were reputed to be, entering the quarter nevertheless provided a "cultural experience" for Han visitors. Visual and aural markers rendered the quarter a distinctive space in the city (see Chapters 2 and 3); "traditional Hui cuisine" provided another sensory experience to titillate and satisfy the tastes of non-Hui "outsiders" who wanted something a little different from their ordinary repast.

Traditional Food and the Discourse of Race

Hui food was implicated in the discourse of race in mid-1990s China. Local residents and the government shared the opinion that food differentiated Hui from Han. However, residents differed from officials in their interpretations of qingzhen. Residents related qingzhen to Islam and to indices of purity that were rooted in religious practice. They saw qingzhen as evidence of their superiority to Han. By contrast, the state related qingzhen to race and saw it as a sign of Hui primitiveness relative to the more advanced and "cultureless" Han nationality.

Although the Xi'an Hui understood qingzhen differently than government officials did, they nevertheless turned the government's position to their advantage. Residents benefited from the state's promotion of their "nationality cuisine" and collaborated with the state by marketing their food as "traditional." "Traditional Hui cuisine" sold in Xi'an, and the outcome of its popularity was a dramatic rise in local incomes—something that residents and officials both desired.

Chapter Five

FACTORY FOOD, MODERNIZATION, AND RACE

One warm spring afternoon in 1995, I rode my bicycle over to Aifeng's house, as I did every two or three days during the eighteen months that I lived in Xi'an in 1994 and 1995. Aifeng had plans to visit a wholesale market and asked me to accompany her. With an extra hand to carry packages, she would be able to buy more of the items her family needed. I had gone shopping with Aifeng many times, but we usually went to the street market behind her house, where ten to twelve farmers from the nearby countryside gathered daily to sell fruit and vegetables. This time we rode our bicycles for ten minutes outside of the quarter until we reached a busy wholesale market just east of the Xi'an city wall.

The market was a large, concrete-paved lot, studded with several roofed, wall-less edifices and encircled by small shops. In the stores, under the covered areas, and out in the open, several dozen vendors displayed boxes and bags of packaged foods, soaps, paper products, and other factory-produced goods. Aifeng had clearly visited the market many times before; she knew exactly where to buy the cheapest bulk toilet paper and powder laundry detergent. I helped her load the household goods she bought onto our bicycles and then followed her toward the food vendors.

Although the offerings were plentiful, Aifeng bought only two types of food from the vendors. First she meticulously checked through the many brands of factory-produced, individually packaged instant noodles (*fangbian mian*) for sale, until she finally found a large box labeled "pure and true" (*qingzhen*). Then Aifeng bought some packaged snacks for her granddaughter, a one-and-a-half-year-old girl who, along with her father (Aifeng's son) and his wife, lived in the upper two floors of Aifeng's house. A vast array of mass-produced, packaged snacks were for sale at the market, including candied nuts, puffed rice, chocolates, chips, biscuits, and hard candies. Most of these foods were packaged in single portion-sized servings colorfully decorated with cartoon figures. Aifeng purchased enough of these snacks to fill two large bags. Later, when we returned to her house, she immediately gave some to her granddaughter and offered others to her school-age nieces who had stopped to visit.

It was not until months later that I realized the importance of Aifeng's and my trip to the wholesale market. At the time I simply noted what goods Aifeng purchased; only afterward did I realize that the snacks she bought for her grandchild were not labeled qingzhen. Furthermore, although Aifeng had spent a great deal of time studying the labels of the instant noodle packages, she had paid very little attention to the labels of the snacks that she had bought for her granddaughter. Based on everything I had seen and been told about the quarter's residents, Aifeng had violated the local standards for Islamic dietary observance when she purchased food for her granddaughter that was not qingzhen.

Such an act was difficult to reconcile with what I knew of Aifeng and her family. Aifeng sold qingzhen stuffed breads (*baozi*) in a small restaurant she operated with her family on Barley Market Street. She was very careful to adhere to the Islamic dietary proscriptions and never ate or drank in a Han restaurant, eatery, or household. Her religious observance went far beyond the minimum level of eating qingzhen. Although her business and family obligations prevented her from worshipping five times a day as stipulated in the Qur'an, she worshipped regularly at home and attended the mosque whenever she could. Aifeng donated money, food, and other goods regularly to the mosque; upheld Islamic precepts of dress; and fasted during Ramadan. Why did she buy snacks for her granddaughter that were not "pure and true"?

Children's Food in China

Foodways in China have undergone significant transformations in the wake of Deng Xiaoping's economic reforms (see Jing 2000). One obvious effect of the reform policies has been the appearance of new foods on the market, including a wide variety of mass-produced, packaged snacks such as chocolate, chips, puffed rice balls, biscuits, ice cream bars, and various types of candy. These foods have had a profound impact on nutritional intake in China, most particularly that of children (see Guldan 2000). Equally dramatic have been the sociological consequences of these new foods. Examinations of the consumer practices surrounding these products reveal that the balance of power between older and younger generations in China, especially parents and children, has shifted (see Guo 2000, Chee 2000; see also Stafford 1995 for a discussion of shifts in intergenerational power relations on Taiwan).

Both of these changes were found in the Muslim district. During June 1997, I asked Peng, an eleven-year-old resident, to record his total dietary intake for seven days (see Figure 15). Peng's food diary reveals that he ate mass-produced snacks similar to those that Aifeng purchased for her granddaughter on a daily basis (see Appendix). Xin, Peng's high school–age brother, was the only other member of his immediate (nuclear) family who ever ate these foods, but he and his parents agreed that Peng ate far more of these snacks than his brother did, both in June 1997 and before that time. The level of Peng's consumption was by no means extraordinary; it matched that of many other children I observed.

Peng was able to snack on the new factory foods because his parents provided him with a de facto allowance of about 3 yuan per day—a fact that they had not been fully aware of until we

FIGURE 15. Peng.

examined his food diary together. When we totaled his snack expenditures, Peng's parents and his brother realized that Peng was the first member of their family to receive a regular, daily allowance. A qualitative (and quantitative) shift had occurred in Peng's family relationships: Peng directly influenced the household budget and even completely controlled a small portion of it. Peng's parents, and many other residents, believed that this kind of child-directed input into the family's affairs was completely new.

Consumption of mass-produced snacks also evidenced an ideological and behavioral shift in residents' Islamic observance. The combination of religious devotion and unthinking disregard for qingzhen seen in Aifeng, Peng and his family, and most other Xi'an Hui reveals that local standards for dietary purity were not entirely applicable to the new foods. Residents used a different set of standards to evaluate mass-produced industrial foods, largely because these foods represented something that most Xi'an Hui desired: modernization.

Non-qingzhen Food

The foods that Aifeng bought for her granddaughter and that Peng consumed were diverse in flavor and ingredients. Most were recent arrivals to the area; residents said that the vast majority of these mass-produced snacks had only been available for ten years. Soda was the exception to this rule. Mingxin, a butcher, remembered seeing Chinese-made sodas for sale in the quarter during the late 1970s. At that time soda cost eleven *fen* per bottle, a price no ordinary person could afford, so only the children of government officials and important people drank it.[1] Nevertheless, although soda had been present in the quarter for a longer period, Mingxin placed it in the same category as candy and chocolate: all were "foreign" (*guowai de*) foods, made by "foreign" machines in "foreign" factories. He pointed out that although many Chinese factories now produced such foods, they had "learned about them from the West."

Even though Mingxin characterized the new foods as "foreign," the majority of mass-produced snacks that residents ate were made in China. Few imported foods were available in Xi'an, and their prices tended to deter most residents from buying them. However, a number of foreign-brand foods were produced in Chinese factories, some even in Shaanxi Province. For example, popular and well-known products such as Coca-Cola were made and bottled in Shaanxi. When local production of Coca-Cola began in 1997, it caused the price of a can to drop from eight yuan to one and a half yuan.

In addition to industrial production techniques, media representations also caused the factory foods to be perceived as "foreign," and more specifically Western. Residents called a number of foods "Western" because they saw them served and consumed in media images of the United States, Canada, and Europe. Television programs, both those made in the United States and those made in China, played an important role in disseminating ideas about "Western" cuisine (and other aspects of "Western" life) to residents of the quarter. One such show was "A Beijinger in New York" (*Beijingren zai Niuyue*), which aired during the early months of 1994. This program was extremely popular throughout Xi'an and occasioned much discussion about American society. Television, movies, magazines, news clips, and articles published in newspapers all made "the West" a meaningful category in the imaginations of my informants, none of whom had ever traveled to the United States or Europe.

Residents also learned about "foreign" foods from the products available in Xi'an's department stores, wholesale markets, convenience stores, and supermarkets. Many of the products available in such shops were specifically marketed as "Western." They included beverages such as Coca-Cola, Sprite, Tang fruit drink, Nestle powdered milk, and Nestle instant coffee and foods such as Snickers, M & Ms, McVitie's Digestive Biscuits, and several kinds of Keebler cookies and crackers, many of which (for example, mango-flavored sandwich cookies) were designed specifically for the Asian market. They also included a variety of Japanese and Hong Kong imitations of these foods and others that were produced in the PRC. Khong Guan and Garden biscuits and crackers were particularly popular among the Hong Kong brands and tended to be cheaper than the comparable American and European goods made by Keebler and McVitie's. Cheapest of all were the PRC-made spin-offs, which included carbonated drinks, crackers, crisps, cookies, ice cream bars, and candy made in Guangzhou, Shenzhen, Tianjin, and Shaanxi. It is worth noting that supermarkets (*chaoji shichang*) themselves were a foreign phenomenon and had only arrived in Xi'an in January 1994. A Hong Kong company called the Seastar Overseas Company (*Haixing Haiwai Gongsi*) had newly opened two supermarkets near the city center when I arrived; by the time I left in August 1995, they had opened at least two more stores. One of these supermarkets was quite close to the Muslim district, and some residents patronized it.

Another reason residents considered the mass-produced foods "Western" was because of the ingredients such products contained. From a Chinese perspective, butter and milk were typical ingredients in Western food. The use of dairy products in many of the Chinese-made snacks, coupled with advertising, processing techniques, and media stereotypes, gave them the aura of Westernness. Dairy products also made these foods luxury goods, at least from the perspective of Hui who were in their 30s and older. Because very few milk products had been available in China before the 1980s, many adults associated them with prosperity. For example, Mingxin remembered craving milk as a child, but little was available for consumption and his family was too poor to buy it. Mingxin attributed the high price and small quantity of milk to low levels of milk production in China during the 1950s, 1960s, and 1970s. However, he said, since the market reforms, China's cows had been "scientifically modernized" (*kexue xiandaihua*), causing dairy products to become readily available and affordable.

Several enterprises in Xi'an sold foods such as fresh yeast bread and cakes that residents and other urbanites associated with the West. Like the mass-produced foods, residents had seen yeast bread and cake in media representations of the United States and Europe. They knew such foods were made with ingredients they considered typical of Western cuisine, and they regarded the food preparation techniques that produced these foods, such as baking in an oven, as Western. Between 1992 and 1998, the number of restaurants and bakeries in Xi'an that made and sold these foods increased rapidly. Residents of the quarter refused to consume most of these products; they limited their consumption to the fresh yeast bread and cake that Hui produced locally. They avoided the Han bakeries; the Chinese fast-food chains that sold such Western-style foods as hamburgers, hot dogs, pizza, and fried chicken; and the American fast-food chain Kentucky Fried Chicken. Residents also abstained from carbonated beverages that came from soda fountains rather than cans or bottles. They justified these practices on the grounds that the locally produced Western-style foods that were not prepared by Hui did not meet the Islamic criteria for dietary purity; only the yeast bread and cake baked by Hui qualified as qingzhen.[2]

Residents ate the "foreign" foods that were industrially processed and that Hui produced. The Western-style food made by Hui was qingzhen according to local definitions: it had been prepared by a believer and a member of the Hui nationality. The factory-produced Western-style snacks, on the other hand, were not made by Muslims nor by members of the Hui nationality. Residents ate them because of three closely related factors. First, they were not made with pork. Second, they were not, conceptually speaking, "Chinese" (which was of course related to the absence of pork). Third, they were the product of industrial production techniques that residents associated with the West and with modernization (both of which contributed to the perception that the snacks were non-Chinese). Because of these factors, most residents did not apply the normal qingzhen rules to the factory snacks.

If the mass-produced foods had contained pork Xi'an Hui would not have considered eating them, regardless of how they had been produced or whether they seemed Western in appearance or content. Several conversations I had with residents indicated that the absence of pork or lard was the baseline for Hui consumption of the new foods. For example, on one occasion I asked Peng's father, Guangliang, whether Hui could eat chocolate. He responded with a puzzled look. "Of course," he replied. "Chocolate? There is nothing in that" (*mei sha*). The "nothing" Guangliang was referring to was pork: chocolate was not made with pork or lard. On another occasion, I discussed the mass-produced foods with Aifeng's daughter Xue, a young woman in her twenties who worked in a department store. Xue had traveled to Beijing with her co-workers on a trip sponsored by her work unit. When she came back from her visit, she complained about how difficult it had been for her to find food to eat while she and her co-workers, all of whom were Han, were sight-seeing. Because her Han colleagues ate in places that were not qingzhen, Xue often went hungry. Indeed, she chose to sit outside during meals, so determined was she not to violate qingzhen. Upon hearing her remarks, I asked her whether she could eat in Western restaurants such as Kentucky Fried Chicken. Xue replied that she could not enter or eat in fast-food restaurants because they were not qingzhen. "And what about the ice cream bars they sell on the street, could you eat them?" I pressed her. "What about when you got thirsty?" "Some foods it is hard to say (*shuo bu qing*)," she responded. "I could eat an ice cream bar, or drink a soft drink, or even eat packaged biscuits (*binggan*) if they didn't have lard in them."

Critical to residents' ability to eat the factory foods and related to the absence of pork products was the residents' perception of these snacks as Western and non-Chinese. As Guangliang's and Xue's remarks suggest, Western-style mass-produced foods occupied a neutral zone or gray area that was "hard to say" was not qingzhen. Chinese food, on the other hand, was never neutral, even when it was industrially processed. An event from Aifeng's and my shopping trip clarified the importance of the residents' belief that the new foods were not Chinese. While Aifeng was looking through the snacks for her grandchild, I began sorting through the piles of factory foods to buy some for myself. I was drawn to a different sort of cuisine than Aifeng was; the foods that I considered buying were factory-produced versions of such Chinese foods as mung bean cakes (*lüdougao*) and peanut cakes (*huashengsu*).[3] Seeing me rummaging through the boxes and sacks, Aifeng came over to examine what I planned to buy. When she saw the factory-made mung bean cakes I was holding, she shook her head. "We can't eat those," she said. "They aren't qingzhen."

Aifeng perceived the mass-produced mung bean cakes and the instant noodles she bought for herself as different from the packaged snacks she bought for her daughter. The reason was that the cakes and noodles were recognizably Chinese and, as such, associated with pork. Aifeng knew that when Han prepared mung bean cakes or noodles they made them with lard; only Hui made such foods with vegetable oil. Her experience and upbringing told Aifeng that she could only consume the Chinese foods made by Hui. Factory production did not affect her understanding. Equally irrelevant was whether such foods actually contained lard—and many of the non-qingzhen instant noodles (including the vegetarian ones I liked to eat) did not. For Aifeng and for other Hui, mung bean cakes and noodles were either permitted Hui food or prohibited Han food. When greeted with industrially processed Chinese foods, residents applied the same standards that they used to measure any other Chinese food.

Although industrial processing alone was not enough to cause residents to eat a "Chinese" product, it nevertheless was a critical component that helped render the "foreign" packaged snacks edible. Factory production meant that the foods were prepared by machines, and this caused many residents to allay their normal concerns about the cleanliness of the foods they ate. A conversation I had with Zenglie shed light on the significance of mechanization to the residents' ability to consume the mass-produced snacks. Zenglie explained the popularity of the factory foods in the quarter as one more stage in a historical development whereby Hui gradually came to eat foods that they had once avoided. It used to be, Zenglie said, that Hui would not drink water that did not come from wells owned by Hui; now everyone drank the water that came through the pipes the government had set up. Sweets (*tianshi*) and nonalcoholic beverages (*yinliao*) were also foods that had once been prohibited. However, Zenglie noted, in the past such foods were all made by hand. Now they were made in factories, so Hui widely accepted them as edible.

Mechanization, whether in the form of factory production or public water pipes, shifted production from an intimate, hands-on mode to one that was farther removed from personal contact. Machine production alleviated the possibility of contamination through contact with the residue of pork, lard, and dirt that Hui believed accrued to Han utensils and hands. Because industrial food processing was disassociated from the person, Hui perceived the qingzhen rules that applied to handmade foods as inapplicable and irrelevant.

Industrial processing also contributed to the association these new foods had with modernization. The CCP held up mechanization as one of the hallmarks of progress. Under Mao, industrialization was a key component of the government's plan for modernization; under Deng, the state had pursued technological advancement as one of the four modernizations. The new mass-produced foods represented modernization because they came from the part of the world that had modernized first and were the products of advanced technology.

Local Food Industries and Industrial Food

In 1994 and 1995, most of the foods for sale in Xi'an were handmade. This was true of the quarter and of the city at large. Inside the city wall and in the residential areas just outside it, hundreds of restaurants, eateries, and food stalls dotted the streets and alleys. The more distant suburbs had smaller and fewer pockets of food enterprises, but even the newest parts of Xi'an had "free markets" (*ziyou shichang*) that included various kinds of private food businesses. The vast majority of these establishments produced handmade food. "Handmade" in this context meant more than just the personalization that this phrase denoted in the contemporary United States. It entailed the absence of any kind of food processing machines in the production process. Mechanized tools for food preparation were very rare in Xi'an. Thus, "handmade" denoted the extensive and intensive use of the hands during all stages of food preparation.

As described in Chapter 4, cleanliness figured highly in the Hui concept of "pure and true." Hui criticized Han for being dirty not only because they consumed pork, but also because they considered the Han to practice inadequate personal hygiene. Because local food preparation techniques relied heavily on the use of hands, the potential for food to become dirty was great. For Xi'an

Hui, of course, "dirty" also included metaphysical contamination. The Han race was metaphysically dirty because of their failure to practice the "one true religion" and their innate immorality. This kind of contamination (and purity as well) was also spread through physical contact, as the discussion of food's "sympathetic magic" in Chapter 4 makes clear.

Noodles were one of the most popular foods for sale all over Xi'an. Both Hui and Han made noodles by hand. Noodles were sold in establishments that ranged from fancy hotel restaurants to tiny street stalls that seated fewer than ten customers at a time. In most restaurants and stalls, noodles were cooked to order in the sight of the customer. Quite a few of the Xi'an urbanites I knew claimed that they could differentiate between the flavor of machine-made and handmade noodles, and they preferred the taste of the handmade ones. Handmade noodles were pulled, rolled, and cut in an assortment of shapes and sizes, but all involved significant use of the hands (see Figure 16).

Noodle preparation typically began with making the dough. The cook poured flour and water into a large basin and then stirred the mixture with chopsticks. As the dough thickened, the chopsticks were abandoned in favor of hands. Once the right proportions of flour and water had been achieved, the cook then removed the dough from the basin and kneaded it by hand. Kneading took anywhere from ten to twenty minutes. Then, if the cook were preparing cut noodles (the simplest sort to prepare), he or she flattened the dough with a rolling pin, continually stretching the flattened dough with his or her hands. Once the dough had been rolled to the desired thinness, the cook cut it with a knife. He or she would cut the right amount of dough for a single bowl, stop, pick it up, and put it to the side in a pile. This would continue until all the dough was cut and separated into individual portions.

At this stage the noodles were ready to be boiled. When a customer appeared, the cook would grab one of the piles of noodles with his or her hands and throw it into a big wok filled with water that was heated by a large, round coal-burning stove (these stoves appeared to be made from oil drums). After a few minutes, the

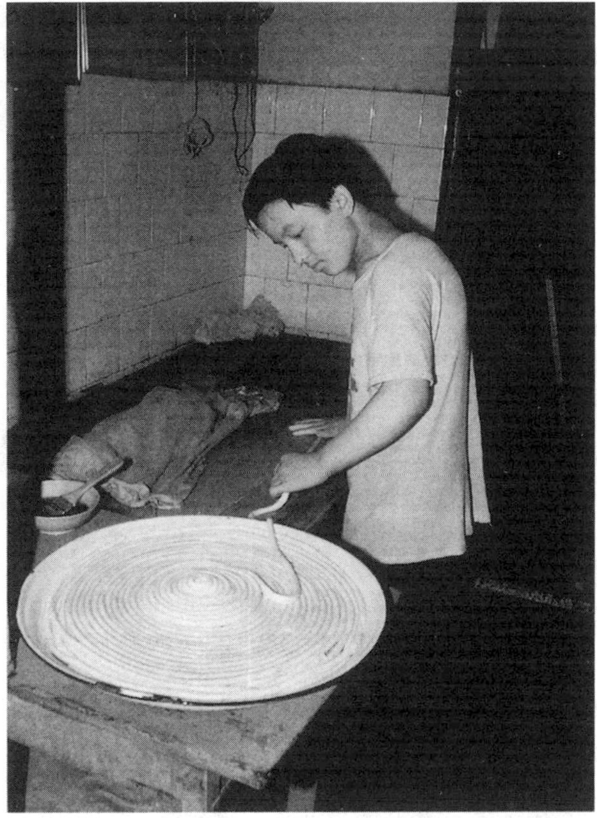

FIGURE 16. A young man rolling noodles in one of the quarter's many food stalls.

noodles were removed with chopsticks, placed in a bowl, and seasoned to the customer's preference. If the customer wanted them with meat, the cook would cut a few slices of precooked meat, pick them up by hand, and place them in the customer's bowl. Next, green bean threads, cilantro, and spring onions would be added, also by hand. Then the cook would ladle broth into the bowl and serve it to the customer.

Much of the food sold in Xi'an (or made at home) involved

such extensive and intensive use of hands. Steamed stuffed buns (*baozi*), dumplings (*jiaozi*), pan-baked flatbreads (*tuo tuo mo*), deep-fried cakes (*yougao*), crullers (*youtiao*), and a wide variety of other foods sold on the streets of Xi'an all required hands-on preparation. Very few entrepreneurs purchased machines to make these foods; machines required a significant capital investment, and a proprietor could cheaply hire laborers to hasten and increase food production. I knew of only a couple enterprises among the hundreds of food stalls and eateries in the quarter that possessed machines for food preparation. Many of the bigger restaurants also preferred to hire multiple laborers to meet their production demands rather than mechanize.

The contrast between the local foods and the mass-produced factory foods could not be more distinct. The foods that restaurateurs and families made were produced by hand, on site, while the customer watched. Industrial foods, on the other hand, were made by machine, in locations far from the quarter and beyond the consumer's range of vision. The use of machines to make the new snacks rendered them atypical; the physical distance between where such foods were made and where they were consumed and the invisibility of the production process further defamiliarized them.

Industrial processing also resulted in products that looked significantly different from the foods that Hui and Han made by hand. The machine-made Western-style foods were standardized in color and shape. Many were dyed. Some were dried and coated; as a category they tended to be crisp. Handmade Hui foods, by contrast, were irregularly shaped and varied in size. They were made without artificial colorings and tended to be soft. These visual and textural differences were accentuated and increased by industrial packaging. In Xi'an, handmade foods tended to be packaged casually. They were wrapped in paper and tied with string or put in flimsy plastic bags tied by their handles. Often consumers would bring their own dishes or bowls to transport their purchases home or eat the food on the spot. By contrast, the mass-produced foods were sealed in plastic, glass, or aluminum, expensive materials that could not be produced in the quarter.

Industrial processing produced foods that looked unfamiliar and, more significantly, modern.

The Consumers

Many residents of the quarter bought Western-style industrial foods, but fewer consumed them than purchased them. Most of these foods were eaten by children. Hui adults by and large limited their intake of mass-produced foods to carbonated beverages, coffee, and juice-based drinks. None of these beverages were popular with adults over 30, and they did not form a part of most adults' daily food intake. They were generally reserved for children and for hosting visitors and guests. Soda, for example, was an indispensable part of any formal banquet at a restaurant, and residents also served it with the meals they provided for guests at circumcisions, engagements, and weddings. When the Barley Market Street Antialcohol Committee, a grassroots organization dedicated to keeping alcohol out of the quarter, hosted a public rally, it provided soda for everyone who attended (see Chapter 6 for a fuller discussion of this organization). Most families I knew kept bottles of soda or boxes of juice drink on hand in the refrigerator for children and for guests, especially during the summer when temperatures in Xi'an soared above 100 degrees Fahrenheit.

The other mass-produced Western-style food that occasionally formed part of the adult Hui diet was candy. Like the Western-style beverages, mass-produced candies were not eaten daily by the Hui adults I knew, but rather were given to children and used to host company. Packaged candies were placed out on trays for guests to eat casually during the lengthy local celebrations of life cycle rituals or brought out during formal visits. Candy was also an item of exchange during marriage transactions. Families whose children became engaged or got married participated in formal rites of gift giving (similar to those described in Yan 1996: 176–209). In the quarter, a number of these exchanges involved food. To give one example, at one point during the process of formalizing a marriage arrangement, the bride's family presented the groom's family with gifts of nuts, dates, and other fancy sweets (*gaodian*). A wide variety of traditional pastries were used for this ritual, but packaged hard candy was frequently one of the items exchanged.

Although residents served and exchanged soft drinks and candy at special occasions, most Hui adults found these foods unpalatable. An adult would drink a can of soda or take a piece of candy that he or she was offered out of politeness, but no Hui adults I knew ever bought such foods to eat for themselves. A frequent comment adult residents made was that they "could not get accustomed to" (*bu xiguan*) the taste of candy, soda, or other Western-style foods. They complained that "Western" foods, not only the factory-produced snacks but also yeast bread and cake, were "too sweet" and "not filling" (*chi bu bao*). Flavor was not why Xi'an Hui used Western-style foods for gift giving and hospitality. Adults purchased, exchanged, served, and occasionally ate these foods because they were luxury goods and associated with modernization.

Although adults rarely chose to eat the new foods themselves, they frequently encouraged their children to do so. Parents and grandparents regularly purchased packaged Western-style snacks for children to consume between meals, and many families I knew kept supplies of these foods at home. Aifeng, for example, frequently fed mass-produced treats to her granddaughter when the little girl cried or when she started playing with something that Aifeng did not wish her to play with—in short, when Aifeng wanted to distract her. Guangliang bought large cases of soda for his two sons to consume; he explained that this practice was one of the ways he rewarded and encouraged his children to work hard in school.

As was the case in Peng's family, most parents in the quarter enabled their children to eat snack foods by giving them spare change. I frequently saw children run to their parents and ask for a few mao so they could buy one of the cheap Chinese imitations of the Western snack foods (see Appendix for the prices of some of these snacks).[4] The usual parental response was to pull out a little money and send the children away. A number of families in the quarter operated small dry goods and convenience stores where children could conveniently spend this money. Quite a few of these stores were near primary and middle schools.

When school-age children made trips to the convenience store together, they compared who had tried which snacks, discussed which snacks contained toys, and judiciously expressed their tastes and preferences. Children frequently bought snacks on the way to and from school and often ate them in or around school property. This made the school yard an important venue for the dissemination of information about mass-produced food. This knowledge was almost entirely the purview of children under fourteen. As Peng's father teasingly said in his son's hearing, "Peng may not know much about anything else, but when it comes to these snacks, he is an expert."

A few residents of the quarter, mostly the older ahong and "men of religion," questioned the propriety of consuming Western-style foods. Jishu, the Small Mosque's religious specialist, refused to drink carbonated beverages or eat any foods associated with the West because he believed they were not qingzhen. Jishu was more careful than many Xi'an Hui; when he made the pilgrimage in 1996 Jishu did not eat any of the food he was served on the airplane because he feared it was not pure. Although he did not directly criticize others for eating Western-style foods, he said that he hoped his abstinence would inspire other Hui to emulate him.

Ordinary residents tended to avoid offering Western-style foods to ahong and members of the community considered to be particularly devout. For example, at the weddings, funerals, and engagements I attended, the ahong and other "men of religion" were not served Western-style soft drinks, though the rest of the guests were. Similarly, the banquets provided by the mosques for collective religious rituals (such as the annual summertime mourning for the late nineteenth-century massacre of Shaanxi Hui or the wintertime celebration of the Prophet's Birthday) did not include any foods associated with the West: no factory-produced snacks, canned or bottled beverages, or local Hui-produced yeast breads or cakes.[5]

Consuming Modernization

The mass-produced snacks that Hui children and adults consumed were pork-free, non-Chinese, and machine-made. They contained ingredients that residents regarded as Western, and their association with the West was strengthened by media representations that depicted Westerners eating such foods. They were the product of industrial processing techniques that epitomized advanced technology and modernization. All these factors played a part in rendering Western-style mass-produced snacks attractive to local residents. By consuming these foods, residents made the West, prosperity, advanced technology, science, and modernization their own.

Most adult Hui did not like the taste of ice cream (and had trouble digesting it), soda, chocolate, or chips, but they liked to think of themselves and be thought of as modern, progressive, and sophisticated. As previous chapters have demonstrated, they created such an image through consumption practices related to housing, mosques, education, and religious observance. Purchasing Western-style foods, giving them as gifts, keeping them around the house, serving them to honored guests, and feeding them to children also gave residents access to modernization and helped project an image of themselves as modern.

Mass-produced Western-style snacks were more suitable for this task than the locally made Western-style food. Residents could use the yeast bread and cakes made in the quarter to convey messages about their modern tastes, but the limited quantities and highly perishable nature of these foods made them less attractive. Only two families in the quarter made Western-style foods, and their products were limited in variety and could keep for only a few days. Furthermore, even though at least one of these families advertised their products as Western by the posters of blonde-haired women dressed in the American flag that they hung in their store, the foods were obviously locally produced. This may have caused them to lose authenticity in the eyes of consumers. Residents who wanted to use the contents of their pantry to participate in modernization could most effectively do so by buying factory-made products.

Modernization, along with its corollaries science and technology, was enormously influential in mid-1990s China. Residents saw modernization as the future for themselves and their children. As parents, Xi'an Hui were particularly concerned that their children be equipped to live in a modern society. They wanted their children to ascend higher on the social ladder than they had, to enjoy a more comfortable life, and to have wider opportunities. This desire was clearly manifest by the discourse surrounding "culture" and education that existed in the quarter, the efforts that parents who had the resources made to get their children into good schools, and the preference for children who did attend high school and college to study science, which parents saw as the key to their children's success (see Chapter 2). Western-style mass-produced foods were another, easier way for parents to prepare their children to live in a modern, technologically advanced, developed society. These snacks helped parents to instill in their children the taste for modernization.

Bourdieu writes that "taste classifies, and it classifies the classifier" (1984:6). Residents of the quarter wanted to be classified as modern. Their pursuit of secular education, their enthusiasm for living in high-rise apartments, their preference for Qur'anic education that used modern technology, their efforts to achieve economic development and exposure abroad, and their consumption of Western-style factory foods all demonstrate that residents saw modernization as desirable. Their consumption of mass-produced foods and the other commodities of modernization suggests that Bourdieu's model of taste, in which taste is in "logical conformity" to social position and people choose goods and services that express their existing social class, requires rethinking (1984:471; see also 1990). Hui consumption of Western-style mass-produced foods was an instance of people exhibiting a taste and inculcating a taste in their children for what they wanted to be: technologically advanced, prosperous, modern.

The Government and Mass Production

For residents of the quarter, what made industrial food edible was what it contained—pork products or no pork products, dairy products or no dairy products—and what it represented—the cuisine of the "modern" West or of "traditional" China. Government officials, however, took a different position; they recast Hui consumption of factory foods in racial terms. The state created a policy for classifying mass-produced food as qingzhen and, in so doing, acted to limit and direct residents' access to the taste of modernization. During the summer of 1996, the Hui official Liangxun told me that the provincial Religion and Nationality Affairs Commission (of which he was vice-director) was debating a policy for certifying factories as qingzhen. Officials had decided upon four criteria for qingzhen factories: (1) the cook must be a member of the Hui nationality (Liangxun did not elaborate upon who, in the factory production process, would be considered the "cook"); (2) the ingredients must not contain pork or pork products; (3) the heads of the factory must belong to the Hui nationality; and (4) at least 25 percent of the factory workers must be members of the Hui nationality. This last point was revised during the week I was visiting; a few days after our initial conversation Liangxun told me that the percentage of factory workers who must be Hui had been increased to 45 percent. He explained that if this policy went into effect, it would apply to many enterprises, including those that did business with Islamic countries. Fears that Muslims from outside China would disapprove of the criteria had caused the provincial government to raise the required percentage of Hui nationality employees. When I returned to the quarter in June 1997, the policy had passed through all the necessary administrative channels. Details had been published in the Xi'an newspaper, but no further actions to implement the policy had been taken.

The state's regulations encouraged residents to reconceptualize qingzhen. Neither the government nor local residents questioned that factory foods could be "pure and true." From my perspective, machines failed to meet the local standards for "pure and true" (which were mostly religious and cosmological), but this was by and large my own problem, a view shared only by a few religious specialists. The government's intervention supported the already existing trend whereby residents incorporated mechanization, advanced technology, and other "Western" products into their lives without fear of violating Islamic observance. The official qingzhen certification policy, however, differed from local understandings and practices in that it was predicated on race and functioned to increase the significance of racial divisions, separate Hui and Han, and restrict Hui access to the foods of modernization.

As with the district government's policy for licensing qingzhen businesses, the provincial government's qingzhen factory policy used racial criteria to classify factories and their products. The regulations extended the use of *minzu* categorization to industrial foods and encouraged Hui to orient their behavior around their racial label. The policy strengthened the association that residents, officials, and the populace at large made between the "nationality custom" of qingzhen and the Hui race. By widening the application of qingzhen—officially defined in racial terms—and increasing its public use, the government promoted the perception of the Hui as different and more "traditional" than the Han. The policy also fostered the separation of Hui and Han by encouraging Hui to restrict their consumption of industrial foods to only those products that officials had determined were appropriate for their nationality.

By classifying factory foods as qingzhen, officials acted to regulate Hui consumption of mass-produced cuisine. In the absence of government intervention, residents had determined for themselves which factory foods they could consume and still be good Muslims. When officials created a qingzhen factory policy, however, they directed residents to consume only those foods that the state had defined as fit for Hui to eat and so acted to limit the range of industrial foods that residents would consider edible. It was inevitable, given the official policy, that fewer factories would qualify as qingzhen than those that did not. The regulations made it likely that residents' consumption of Western brands in particular would decrease, because Keebler, Coca-Cola, and Nestle were unlikely to set up factories that had the requisite number of Hui nationality members needed to produce qingzhen foods. If the policy took hold, the state would have effectively assumed control of residents' consumption of "modern" foods.

Factory Foods and Hui-Han Sociability

Although the government's policy functioned to separate Hui and Han, as the situation stood in the mid-1990s the mass-produced snack foods increased the opportunities for Hui and Han to eat together. Whereas residents rejected the food that Han made locally and the Chinese-style industrial products, they ate and encouraged their children to eat the factory-made Western-style foods. These new snacks were also extremely popular among Han Chinese, and for many of the same reasons that Xi'an Hui consumed them: they were associated with modernization, the West, science, and social advancement (see the articles in Jing 2000 for examples). As the mass-produced foods became a regular part of Hui children's diet, they made it easier for residents to interact with Han by providing a common ground for Hui and Han to eat together. Although the consumption of mass-produced snack foods provided more such opportunities children than for adults, the industrial Western-style foods also broadened the possible scope of interactions for Hui adults in Han settings. Residents who visited Han households could accept a can of soda where they rejected tea served in cups. In so doing, they acquiesced to Han hospitality and made Hui-Han relations bilateral rather than unidirectional. Hui and Han shared the taste for modernization, and this brought them together. When the state created regulations to define qingzhen factory food, however, it acted to separate the two "races" and keep the Hui in their proper "traditional" position.

Chapter Six

ALCOHOL AND "BUILDING A CIVILIZED SOCIETY"

Alcohol is one of the four substances that the Qur'an decrees Muslims must not consume. Residents of the quarter believed that alcohol was "dirty" (*zang*), some said even dirtier than pork. All of the Xi'an Hui I knew, both men and women, steadfastly abstained from alcohol. Some were not merely personally abstemious, but also rejected all contact with alcohol; for example, one man told me that he would throw away a glass that had ever contained alcohol, even if it had been washed. Others said that they would refuse to sit at a table that had alcohol upon it. However, not all Hui felt equally strongly about this issue. Residents were aware that Hui in other places were less strict in their behavior. For example, many Hui who lived in other parts of Xi'an sold alcohol in their restaurants, and several locals commented on the fact that young Hui men in Ningxia drank beer under the pretense that it "wasn't really alcohol" (this position can be justified, depending on how one interprets the Qur'anic passages concerning alcohol). A young Hui man who worked as a custodian at the Hui Middle School had traveled to a Hui community in northeast China, because his wife's family came from there; he told me that Hui there drank hard liquor and admitted to trying some while visiting his in-laws.

Alcohol had become both more available and more affordable during the 1980s and 1990s. Residents spoke of the new, Western liquors for sale on the market and described reports they had read about the conspicuous consumption of alcohol by China's new rich. Like the Western-style mass-produced food or the new mosque styles, alcohol was a commodity that residents associated with modernization—but they did not see alcohol as desirable. On the contrary, alcohol violated residents' notions of what it meant to be civilized.

The Antialcohol Movement

Many residents stated with conviction that the Hui who lived in the Muslim district did not drink alcohol. However, a number of people told me that in the early 1980s, when large numbers of families entered private enterprise, many sold alcohol in their restaurants and shops and allowed their customers to consume alcohol in their stores. The food businesses of the quarter depended on Han patronage for success, and Han, particularly Han men, were said to prefer to drink when they ate. My own experience bore out this stereotype: the Han men that I knew in Xi'an (and many that I had observed elsewhere in northwest China) regularly drank beer or other forms of alcohol at lunch and dinner. At mealtime the laughs and shouts of small groups of Han men playing drinking games over their food serenaded passersby and fellow diners in restaurants all over the city. Aware of this pattern, many Hui entrepreneurs tolerated the presence of alcohol on their premises because they thought it would increase their custom.

Most of the quarter's private food businesses quickly became profitable. The entrepreneurs I knew best generated three or four times as much money in a single day than they had earned in a month at the state-owned factories and work units where they were once employed. As the economic reforms proceeded and the government continued to permit "normal religious activities" (*zhengshi zongjiao huodong*) to occur without attack, a few men who operated restaurants on Barley Market Street began to criticize alcohol's presence in the quarter. These men felt strongly that it was inappropriate for Hui to tolerate alcohol, and they resented the social disruptions, such as fights and shouting, which often resulted from Han drinking. According to Chen, who ran an eatery that sold prepared meat and vegetable dishes, in 1984 and 1988 he and a couple of men held a series of discussions with other local businessmen about getting alcohol out of the area, but to no end. In 1990, Chen and his associates successfully gathered all the Barley Market Street entrepreneurs to a meeting where they encouraged the shopkeepers to forbid customers from bringing alcohol into their establishments, but, as Chen put it, the meeting "had no long-term effects."

In 1992, on the other (eastern) side of the Muslim district, Yingchun, ahong of the Dapiyuan Mosque, began speaking out about the evils of alcohol at the exhortations he gave during *zhuma*. Because the Friday collective worship services drew big crowds, his explanations of the Islamic alcohol taboo reached a large audience. Yingchun strongly advocated that all Hui cease selling alcohol or permitting customers to drink it in their establishments. As the weeks passed, he targeted individual entrepreneurs and denounced by name those residents who sold alcohol. His bold attacks motivated religious specialists at other mosques to criticize publicly the presence of alcohol in a Muslim area.

As the censure of alcohol grew more public, some residents decided to take stronger action. A group of ahong and entrepreneurs visited the district government to petition that officials make alcohol illegal in the quarter. The government refused. Officials explained that alcohol was legal in the People's Republic, so such a policy would contravene national laws. The group was told that the residents of the quarter would have to resolve the problem of alcohol by themselves.

Although the ahong and businessmen failed to persuade the government to intervene, the increasingly vocal cries against alcohol did have an effect. All over the quarter, especially on Dapiyuan Street where Yingchun had exposed specific alcohol-selling entrepreneurs by name, Hui stopped selling alcohol or letting their customers bring it into their restaurants. Guangliang, who lived on Dapiyuan Street, remembered that public sentiment against alcohol became so intense that violence was threatened;

many local restaurateurs feared that other residents would smash their stores if they did not immediately ban alcohol from their premises. Meanwhile, to foster support of the ban, the Dapiyuan Mosque had signs printed that read "Qingzhen, alcohol prohibited. Thank you for your cooperation" (*qingzhen jinjiu, xiexie hezuo*) and had them distributed to local owners of food establishments. However, after a short time, the movement to ban alcohol lost momentum. Gradually, local restaurateurs returned to their policy of allowing customers to drink, and some Hui began selling alcohol again. Residents cited profit as the main motive: entrepreneurs feared losing their Han customers.

Although Dapiyuan Street did not sustain the ban, on Barley Market Street Yingchun's words sparked the few local entrepreneurs who had previously wanted to expel alcohol to try again. Ten businessmen, including Chen and his associates, formed an antialcohol committee (*jinjiu xiehui*). The committee defined its goal as making Barley Market Street completely alcohol-free. To do this, the ten members engaged in what, echoing CCP rhetoric, they called "thought work" (*sixiang gongzuo*): the group visited every restaurateur, food stall keeper, and convenience store owner on Barley Market Street, sat down with them, and discussed why they should prohibit alcohol from their establishments. Some entrepreneurs agreed immediately; others were more difficult to persuade. Meat-skewer (*rouchuan*) sellers were particularly resistant to the idea of a ban on alcohol, insisting that its consumption was crucial to their sales. The members of the antialcohol committee also recalled that the few Han businessmen who operated convenience stores on Barley Market Street were extremely difficult to convince. These entrepreneurs believed that since they were not Hui, they should not have to participate in the prohibition. In each case, the committee members persuaded these entrepreneurs by persistent, relentless pressure. They returned repeatedly to those businesses whose owners were unwilling to participate and described the importance of removing alcohol from a "Hui people area" (*Huimin diqu*) and the increasing numbers of businessmen who had agreed.

Finally, all 88 shop owners on Barley Market Street promised not to sell alcohol, permit its consumption on the premises of their establishments, or tolerate its presence on the street.

After obtaining their business associates' compliance, the committee decided to launch a propaganda campaign to promote awareness of Islam's position on alcohol and encourage continued support of the ban. Using money that they had earned from their private businesses, the members of the committee made signs and banners to hang on Barley Market Street (see Figure 1). These signs explained what qingzhen meant, listed the Qur'anic injunctions on alcohol, and described Muslims' obligation to avoid all contact with alcohol. The committee also paid to reprint a pamphlet written during the 1950s that explained the evils of alcohol, which they distributed to the Barley Market Street entrepreneurs. In addition, the members of the committee acted as Barley Market Street's unofficial alcohol police, watching for people carrying alcohol and asking those who did to leave the area.

I first learned of the antialcohol committee in 1994, two years after its founding. At this time, the group would hang propaganda banners and signs over the street each week. They organized at least four antialcohol rallies between February 1994 and July 1995 that were attended by residents who lived in the neighborhood of Barley Market Street and by some Hui from other parts of the quarter. In May 1995, the committee sent a letter of appeal to the quarter's ten mosques. This letter explained the nature of committee's work and asked the ahong to use their exhortations to persuade Hui to keep alcohol out of the quarter. Word of the group had spread far beyond Barley Market Street and the Muslim district: a Henan Hui newspaper published an article about the committee, and a group of Hui in Sichuan sent the men a large wooden plaque to commemorate their efforts. When I left Xi'an in August 1995, some residents in other parts of the quarter allowed their customers to drink in their food establishments, and a few stores sold alcohol, but Barley Market Street remained an alcohol-free zone.

Reasons for the Movement

When I asked members why they had formed an antialcohol committee, they spoke first about the Qur'anic prohibition. Several of the men explained that alcohol was forbidden because it confuses people and leads them into trouble. As one man put it, a person who drinks alcohol speaks wildly and forgets about God. Ma, the spokesman for the group, continued the conversation by saying that all the members of the committee ran businesses on the officially designated "Hui food and drink street" (*Huimin yinshi jie*). Having a Hui food and drink street, Ma said, meant "meeting the standards of the Hui people" (*Huimin*), which included prohibiting alcohol. At this, Chen objected. "You mean meeting the standards of *Muslims*" (*Musilin*), he said. "The law prohibiting alcohol is an *Islamic* law." In a fine example of how local definitions of Hui extended beyond the state's racial definition, Ma dismissed Chen's comment by saying "Here in China we say 'Hui people.'" Ma went on to state that they could not control what happened elsewhere in Xi'an, but "this part of town is a Hui people district" (*Huimin diqu*), so Hui standards should be enforced.

Ma and the other committee members were proud that they were playing a role in "propagating Islam" (*chuan jiao*). They saw alcohol's appearance in the quarter as symbolizing the decline of religion: "Hui people" were no longer adhering to the laws of Islam. The men described their acts as "doing a service" for Islam. Several members stressed that the committee wanted to prevent the younger generation from turning to alcohol. This was their duty as Muslims and as children of their parents. As Mingjie, one of the group's founding members, explained, "Our parents in the 1950s and 1960s passed on what they knew about Islam to us, even though no one dared worship or talk about religion then. It is our responsibility to ensure that the young people today follow Islam."

Several committee members and a number of other residents commented that the change in material conditions that had occurred since the early 1980s made it difficult for youth to observe Islamic precepts. They attributed the problem to the sharp increase in disposable income and the wider availability of alcohol. Some residents also pointed out how the media glamorized alcohol consumption, associating it with prosperity and a modern lifestyle. Children saw alcohol consumed on television programs and in the movies, and news reports detailed the vast expenditures of China's new rich on imported liquor. Worse yet, Han students encouraged their Hui classmates to drink. "Hui youth today don't know why they shouldn't drink," Ma said. "It is very easy for young people to get involved with drink, drugs, and gambling. If we allow alcohol in the quarter, young people will think it is just another beverage."

Related to the committee members' concerns about their children was their desire to make the quarter a clean, safe place to live. Members said that the alcohol ban had made Barley Market Street more peaceful and orderly. According to Ma, once alcohol was no longer available, street fighting had diminished, and the families who lived in the area were able to sleep peacefully at night. The committee members believed their efforts had greatly enhanced Barley Market Street's reputation. "Customers know that Barley Market Street is clean and safe, a place to find qingzhen food in a wholesome environment," Ma stated. The members argued that the ban had not caused economic decline, and suggested it had even been good for business. Although Ma acknowledged that food enterprise incomes had decreased when the ban first went into effect, he insisted that all losses suffered had been temporary. Certainly, food sales on Barley Market Street were booming during 1994 and 1995. However, the street had very few meat-skewer sellers, only one or two compared to the dozen or so on North Court Gate, for example. Though Ma neglected to mention this, apparently those Hui who ran shish-kebab businesses had vacated Barley Market Street in favor of places where alcohol was not banned.

The members of the committee hoped that the effect of their efforts would not simply be local. As Ma put it, the committee believed that Barley Market Street should serve as a model for the quarter, the nation, and foreign countries, too. By carrying out the antialcohol movement, the committee members were "building a civilized society" (*jianshe wenming shehui*). "Building a civilized society" was one of the CCP's official goals for China; I frequently saw this phrase in government documents, in propaganda promoting the national birth control policy, and on signs urging citizens not to litter, spit, or engage in other "uncivilized" behaviors. Officials also gave "civilized work unit" (*wenming danwei*) awards to factories, schools, and other institutions, and "civilized village" (*wenming cun*) campaigns had been carried out in rural China (see Anagnost 1992, 1997a; Litzinger 1995:121; see also Huang 1989:168–9). The antialcohol committee saw the cessation of alcohol consumption as a critical component of a "civilized society." By enforcing the ban on alcohol, the committee would make Barley Market Street an exemplar of "civilization."

The Members of the Antialcohol Committee

In 1995, twelve men constituted the antialcohol committee. Three new men had joined the original ten, one of whom had died. Each member of the committee ran a restaurant, food stall, or store that sold packaged food and drink in an establishment he owned or rented on Barley Market Street. As petty entrepreneurs with businesses adjacent to or close by one another, the men had similar concerns and tended to rely on each other for business contacts. All the committee members lived in close proximity to one another. Several lived with their families behind or above their businesses on Barley Market Street; the rest lived in the neighboring alleys. All were married with children and were between the ages of 30 and 55.

Each of the twelve men belonged to one of the three mosques that were near Barley Market Street. These mosques were associated with different religious factions: the Western Mosque was Sunnaiti, the Middle Mosque was Gedimu, and the Yingli Mosque was Santai. The men's differences in religious practice were not a bar to the committee's cooperation, however. Similarly, the activities they organized were for the benefit of all those who lived, worked, and ate on Barley Market Street regardless of factional differences or nationality affiliation.

The committee members described themselves as "middle class" (*zhongceng*), neither the wealthiest residents of the quarter nor the poorest. In terms of city-wide incomes, they earned well more than the average urbanite. The homes of those committee members I visited varied in size, but they were universally replete with the consumer goods that marked the attainment of a comfortable standard of living: televisions, videocassette recorders, stereos, refrigerators, and in several cases telephones. Each member possessed sufficient disposable income to contribute money for the group's activities. The antialcohol committee did not receive support from any government body, including the state-instituted Islamic Association. When I spoke with committee members in 1994 and 1995, they repeatedly emphasized that the group's activities were privately funded by the members. This characterized at least the first four years of the committee's operations. During late 1996 or early 1997, however, the quarter's ten mosques made a 5,000-yuan donation to the group. This contribution did not affect the committee's autonomy. The members continued to exercise complete control over what antialcohol activities took place on Barley Market Street.

Membership in the committee provided these men with an important opportunity to earn good reputations in the quarter. Having a "name" (*ming*) was a valuable resource for these entrepreneurs, as was true for most Chinese involved in public life.[1] The most successful businessmen in the quarter were described as "having a name" (*youming*), and residents believed that a good reputation improved business. Xi'an Hui could achieve a good reputation through several methods. One way was through the longevity of their businesses. For example, Lanying, when describing her family's noodle stall, said her father "particularly had a name" (*te youming*) for his noodles. This fame was based on the family's history: her father had sold noodles before 1949, as had his father before him. The family's business was excellent, largely because of their product's enduring reputation for consistent good quality. Lanying's family made so much money that they could afford to operate their eatery on a seasonal basis. Unlike other noodle stall owners, Lanying's family opened their eatery for business in March and closed by late October.

Residents also gained a name through good works. Three of the quarter's wealthiest entrepreneurs contributed money to the local middle schools, gave scholarships to students who passed the high school and college entrance exams, and occasionally funded academic contests. These men also funded and participated in religious activities; for example, all three were key donors at a ceremony commemorating the Ming dynasty teacher Hu Dengzhou that was organized by the Great Mosque and the provincial Islamic Association. The principle at work behind these activities was the same as any instance of corporate sponsorship or philanthropy. The reputation that the men gained from such charitable activities heightened their prestige and was good for business.

The members of the antialcohol committee could not compete with the quarter's three "big bucks" entrepreneurs in the size or frequency of their donations. The committee members could, however, use the antialcohol movement to build their reputation as devout and civic-minded businessmen. By donating their time, energy, and incomes toward the promulgation of one of the basic tenets of Islam, the twelve committee members acquired a degree of renown on Barley Market Street that increased their ability to influence local affairs and built up their business reputations.

Three of the committee's members specifically harnessed their participation in the antialcohol movement for their economic advantage by establishing a "Hui Quarter Antialcohol Committee Food Processing Factory" (*Huifang jinxie shipin jiagongchang*). They set up this steamed bread factory on Barley Market Street during the fall of 1995. When I interviewed the three co-proprietors during June 1997, they stated that the factory "had no relationship" to the antialcohol committee, despite its name. As our discussion continued, however, the men demonstrated that they connected the factory's activities with the committee. For example, in 1996 they hosted a one-year anniversary celebration of the factory's founding at which they gave 6,000 yuan to local handicapped people. Ma described this donation as "one of the antialcohol committee's small-scale activities" that had been carried out in my absence. Mingjie, a member of the antialcohol committee who had not become a proprietor of the steamed bread factory, sourly characterized the three committee members as "using the name of the antialcohol committee to benefit themselves and make a profit." According to him and other local entrepreneurs, the committee's evangelical and philanthropical activities had paid off: the Hui Quarter Antialcohol Committee Food Processing Factory was extremely profitable.

No women were formal members of the antialcohol committee, although a few wives of the members occasionally attended group functions and helped clean up afterward. Two women, one a wife and the other a daughter of men who had founded the committee, said that the group's affairs were "men's business" (*nanren de shi*). The committee's masculine bias arose from two local expectations: first, that only men spoke out in public, and second, that men were more likely to consume alcohol.

Generally speaking, in the quarter men were acknowledged as heads of households, proprietors, and mosque representatives. Even when, as was the case with Lanying's family, a family business was operated entirely by women, a male member of the family (in this case, Lanying's elderly father) was credited as being the owner and decision maker. Most female residents regarded their families as their primary concern. Women's public roles, whether these were attending parent-teacher meetings at school, working in the family enterprise, or supporting their husbands' participation in the antialcohol movement, were more limited in scope because of women's domestic orientation.

Most residents perceived women to be less vulnerable to alcohol's lures. Several factors accounted for this perception. Hui women were far more likely to spend the majority of their time in the quarter than were men. This meant that female residents had fewer close contacts with Han and fewer opportunities to eat in restaurants or socialize outside the quarter. In the private businesses with which I was familiar (both food and other types of enterprise), women acted as laborers and in-store managers while men assumed the task of procuring resources, making business connections, and distributing the goods produced. For example, one family I knew operated a trucking concern. Two brothers drove the truck and their mother and sister attended the telephone and took requests for future loads. Similar social and occupational differences between the sexes have been recorded in many other Muslim societies (see, e.g., Abu-Lughod 1986:72–4; Boddy 1989: 36–7, 41–6). In my experience, they were more true of the quarter than other parts of Xi'an, probably because Xi'an Han women were more likely to work in work units.

Propaganda and Rallies

"Thought work" in the form of public propaganda was the primary form of committee activity. Committee members hung signs in their establishments proclaiming that alcohol was prohibited and thanking customers for complying with the ban. The large banners that they strung over Barley Market Street were inscribed with messages such as "qingzhen does not mix with alcohol" or "respect the Muslim traditions." Barley Market Street was bedecked with at least one antialcohol banner during the entire eighteen months I lived in Xi'an. The antialcohol committee wrote their name in the corner of every banner or sign, a tactic that ensured that the group's members were credited for their efforts. Although other associations, such as the Dapiyuan Mosque management committee (*siguanhui*), occasionally hung signs in their neighborhoods that denounced alcohol, only the Barley Market Street Antialcohol Committee maintained continual publicity for the cause. This was a source of pride for the committee's members, for the mosques to which they belonged, and for the Barley Market Street neighborhood—referred to as the "Western" (*xitou*) half of the quarter—whose residents saw themselves as being at the forefront of the movement to eradicate alcohol.

At the antialcohol meetings and rallies, committee members supplied participants with food and soft drinks from their enterprises. They used their businesses' tables and chairs to set up a meeting place in the street in front of their stores. One rally I witnessed in April 1995 included guests from two local mosques. Originally, the antialcohol committee had prepared to host only the Middle Mosque congregation. Committee members had organized a meeting where one of the Middle Mosque's religious specialists would speak to the Middle Mosque congregation and the shopkeepers on Barley Market Street about the Islamic prohibition of alcohol. However, at the last minute the neighboring Yingli Mosque congregation asked if they could also attend, and the committee had agreed. Aside from funerals or meetings organized by government institutions, the resulting interfaction mass rally was the only public event in the quarter that I knew of that included both Gedimu and Ikhwan adherents.

The two congregations marched toward the meeting site in two separate processions. First, the Middle Mosque congregation lined up its male members inside the mosque and paraded along a circuitous route until they reached the site of the rally. At the front of the procession, several members of the congregation carried a large wooden plaque inscribed with the phrase "the glory of the believers" (*mumin zhi guang*) that the mosque had prepared to commemorate the antialcohol committee. Other men carried flags that read "Middle Mosque." Heading the whole ensemble was a parade leader swinging a baton. The clamor of the local markets surrounded the procession as the group paraded toward Barley Market Street. Contrary to the committee's original intentions, no women from the Middle Mosque participated. When the Yingli Mosque had petitioned to attend the rally, the antialcohol committee asked the female members of the Middle Mosque congregation not to come for fear that there would not be adequate space for everyone to be seated.

After the Middle Mosque had completed their procession, the

Yingli Mosque's began. Although the Yingli Mosque and the Middle Mosque were located on Small Study Street only a few blocks apart, the Yingli Mosque congregation began in their own mosque and paraded along a different route toward the meeting site. Because the Yingli Mosque's participation was rather last-minute, the congregation had not been able to commission a plaque for the committee. Not to be outdone by the Middle Mosque, however, they purchased and framed a large poster instead, inscribing it as a gift from "the entire peoples of Small Study Street" because only those members of the Yingli congregation who lived on Small Study Street attended the rally.[2] Rather than displaying banners and wielding batons, the Yingli Mosque group instead shouted "God is great!" together in Arabic (*Allahu akbar*) as they walked to the rally site. Both the purchase of the poster and the shouting of Islamic praises were examples of the quarter's factional competitions. Although the Yingli Mosque's gift may have looked second-class compared to the Middle Mosque's specially made plaque, the Yingli Mosque subtly asserted their superiority and greater authenticity through their Arabic calls, which were in "standard" Arabic learned through what the congregation touted as "scientific" educational methods.

After both processions arrived at Barley Market Street, the two congregations were seated, with the men from the Middle Mosque on one side of the tables and the men from the Yingli Mosque on the other. The Yingli Mosque women seated themselves together at a couple of tables at the end of the two rows of men (see Figure 17). The crowd listened patiently under the hot midday sun as a number of men made speeches. First, a representative of the antialcohol committee spoke, then the head of the Middle Mosque management committee, and then the ahong of the Middle Mosque. The first speaker gave a brief history of the antialcohol committee's formation and activities, after which discussion focused on the Islamic prohibition of alcohol and Muslims' duty to avoid it. After the speeches, the committee members, helped by their wives and adult children, served their guests sweets, pastries, tea, and soft drinks. The guests ate quickly and left, the Middle

Mosque congregation leaving together in one direction and the Yingli Mosque members heading the opposite way.

Although the joint Middle Mosque–Yingli Mosque gathering was a success, not all of the antialcohol committee's events proceeded so smoothly. Shortly after the Middle Mosque–Yingli Mosque rally, members of the Western Mosque (the other mosque in Barley Market Street's immediate vicinity) informed the group that they also wanted the opportunity to express their appreciation for the committee's efforts. The Western Mosque's request was clearly an effort to stake their congregation's position in the ongoing status competition that occurred among the mosques and factions. Members of the antialcohol committee offered to sponsor another public rally at which the Western Mosque congregation would be the guests of honor. On the day of the event, however, I arrived to find Barley Market Street set up for the meeting, but no participants in sight. A few others who had shown up for the rally were equally confused. Finally, one committee member's wife came by and said that at the last minute the men had gone to attend the reopening of the Yingli Mosque, which had temporarily been closed by the government. Whether because of inertia, the expense of hosting such an event, or for some other reason, the meeting was never rescheduled.

Building a "Civilized Society"

In the Chinese Communist Party's vision of progress, the roots of which lay in anticolonialist sentiment, social evolutionism, nationalism, and Marxism, "civilization" was viewed as the end point of modernization and the outcome of history. In government rhetoric since 1979, the party has divided "civilization" (*wenming*) into two parts: "material civilization" (*wuzhi wenming*) and "spiritual civilization" (*jingshen wenming*). Deng's program of modernization, in which the party promoted marketization, privatization, and the creation of a consumer economy as necessary steps for China's development, brought about the rising standards of living and material changes that were characterized

FIGURE 17. Antialcohol committee rally on Barley Market Street.

as "material civilization" or at least progress toward this goal. "Spiritual civilization," on the other hand, was more elusive, but nevertheless an essential concern after 1979 (Anagnost 1992:182; see also Anagnost 1997a). One facet of "spiritual civilization" was Marxist or socialist. Deng's economic reforms created a kind of capitalist economy in China, but the party saw capitalism as only a passing stage en route to true civilization, which meant communist utopia. One of the CCP's concerns after 1979 was to avert the rise of "bourgeois individualism" that accompanies the capitalist stage of development and to inculcate socialist ethics. Augmenting this aspect of "spiritual civilization" was the need to develop the racial capacities and performance of China's population, which was couched in terms of improving the "cultural quality" (*wenhua suzhi*) of Chinese citizens. In addition, a Confucian or "Chinese" definition of civilization infiltrated notions of "spiritual civilization," such that the party held up the Han race as a model of civilization for the other *minzu* to emulate (Harrell 1995b:26–7).

The blending of Marxist, racial, and Confucian components made the CCP's push to build "spiritual civilization" a multifaceted program. Educative campaigns and propaganda to improve etiquette and sanitation were one element of "building a civilized society" (*jianshe wenming shehui*). Compliance with the official birth control policy, described in eugenicist terms as "quality births" (*yousheng*), was another. Orderly behavior, effective conflict management, the eradication of prostitution, and good relations between party members and ordinary citizens were also elements of the government's ethical campaigns to create a "civilized society" (see Anagnost 1992; Litzinger 1995:120–1). In each case, the government positioned itself as the arbiter of civilized behavior and the nation's guide to civilization.

Residents of the quarter accepted the idea that they needed to develop a "civilized society." They believed that "civilization" was the ultimate outcome of history. When, during the early stages of the antialcohol movement, a group of residents petitioned the government to make a law prohibiting alcohol in the Muslim district, they acted in a way that affirmed the government's paramount role in developing a "civilized society." The Barley Market Street Antialcohol Committee, however, went beyond the CCP's program for "building a civilized society." The members of the committee took the initiative as private citizens to ban alcohol, which was legal in the PRC. They condemned alcohol consumption as immoral and causing uncivilized behavior. Their private prohibition worked against modernization from the state's point of view, because it restricted and had the goal of totally eliminating a form of consumption that generated money for the economy. Just as bad was the committee members' failure to take the party as their guide for dealing with alcohol; rather, the model of civilization that the committee adopted was an Islamic one. The antialcohol movement pointed to Islam as the true locus of civilization. Their Islamic vision of "civilized society" challenged the government's monopoly on civility and modernization and upset the state's evolutionary hierarchy that defined Hui as less civilized than Han. Instead, the antialcohol committee held itself up as a model for others to imitate, and members took upon themselves the role of purveying civilization to local, national, and international communities.

The case of the Barley Market Street Antialcohol Committee provides an example of how Islam can serve as an ethical guide, stimulate political action, and provide the basis for a utopic vision of the future. Watts (1996) describes an analogous case in Kano, Nigeria. His study focuses on a charismatic leader who, in response to the rapid economic transformations occurring in Nigeria after the oil boom, used the Qur'an to critique rampant materialism, social inequities, and government corruption. Ultimately, this leader's calls for reform led to military opposition to the government and an attempt to seize control of the key institutions in Kano city. The Barley Market Street Antialcohol Committee was far less radical than the group that Watts studied, but important similarities exist. Both movements arose in response to "modernization." Both were grassroots crusades inspired by

Islamic doctrine. Both looked to Islam as the ultimate ethical source and found a model for a "civilized society" in Islamic observance.

Although the antialcohol movement's vision of civilization was not isomorphic with the government's, the methods that residents used to achieve a civilized society and the nature of that society were strongly influenced by the state. These characteristics were shared by other social movements that occurred in China after 1979. For example, Wasserstrom and Liu point out that during the 1989 Beijing protests, the students used state-created student organizations to order the movement, and the student leaders emulated the managerial techniques of party officials (1995). In the quarter, Yingchun's public censure of residents who sold alcohol resembled the public denunciations and scapegoating that the party used under Mao. The social pressure exerted though threatened physical destruction of local establishments that sold alcohol mimicked but did not fully reenact the repressive Cultural Revolution tactics whereby Red Guards destroyed the property of nonconforming "enemies of the people." The coercive techniques of social persuasion that the committee members adopted to convince the entrepreneurs on Barley Market Street to ban alcohol are strongly reminiscent of the "thought work" carried out during the Maoist era, when teams of cadres used group pressure and barrages of propaganda to "persuade" dissenters to adhere to the party line. Once the ban was in place, the committee's stress on propaganda, mass rallies, and ideological indoctrination was also borrowed from the CCP.

The form of the "civilized society" that the committee built was also heavily influenced by government policies. Even though the men legitimated their activities in Islamic terms, the society they created did not adhere to Middle Eastern models. For example, women participated in the movement, and public events were not gender-segregated. A number of the committee members considered their wives to be part of the movement. When the committee commissioned me to take formal photographs of the group, the members made certain that I photographed their gathered wives as well. They relied on their wives to work at and help oversee the rallies. At many of their public meetings, the committee also welcomed the participation of both men and women. The exclusion of the Middle Mosque's women from the April 1995 meeting was, Ma's wife stated, an unfortunate exception, and several women from the Yingli Mosque had attended. The committee's inclusion of the women evidenced their belief that women were important social actors with public roles, a position that the CCP had promoted since the party was first formed.

The committee also followed the government's lead in designing activities that crossed the diverse loyalties to mosque, religious faction, neighborhood, and place of origin that characterized the quarter (and most other Hui communities in northwest China; see Lipman 1984). The joint Middle Mosque–Yingli Mosque rally was an event that brought together members of different congregations and factions. The letter of appeal that the committee sent to all ten mosques in the quarter also exemplifies the breadth of their social vision. When committee members invited Yingchun, the Dapiyuan Mosque ahong credited with instigating the antialcohol movement, to speak at a meeting of Barley Market Street shopkeepers, they ignored the "East-West" cleavage (*dongtou, xitou*) that characterized the district. Such acts went against local prejudices and behavioral patterns. Residents of "the East" and "the West" tended to distrust one another and had limited social interactions unless they were linked by kinship ties. The families who lived in "the East" saw themselves as more civilized than those who lived in "the West." Several families who lived on Dapiyuan Street encouraged me not to visit the Barley Market Street neighborhood, because "those people had low cultural quality" (*naxieren wenhua suzhi di*). The Barley Market Street Antialcohol Committee overrode these parochial loyalties and stereotypes. When I left Xi'an in August 1995, the committee was making plans to organize a quarterwide rally that would include representatives from all ten mosques (and all three factions).

The Antialcohol Committee and the Government

During the first four years of the antialcohol committee's existence, the government did not interfere in the movement. This lack of official response was related to a number of factors. First, residents had asked the government to intervene. This reaffirmed the state's authority. Second, many government officials were reluctant to involve themselves in the Muslim district's affairs because of the reputation that residents had for being "troublesome" and "sensitive." Third, district officials were primarily concerned with economic development and so may have regarded the antialcohol committee's propaganda efforts as harmless. Because the committee organized public rallies sporadically, it was possible that the district government was unaware of them or that district officials could pretend to be so. Fourth, the goals of the antialcohol movement, defined as "building a civilized society," were not overtly incompatible with the government's program.

When I returned to the quarter for a brief visit in June 1996, however, the situation had changed dramatically. According to Chen, some "unbeliever" who sold alcohol had complained about the antialcohol committee to local officials. Once a complaint had been registered, the government was forced to do something about the group. Officials reacted by declaring the committee an "illegal organization" (*feifa zuzhi*) on the grounds that it had not received state permission to form. Some members of the committee ceased participating when the group was declared illegal; Mingjie, once an extremely enthusiastic member (and the person who had first told me about the group), was one. The remaining committee members petitioned all the mosques in Xi'an, including the eight mosques that were outside the quarter, to express their support for the committee to the government. Confronted by the mosques' advocacy, the government designated an official to investigate the committee and its activities. Until these investigations were concluded and officials reached a decision, the remaining committee members decided to remain quiet. Chen said they did this so that the government would not perceive them as having an "antagonistic" (*duikang*) attitude.

When I visited four members of the antialcohol committee during June 1997, the government had concluded its research. An official had interviewed seventeen businesses, work units, and homes in the quarter to ascertain their opinions of the antialcohol committee. Twelve of these had been Hui, and five were Han. All those interviewed had been extremely supportive of the group. The committee members said that everyone the official had spoken to "had a relationship" with members of the committee, a testimony to the group's influence and its members' strong social networks. After the interviews were concluded, the government convened a meeting for the committee members, the district government officials, city government officials, and the provincial Islamic Association. Many spoke out in the committee's defense; Ma told me that a high-ranking member of the provincial Islamic Association praised the group for its activities and strongly urged that the government withdraw the label of "illegal organization" that had been applied to the group. The officials responded by praising the "civilized spirit" (*wenming jingshen*) of the committee. However, they chose to adhere to the letter of the law: the organization was illegal and could not receive official permission to exist unless it accepted a representative of the CCP who would report to the state as a member.

The committee's reputation suffered from these events. According to Xijuan, who ran an eatery with her husband on Barley Market Street, the committee had "scattered" (*san le*) and the antialcohol movement was in disarray. She and some other residents stated that the group had not hosted any events for a few months. Xijuan claimed that alcohol had reappeared on Barley Market Street. Some of the local entrepreneurs were once again allowing their customers to consume alcohol, and a few even sold it. She said that she and her husband now ran one of the few remaining enterprises that prohibited alcohol.

Mingjie, now an ex-member of the committee, voiced suspicions about the remaining members, whom he characterized as "using the group for other purposes." One complaint he made was that the men used the committee's name on the steamed bread factory; Mingjie saw this as a moneymaking venture that had nothing to do with the committee's original purpose. Mingjie also suggested that the other committee members were less than honest in their organizational accounting. The group had received 500 yuan from each of the quarter's ten mosques to support the committee's antialcohol propaganda. Five thousand yuan was a large sum, Mingjie stated, but "no one knew" to what uses the money had been put. The implication was that the remaining committee members had pocketed the money.

When I left Xi'an in late June 1997, the men who continued to associate themselves with the committee disagreed about what they should do next. Chen was very excited by a recently published newspaper article that described the regulations on qingzhen foods that the provincial government had developed. Chen interpreted the new regulations as an official recognition of qingzhen and its worth (despite the fact that the policies had nothing to do with Islam) and wanted the group to offer to publicize the new policies. Other members refused to have anything to do with the government, stating it was "untrustworthy" (*bu shou xinyong*). Ma explained that official propaganda and official actions had diverged too many times, and if the group were recognized by the government, state officials would interfere with their ability to convey their message. The presence of a party member in the committee would prevent them from even being able to talk to me. Regardless of these disagreements, the men agreed that at the moment nothing could be done: the "glorious return" of Hong Kong was fast approaching, and "it was a bad time to do propaganda work."

Alcohol and Civilization

Residents generally applauded and looked forward to modernization. They embraced many aspects of the consumer lifestyle that the Deng reforms had made possible. Yet the problems with alcohol developed in response to Deng's modernization program. Privatization provoked the need to make a profit, which residents blamed for alcohol's appearance in the quarter. Privatization and marketization produced the increase in disposable incomes that made it possible to buy alcohol and to buy the newspapers, magazines, and televisions that depicted alcohol-drinking Chinese "big bucks" and Westerners. These media representations and the kinds of knowledge they engendered were also results of Deng's reform policies. The state's promotion of personal consumption since 1979 compounded the problem, because a ban on alcohol could be interpreted as counter to official goals.

Rather than allowing themselves to be perceived as reactionary, unprogressive, or antistate, the members of the Barley Market Street Antialcohol Committee co-opted the government's rhetoric of civilization and promoted the ban on alcohol as good for economic development. They presented the alcohol-free Barley Market Street as a clean, wholesome place that was more attractive for customers. They claimed that the ban had minimized drunken brawls and disorderly behavior, making Barley Market Street a more civilized place to live, work, and eat. The committee members used the movement to build reputations for themselves that improved business, with the most obvious financial gains coming from the "Hui Quarter Antialcohol Food Processing Factory." The committee's activism broadened members' social networks within the quarter and to Hui communities elsewhere in China, which could also yield economic benefits (as well as increasing the committee members' prestige, influence, and social standing).

Committee members saw themselves as promoting a form of civilization that was guided by Islam. They conceptualized their acts in terms of Islamic standards rather than "socialist ethics" or Han society. By forming an antialcohol organization, the committee challenged the CCP's monopoly on progress and morality and the leadership role that the state apportioned to itself—however unwillingly at the start. When the committee members positioned themselves as exemplars and condemned the Han practice of drinking, they also upset the official evolutionary hierarchy that ranked the Han as more civilized than the Hui.

In June 1997, it appeared that the government had quashed the threats posed by the antialcohol movement and muzzled those who had usurped the official role of "building a civilized society" in the quarter. Yet the state's efforts produced no conclusive results, largely because officials had not succeeded in changing anyone's mind about the committee or about alcohol. The persistence of a local vision of civilization was perhaps best symbolized by the name of the steamed bread factory that some of the committee members had formed. When the government tried to eliminate the antialcohol committee, officials demanded that the name of the factory be changed. The owners were not willing to refuse for fear that local officials would shut down the business, yet at the same time, the men did not want to give in meekly to the government's request or admit that the committee was anything other than temporarily dysfunctional. Instead, they found a resident who could translate the factory's name into Persian and submitted the Persian translation, which they said also meant the "Hui Quarter Antialcohol Committee Food Processing Factory," to the government's registration bureau. The sign bearing the name in Chinese they left hanging over the entrance to the factory.

Chapter Seven

WEDDING GOWNS AND MODERNIZATION

In the 1990s, a new trend in wedding gowns and bridal appearance swept the People's Republic of China (see Faison 1996; Agence France-Presse 1997). Dresses that imitated Western bridal gowns became the fashion as the PRC's urbanites followed trends that had begun a decade or more earlier in Hong Kong, Taiwan, and Japan (see, e.g., Yang 1981; Wolf 1972:134; Goldstein-Gidoni 1997). Xi'an and the Muslim district were no exception. There, young women chose to wear elaborate pink or coral gowns with long skirts and tight bodices on their wedding day and for commemorative wedding photos.

Chinese wedding attire had changed dramatically and repeatedly during the 50 years before this trend. These fashion shifts followed the changes in government policies for modernizing China. For many residents, the new wedding gowns epitomized the heights of modernization, evoking such exemplars as Hong Kong, the United States, and Western Europe. Yet modernization in the guise of a wedding gown had many meanings for young women, their older female relatives, the quarter's religious specialists, and government officials. The goods and services that a young woman consumed for her wedding made visible her self-image and goals, her economic capacity and the economy within which she functioned, her position and decision-making power within her family, and her religiosity and relationship to the mosque. Wedding gown consumption also revealed that the economic reforms had had some unintended consequences: they had increased Chinese citizens' sense of agency and given them the means to grasp their own modernization. Not surprisingly, government officials found this trend very disturbing.

*Wedding Dress and "Wedding Gowns" (*Hunsha*)*

The clothes that most Xi'an brides, whether Hui or Han, wore in 1994 and 1995 were known as *hunsha*, "wedding gowns." This word referred specifically to the dresses that brides wore in Hong Kong, the United States, and Western Europe, which residents had seen in magazines, on television, and in films. A number of residents made the comment to me that "you Westerners wear *hunsha*." What provoked this remark was the relative novelty of such attire; women who had been married for longer than five years had not worn wedding gowns for their marriage ceremony. They used other terms to describe their wedding clothes: *qipao*, which referred to the tight-fitting, high-necked dress associated with prerevolutionary China; "traditional Chinese clothes" (*Zhongguo chuantong yifu*), which consisted of a tunic and trousers; Sun Yat-sen or "Mao" suits, as they are known in the West (*Zhongshan zhuang*); or Western suits (*xizhuang*).[1]

In the following paragraphs, I provide a short historical reconstruction of wedding attire in Xi'an based on hundreds of discussions about weddings with dozens of women and close conversations with twenty women who served as my key informants. The twenty brides consisted of four women who married before 1949, two who married in the 1950s, three who married in the 1960s, one from the 1970s, three from the 1980s, and seven from the 1990s. With the exception of one 1960s bride and one 1990s bride, all my informants were Hui. Nevertheless, popular articles (Faison 1996; Agence France-Presse 1997), the experiences of other ethnographers in China, and my own observations in cities such as Beijing, Yinchuan, and Xining suggest that few if any differences existed between Hui and Han bridal attire. The most significant variation was that Xi'an Han adopted wedding gowns before the residents of the quarter did.

The women of my acquaintance who had been married before 1949 stated that they wore either the tight-fitting, skirted qipao or a tunic and trousers during their wedding ceremonies. Women younger than 65 also described the clothes that their mothers and grandmothers wore when they were married in this way. Xi'an urbanites especially associated the qipao with imperial China and the wealth and power of the upper classes, despite the fact that the qipao first appeared in China during the 1920s (see Finnane 1996). A bride who wore a qipao before 1949 showed her family's affluence and sophistication. By contrast, most women associated the tunic and trousers with the countryside and poorer lifestyles. Women who married during the 1950s and the one woman I spoke with who married in the Shaanxi countryside during the 1960s also wore tunics and trousers in their weddings. None of my informants characterized tunics and trousers as desirable or fashionable bridal attire; rather, many contrasted the poverty and plainness of such clothing with the elegance and costliness of the wedding gowns popular during the 1990s. A common complaint was that the tunics and trousers strongly resembled everyday wear. Their red color—red being the traditional color for bridal attire in China—rather than their form was the most striking feature demarcating wedding clothing from ordinary clothing during this period.

As CCP policies grew increasingly leftist during the 1960s and the political climate grew more harsh, brides switched their red garb for suits in more austere hues. Several women who had married during the 1960s wore Mao suits of gray or blue at their weddings, as did their grooms. Maoist propaganda, which characterized traditional wedding attire and marriage practices as "feudal," encouraged these changes (see, e.g. Lu [1966] 1969; Zhang 1966). The switch to Mao suits was paralleled by a greatly simplified wedding ceremony that focused on the state rather than on the families of the couple (see Whyte 1993 for a description). Almost without exception, the women who married during this period characterized their bridal attire as impoverished. Aifeng, who married in 1967, recounted that she had had to borrow clothing to wear for her wedding. After 1969, when the worst of Cultural Revolution radicalism had passed, brides exchanged their Mao suits for Western-style ones. During the 1970s and early 1980s, Western jacket-and-trouser suits in cream, pink, and yellow became popular.

According to my informants, wedding gowns debuted in the quarter around 1990. Several residents pointed out that Xi'an Han had begun wearing them even earlier. Xue, a young woman in her early twenties, described the appearance of wedding gowns in this way: "Wedding gowns have only recently sprung up (*cai xing qi lai le*). We saw the gowns on the streets: there were stores selling them, they were displayed in shop windows. That is where we [Hui women] saw them." She and the other women I asked said that Hui started wearing the dresses because they were fashionable and pretty. Several explained the switch by saying "a bride has to look like a bride." Such comments indicate that Chinese ideas about bridal appearance had changed markedly since the PRC's "open door" policies were first implemented in the early 1980s. A "proper bride" in the mid-1990s was defined by fashions associated with the affluence, cosmopolitanism, and "modernization" characteristic of Hong Kong and American elites.

Although residents identified the new wedding gowns with Western and Hong Kong fashions, the dresses that brides wore in Xi'an possessed distinctive characteristics in color and style. Although many brides chose to wear white wedding gowns for their formal wedding portraits (a recent addition to the marriage ritual), at none of the six weddings I attended during 1994 and 1995 and in none of the three weddings I saw on video and in photographs did Xi'an brides wear white. Whereas in the West white symbolizes purity and virginity, in Xi'an and the PRC white was generally associated with mourning. Some of the formal wedding portraits I saw referenced the Western custom, which was also popular in Japan, Hong Kong, and Taiwan, by showing the bride dressed in white. Such photos were set against a luxurious background containing furniture and props reminiscent of elite European houses. However, what brides wore during the actual wedding ritual did not match this fantasy depiction. All the Xi'an brides I observed wore either pink (*fenhongse*), coral (*rouse*), or red (*hongse*) dresses during their wedding ceremonies. Pink and coral bridal clothes straddled red's long-standing association with good fortune, happiness, and prosperity and the white of Western wedding gowns. In addition, the variety of wedding gown styles available to purchase, rent, or model for photographs in Xi'an was quite limited compared to the United States or Hong Kong. Stylistically, the dresses adhered to a standard model: tight bodice, puffy sleeves, and floor-length skirts with petticoats (see Figure 18).

Wedding Rituals

Weddings in the quarter differed from Xi'an Han weddings in duration and the type of ritual events that took place. Some of these differences derived from Islamic regulations about food (including alcohol) and about marriage, but many more resulted from the fact that most Hui did not work in work units but rather engaged in private enterprise. The money that residents made from private entrepreneurship enabled them to engage in more extensive and expensive marriage rituals than most Han. Despite differences, however, Hui and Han wedding rituals shared structural elements related to the relationship that the marriage created between the bride's and groom's families and the establishment of a new conjugal unit.

The Han wedding I attended in Xi'an lasted one day. The main events were the transfer of the bride and her dowry from the home of her birth to her marital home and a large banquet hosted in a restaurant. The dowry transfer and subsequent bride transfer differed from the Hui ritual only in the time of day when these rites took place (earlier in the day during the Han wedding) and the amount of time between them (shorter during the Han wedding). The restaurant banquet, attended by the families and guests of both the bride and the groom, was a ritual feature that weddings in the quarter did not have. At the Han restaurant banquet, the

FIGURE 18. Yan, wearing a wedding gown, sits in the "new house" (*xinfang*) during the second day of the wedding ritual.

leaders of the groom's work unit were specially acknowledged and honored; one read aloud the information written on the couple's official marriage license, which was procured several weeks before the ceremony. Other events included the bride and groom toasting each of the guests with alcohol (*baijiu*) and some teasing of the newlyweds by the groom's best man (*banlang*).[2]

By contrast, Hui weddings spanned a four-day period. On the first and second days, ritual banquets were held at the bride's household and at the groom's household. The bride's family hosted a banquet for their relatives, friends, and neighbors at the bride's house, and the groom's family hosted one for their relatives, friends, and neighbors at the groom's house. At both sites, the banquets opened with a recitation of the entire Qur'an by religious specialists and "men of religion" who could recite in Arabic. Then the guests ate in a prescribed hierarchical order, first the ahong and "men of religion," then the adult male guests, and finally the women and children. After the banquets came a series of food presentations between the bride's and groom's families, including the delivery of an entire meal (at least twelve dishes) to the bride's family.

On the first day of the wedding, another important event took place in the afternoon when the groom, accompanied by his best man, and an ahong from the mosque that the bride's family attended came to the bride's household. The ahong sat with the bride and the groom in a public place, usually her family's courtyard, and asked them formally if they consented to the wedding. These vows were known as "reciting the *yizabu*" (*nian yizabu* or *fan yizabu*); *yizabu* is a Chinese transliteration of the Arabic word *i'jab*, meaning "to make a contract." After this ceremony was completed, members of the bride's family and her friends transferred her dowry from her natal home to her new marital residence (the "new house" or *xinfang*), which was frequently located in the groom's parents' household.

The second day of the marriage ritual was the day that residents regarded as the "wedding day." It was during the afternoon and evening of this day that young women dressed in wedding gowns. The second day had another set of banquets and included the transfer of the bride from her natal home to the groom's parents' residence (this was true even if the couple's "new house" was not part of the groom's parents' home). The groom's family sent a team of ten or more cars to the bride's home to transport her, members of her family, and her guests to the groom's home. After picking up the bride, the team of cars returned by a circuitous route, making sure to drive in a procession down some of Xi'an's main streets and around the Bell Tower in the city's center. After a short stay of fifteen or twenty minutes at the groom's parents' home, the bride's guests adjourned. The remaining events of the day included public teasing of the groom and an extended period during which the bride was displayed to the groom's family and guests.

At about five o'clock in the morning on the third day, before morning prayers, the groom's family presented the bride with gifts, and she returned to her natal household escorted by her brother (or, lacking a brother, a categorical equivalent such as her father's brother's son). She remained at her natal home that night. On the fourth and final day of the ritual, several members of the bride's family escorted her back to the "new house," and the bride presented gifts to her new in-laws. The wedding ritual concluded after the groom's family had served the bride's guests dinner.

Weddings in the quarter were a "big deal" (*dashi*). Residents regarded a marriage ceremony as a once-in-a-lifetime event that marked a young person's entry into social adulthood. Their importance may have been even greater in the quarter than in other parts of Xi'an because so few Hui ever participated in graduation ceremonies or rites hosted by work units. Weddings were a defining moment for the bride, the groom, and their families, a critical time for them to create and present their public image to relatives, neighbors, and other urbanites. Families conveyed messages about their level of prosperity and degree of modernization through the consumption practices that they engaged in when a family member got married.

Dressing for Marriage: Xue's Story

At about 1:00 p.m. on the day of her wedding (the second day of the marriage ritual), Xue was extremely upset. Her sister and brother-in-law had just returned from picking up the wedding gown Xue had rented from a store that was twenty minutes away by car, and the gown was dirty. When she examined the outfit, Xue found mud stains on the gown's hem and headpiece and spots on the skirt. After a few minutes of furious discussion with her maid of honor, the two women (both in their early twenties) determined to take the dress back to the store and exchange it.

It was after 3:00 p.m. when Xue returned, to the consternation of her aunts (her father's sisters) who were guests at her family's home. They worried aloud whether Xue could be ready by the time the cars arrived to take her to the groom's home that evening. Xue was more sanguine, although she remarked that exchanging the gown had made her miss her 2:30 p.m. makeup and hairstyling appointment at Golden Lady, the fanciest beauty salon in the city. More immediately important, however, was that she had successfully changed the dirty pale pink gown for one in better condition. Although the new dress was coral in color, like the other gown it had a floor-length full skirt, large puffy short sleeves, and a tightly fitted bodice embroidered with an elaborate pearl and lace design. The gown's low-cut princess neckline was attached with transparent gauze to a pearl-and-lace collar.[3] With the gown came long gauze-and-lace gloves and a long gauze veil.

Xue left the dress in her room for her aunts and cousins to inspect and immediately set out for the Golden Lady, which was on the other side of town. Her maid of honor, bridesmaid, the bridesmaid's three-and-a-half-year-old son, and I accompanied her.[4] Xue and her fiancé had previously visited the salon when they were photographed for their formal wedding portraits, but none of the rest of us had been there before. Golden Lady was the most opulent beauty salon and studio that I had ever seen. It was packed with young women getting made up, having their hair done, and being photographed in a variety of fanciful bridal costumes supplied by the store. Fortunately for Xue, a stylist was available to tend to her face and hair immediately. Over the next hour, the bridesmaids and I watched the stylist apply makeup to Xue, gawked at the other women being beautified, paged through the books of wedding photographs that the studio provided as samples, and chatted together in the crowded waiting room. The little boy fell asleep on one of the couches, causing the receptionist to complain.

When Xue emerged from the stylist's chair, her hair was swept up on top of her head in a sophisticated style that left two long ringlets hanging down by each ear. Fresh pink carnations and baby's breath artfully decorated the top, with the coral-pink veil draped down the back. Liquid makeup and powder, meticulously applied, made her face look pale and polished. Deep brown eye shadow, black eyeliner, and mascara enhanced her eyes, and bright red lipstick drew attention to her lips (see Figure 19).

By the time we left the salon it was already 5:00 p.m. No one knew exactly when the groom would send the cars to meet Xue (around 6:00 p.m. was typical of the weddings I had attended), but all of us fretted that she would be late. Upon our return to her home, Xue dressed quickly, first donning the gold earrings, necklace, rings, and bracelets she had received as gifts from her husband's family, and then putting on her wedding gown. With her flowers, elaborate makeup, perfect hair, and flowing dress, she reminded me of a fairy tale princess. When Xue emerged from her room, her female friends and relatives rushed to her side, clamoring to have their photographs taken with the bride. Xue carefully posed with all her female relatives according to their generation: one photograph with her grandmother, great-aunt, and grandfather's brother's wife, another with her five paternal aunts, others with her peer-age cousins, and one with all of her cousins' and brother's children.

Xue spent about five hours that day preparing for her appearance as a bride. After the photographs, her formal performance began when the ahong arrived to recite the *qifa*, a prayer of leave-taking. All the guests crowded around her, the ahong, and her

FIGURE 19. Xue, freshly made up for her wedding.

maid of honor in a tight circle in the family's courtyard to watch and hear Xue be blessed. Later that evening, Xue spent seven hours on display in the groom's household. Like all Hui brides, she maintained a silent demeanor with eyes cast down while the groom's relatives and wedding guests came by the room where she was seated to look at and be photographed with her (see Figure

18).[5] Several of her new affines commented favorably on Xue's appearance to the other guests in her (and my) hearing: "Look at what a beautiful new daughter-in-law we have."

Unpacking Bridal Attire: Women, Shops, and Families

Several features of Xue's wedding preparations were striking; among the most notable was Xue's sense of consumer rights. Dissatisfied with the condition of the gown she had originally rented, Xue hesitated only briefly before going to the store to demand a replacement. Her willingness to fight for a clean gown related to the cost of the rental: the 360 yuan that she had paid was greater than a month's salary for a clerical worker in Xi'an's state enterprises. Even though Xue's family (which included eight people at the time of her marriage), as owners of a small private restaurant in the quarter, earned about 500 yuan a day in net income (making them quite comfortable by Xi'an standards), neither she nor her family undertook large expenditures lightly.

Just as important as the size of Xue's investment was the fact that she had procured the dress from a private business. Because Xue helped her family sell steamed stuffed buns (*baozi*) on Barley Market Street, she knew that the quality of the goods and services she provided largely determined how well her restaurant would do.[6] Xue and her family worked hard to ensure that the foods they sold were tasty and attractive. I frequently heard Xue's mother Aifeng criticize her children and the other employees for producing inferior *baozi*. Xue's experience as a private entrepreneur enabled her to recognize that market competition and the general availability of wedding gowns gave her power. When I asked her how the rental exchange had gone, she replied that it had been easy. She pointed out that many stores rented bridal clothes in that part of town, so she could easily have taken her business elsewhere had that store refused to satisfy her demands.

More than two years after her wedding day, Xue and I were talking about her marriage, and I asked her how she had managed to get a replacement. To my surprise, Xue told me that she actually had not successfully persuaded the store to exchange the gown. She and her maid of honor had argued at length with the storekeeper about the gown's condition, but the storekeeper kept making excuses and waffling about how to handle the problem. Ultimately, time pressures caused Xue to abandon her efforts. Xue said she simply rented another, cheaper gown from a nearby store.

This was not the story that Xue had told me, her friends, or her relatives on her wedding day. Perhaps then Xue had misrepresented her trip to exchange the gown in order to avoid criticism and prevent the incident from spoiling her marriage ceremony. Whether or not Xue successfully completed her mission, her story reveals a consumer awareness that was new to the post-Mao era. Xue's attempts mark a significant transformation in the Chinese economy and the powers of Chinese citizens.

Stories that Xi'an residents told me about the Maoist era painted a portrait of scarce goods and lack of choice. Many people in their 40s and older remembered a monotonous diet of sweet potatoes during the late 1960s and 1970s and shuddered at the prospect of ever eating them again. The ration coupons that urbanites received limited the kind and amount of food and other goods (such as clothing or shoes) they could procure. During the Maoist period, Chinese citizens were recipients of the state's largesse. They were the government's clients, not consumers who chose the products they desired from an array of potential purchases. Xue's agency as a consumer shows how the market economy has taught customers that they have the power to both select and reject commodities. Her retelling of her story indicates that this power related directly to the rising incomes that many Chinese citizens experienced since 1979 and was most easily exercised when the customer's pockets were flush.

The second noteworthy feature of wedding gown consumption was the nature of interactions between Hui and Han that it revealed. Golden Lady and the store where Xue rented her dress were both popular among Xi'an brides. Like most of the city's bridal stores, photography studios, and expensive salons, they were located in the northeastern part of Xi'an within the city wall, a good distance away from the quarter. A few other wedding gown establishments and marriage portrait studios were located on the main east-west street that bisected the city's center. In 1994 and 1995, the quarter had no places to rent gowns or have formal photographs taken, but it did have a few beauty salons that styled brides' hair and made up their faces.

Xi'an's marriage-related businesses were privately operated and for the most part run by Han entrepreneurs. Because Xi'an was predominantly a Han city, most of the patrons of these enterprises were Han. When young Hui women rented dresses from wedding gown stores, they wore clothing that had been worn by their Han peers. When they visited beauty salons in the northeastern part of the city, they received beauty treatments from Han employees. Even though residents of the quarter regarded themselves as racially and culturally distinct from (and better than) the Han and tended to limit their contacts with Han, sharing wedding gowns, facilities, and services with Han did not disturb the young Hui women of my acquaintance.

Although the government went to great lengths to establish, classify, and maintain the supposedly distinctive "nationality characteristics" of the Hui, wedding gown consumption patterns (and the wedding rituals) reveal how close Hui and Han were. Yet, residents refused to recognize this closeness. They did not associate wedding gowns with the Han race, even though they imitated styles that Han women had made fashionable and received service from Han entrepreneurs. Rather, Xi'an Hui characterized the wedding gowns as "modern," "trendy" (*liuxing*), and "Western," the opposite of the "traditional Chinese clothing" they equated with China's poor, rural, past (and present, in some places).

Another illuminating aspect of Xue's wedding preparations was her friends' and relatives' participation in creating her appearance. Particularly remarkable were the ways in which her older female relatives collaborated to ensure that she "looked like a bride," because Xue's appearance on her wedding day differed dramatically from the norms of female dress and ideas about modesty that characterized most residents of the quarter. Xue's story reveals that the female population collectively defined Hui bridal fashion in a manner that subverted some commonly held mores.

Xue's bridesmaids and her maid of honor, young women in their 20s and early 30s, participated in her beauty preparations at every stage of the process. Their presence signified their approbation of her appearance, and also gave them the opportunity to critique Xue should she attempt to deviate from how they thought she should look. On the first day of Xue's wedding, for example, when she was preparing for the *yizabu* ceremony, I heard Xue's maid of honor shame Xue into wearing flowers in her hair. At such ceremonies, brides usually wore dressy versions of daily wear, such as a long-sleeved sweater and trousers. What demarcated the bride from her female guests at these events were the flowers she wore in her hair and the scarf with which she covered her head. Xue had been complaining about the flowers she had prepared and suddenly stated that she would not wear them. Her maid of honor was shocked, and insisted that Xue put them on. "Otherwise no one will know you are the bride!" she said. Similarly, Xue's aunts and cousins inspected her wedding attire both before she dressed and afterward. During their examination, they gave their opinions of the gown's color, the way it looked on Xue, the shoes they thought she should wear with it, and so forth. At these moments, older Hui women helped create and maintain an image of the "proper bride."

When Xue's peers and relatives had their photographs taken with the bride, they demonstrated their approval of her appearance. Their acts suggested that Xue as a bride was important and that they valued the way she looked. In general, their comments and actions during the wedding showed an element of possessiveness, as if the bride were a valuable object they owned and were showing off. When Xue was on display at the groom's house, her new in-laws behaved in a similar manner, reinforcing the appropriateness of her appearance by making verbal commentary about her comeliness and taking turns being photographed with her. By participating in Xue's beauty preparations, being photographed with her, admiring her formal wedding photographs, and commenting on her appearance during the ritual, Xue's peers and older women colluded to produce a normative image of how a bride should look and disseminated this image to young, unmarried women.

The proper bridal look was highly standardized. Xue's makeover was more expensive than that of the other six brides whose weddings I attended, but her preparations and appearance (as well as her ritual role) were remarkably similar. At seven of the nine weddings with which I am most familiar, the brides dressed in a manner virtually identical to Xue. All wore long pink or coral gowns with tight bodices, low-cut necklines, fluffy skirts, gloves, and veils. They also wore high heels and flesh-toned nylons. Each had a formal hairstyling session on her wedding day, during which her hair was elaborately coifed: piled on top of the head with two long ringlets left dangling by each ear, crowned with flowers, and sprayed with colorful sparkly confetti (compare Figures 18 and 19). A specialist carefully applied their makeup, which included base and powder to whiten the face, eye shadow, eye liner, and mascara to emphasize the eyes, and bright red lipstick to accentuate the lips. Matching scarlet nail polish was applied to their fingernails. All the brides adorned their ears, necks, arms, and hands with jewelry, much of it gold. Although two of the nine brides chose not to wear long pink gowns, their hairstyles, makeup, shoes, stockings, and jewelry matched those of the other women.[7]

The experiences of one young Hui bride who attempted to wear something other than the standard wedding attire provides further evidence that women created and enforced an image of the "proper bride." Yue was a 24-year-old Hui intellectual, a Ph.D. candidate in computer science at the time I left Xi'an in August 1995. During the eighteen months I had been living there, she set and reset the date for her wedding several times: first it was scheduled for April 1995, then moved to May, and then July. Yue finally married in September 1995, a month after I had departed.

The difficulty with fixing Yue's wedding date sprang from the fact that Yue did not want to have a typical wedding. She did not want to follow the customary four-day wedding ritual, and she was determined to not dress like the other brides in the quarter. However, her fiancé's family and, as Yue told me, her future mother-in-law in particular, believed strongly that Yue and her fiancé should follow the local marriage practices. Perhaps some of their insistence came from their awareness of how exceptional a Hui woman Yue was, with her graduate education and work experience far removed from the petty entrepreneurial lifestyle common to most women in the quarter. Yue needed to procure her affines' agreement that she marry in the style she wished because, like most young Chinese, she depended on her own and her husband's family to pay for the wedding (see Whyte 1993; Siu 1993 for accounts of parental expenditures for children's weddings). While she negotiated to get her own way Yue repeatedly delayed the ceremony. She had been engaged for a year when we first met in the spring of 1994; most Hui I knew thought that after a year it was time for an affianced couple to get married.

I first received photographs and a description of Yue's wedding from her younger sister, who wrote a week after the marriage took place. Opening the letter, I was surprised to see that Yue wore the typical light pink gown, veil, high heels, makeup, and jewelry. Shortly thereafter, Yue herself wrote and sent more photographs. In that letter, and in a subsequent telephone conversation, Yue explained why she had acceded to her mother-in-law's wishes. Her own aunts and female cousins had added their voices to the pressure from her husband's family that Yue marry in the current style, until finally she gave in. Her wedding had been "exactly like the ones" I had witnessed, Yue told me. "Actually," she wrote in her letter, "it was a hard time for me."

The importance placed on being a bride who "looks like a bride" is also illustrated by a trend I observed among married women in early middle age to have themselves photographed in wedding gowns, even though they had been married for several years. Most of the women I knew who had done this were Han.

However, older Hui women were also very taken with the wedding gowns, as the pressure Yue's female relatives and in-laws exerted attests. At one wedding I attended in the quarter, the bride's youngest aunt (father's sister) excitedly tried on her niece's wedding gown (see Figure 20). After she put it on, she called her husband and two teenaged children over and asked me to photograph them together.

Older women's willingness to countenance wedding gowns and their encouragement of young women to wear them was surprising. Under normal circumstances, few Hui women wore skirts, and those who did were almost all younger than 30. Older women and men strongly disapproved of skirts and were extremely vocal in their criticisms of the young Hui women who wore them. Most residents of the quarter said that skirts violated the Islamic code of modesty—known locally as *xiuti* or "shamed body"—which dictates that women's bodies be covered from ankle to wrist.

For most Xi'an Hui, observing modesty dictates meant wearing trousers, not skirts. This was a reversal of the Islamic modesty code practiced in the Middle East, where long skirts were the hallmark of the modest woman. When trousers were introduced in the Middle East in the early twentieth century, they provoked public censure, personal attacks, and even riots. By contrast, in Xi'an, observance of *xiuti* had long meant following Chinese norms for modesty, which entailed wearing trousers. However, *xiuti* was changing in the quarter. During the summers of 1996 and 1997, I saw small groups of young Ikhwan women wearing ankle-length skirts instead of trousers, evidence of Arabization's influence. The long skirts enabled the young women to be modern, more authentically Muslim, and distinctly un-Chinese and non-Han through copying the Middle Eastern style.

Older women and ahong were the two main sources of censure about clothing styles in the quarter. In the heat of June 1995, when Yan decided to wear a dress late in her pregnancy, her aunt disapproved. "Naked, revealed body!" (*chi shen luo ti*), she exclaimed upon seeing Yan's skirts. She then told Yan and me that the ahong of the mosque she attended had criticized a family in

FIGURE 20. Yan's aunt tries on Yan's wedding gown.

public because the women of the family wore skirts. One elderly member of this family had successfully completed the pilgrimage to Mecca, so his family hosted a large celebration in his honor. When the ahong, a guest of honor at the party, saw that some of the pilgrim's female relatives wore skirts, he angrily scolded the man in front of the guests for not ensuring that his own family dressed modestly.

Although women like Yan's aunt strongly disapproved of skirts for everyday wear, they did not object to brides who wore wedding gowns. The calf-length, high-necked dress worn by an overheated and heavily pregnant Yan occasioned her aunt's reproaches, but this same aunt looked on approvingly during Yan's wedding when Yan wore a long pink gown with a low-cut neckline. Indeed, at her wedding, Yan's aunt sanctioned Yan's appearance by being photographed with her and joining in the general admiration of her beauty. Comments like those recounted at Xue's wedding, where affinal relatives bragged about the beauty of the family's "new daughter-in-law," were commonly made at weddings by older women, despite the conflict between the bride's attire and most of the older women's own standards of dress. With few exceptions, when I asked women ranging in age from 35 to 80 if they had worn such wedding gowns, they laughed at the idea and told me that they had never worn skirts in their lives.[8] Middle-aged and older women tended to wear loose long-sleeved blouses and trousers and to cover their hair with a white hat or *gaitou* (the traditional Hui hoodlike veil), in compliance with modesty dictates.

One of the most notable features of wedding gowns was the emphasis they placed on the body. In 1994 and 1995, Hui women rarely wore form-fitting clothes. I saw a few young women wearing relatively tight clothing at festive occasions like weddings, but most preferred to dress fashionably in a manner that did not emphasize the shape of their bodies. No Hui women I knew considered close-fitting attire suitable for daily wear, unlike many of the young Han women I saw in Xi'an. In general, young Hui women wore trousers and shirts (with extra layers in the winter). Women in their 30s, 40s, and 50s usually wore roomy blouses loose over unfitted slacks. Hui women in their 60s and older wore late imperial-style tunics with high collars over wide cotton trousers. Older women were likely to simply wear freshly laundered versions of their everyday clothes at weddings and communal celebrations. Only young women dressed up on festive occasions.

Despite the challenge that contemporary bridal attire posed to Hui notions of modesty, wedding gowns conveyed an image that resonated with and supported certain ideals that residents of the quarter held. One set of ideas the gowns represented were youth and fertility. Wedding gowns were the domain of the young. Neither of the two older women I knew (both widows) who had married in the early 1990s wore this type of bridal attire. One of the gown's undeniable effects was to emphasize the nubility and, through the enhancement of the bust and hips, the fertility of a young bride. This suggests that some of the gowns' popularity, perhaps especially among older women, derived from the role they played in establishing the bride's new identity as wife and mother.

Paradoxically, given the state's birth control policies, mothering had taken on an increased importance in Deng-era China. In her study of home interiors, Davis (1989) points to the large double beds in Shanghai workers' apartments as evidence that, at home, women were creating an identity focused on reproduction and their sexual obligations. She argues that the CCP's population control and residential policies have heightened the importance of wife- and motherhood by making children a limited good. Rofel (1994) writes that young married silk workers in Hangzhou have rejected their worker identities in favor of mothering. She interprets this as an effort by women to assert control over their bodies and lives and resist the workplace discipline imposed by the state.

Although no women in Xi'an discussed wedding gowns in relation to sex or mothering, the dresses were nevertheless connected to the roles of wife and mother. Most obviously, the gowns were worn during the ritual that marked a woman's transition into these roles. It is worth noting that motherhood followed marriage. Most young women that I knew had a baby before their one-year marriage anniversary, and those that didn't were subject to speculation and concern from their families and neighbors. The ways that the gowns accentuated the body and the vast amounts of time and money spent on the bride's appearance indicate the importance that residents placed on becoming a wife and a mother.

Equally if not more important were the symbolic messages that the wedding gowns conveyed about modernization. Young, marriage-aged women contrasted wedding gowns with what they called the "traditional" clothes their grandmothers wore. Women who were married in the 1970s and earlier contrasted their bridal attire unfavorably with that of more recent brides. Female residents of the quarter described the 1990s wedding gowns as "elaborate" (*jiangjiu*), "fashionable" (*liuxing*), and "modern" (*xiandaihua*). They associated the gowns with places they regarded as modern, urban, and prosperous. By choosing to wear wedding gowns, young Hui women appropriated the ideas that the gowns represented for themselves. Wedding gowns enabled a bride to signal her participation in modernization to her family, neighbors, relatives, friends, religious specialists, casual passersby, and the other residents of Xi'an who saw her as she was driven down the main city streets and around the Bell Tower en route to the groom's household.

Wedding dresses represented prosperity on a symbolic level, but they also demonstrated wealth more literally. The young brides I knew in the mid-1990s possessed large amounts of money to spend on their appearance (see Chart 2 for an expense record of Xue's wedding attire). Renting bridal attire in Xi'an cost between 200 and 400 yuan; this included the gown, gloves, and veil. Young women specially purchased the shoes and nylons they wore on their wedding day and paid for the services of the beauty parlor; Xue's makeover, hairstyle, and flowers cost 100 yuan. Brides also wore large amounts of gold jewelry, some of which they had bought for themselves, and some of which had been given as engagement gifts by the groom's family.

A great deal of the money that women spent on their wedding clothes came from the marriage payments made by the groom's family. In 1994, a Hui man who became engaged was expected to give the bride 10,000 yuan in cash and a plethora of gifts ranging from facial cleansing cream to bicycles and motor scooters. The bride was expected to use the money to provide a dowry for herself at marriage, but because her family also gave her cash and household items toward this end, ultimately she had a large amount of money to spend (compare Yan 1996:176–209; compare also Goldstein-Gidoni 1997:128–34). The bride also had her own earnings. Most young Hui women worked after completing junior middle school (at age thirteen) while continuing to live in

Chart 2. Xue's wedding attire expenses, May 1995

Item	Cost
Wedding gown deposit	500 yuan
Wedding gown rental (includes gloves and veil)	250 yuan
Wedding shoes (fake leather)	220 yuan
Nylons	6 yuan
Underwear and bra	20 yuan
Fresh flowers for hair	30 yuan
Makeover at Golden Lady Salon	70 yuan
10.4-carat gold bracelet	1,019.20 yuan
6-carat gold ring	588 yuan
TOTAL (including the deposit)	2,703.20 yuan

Xue also wore a great deal of jewelry on her wedding day that she been given by the groom's family. Most of the jewelry was gold. It included a gold necklace, earrings, bracelet, and ring, and a sapphire ring set in gold. Xue did not know how much these goods had cost or how many carats the gold was, but she knew that the price for a carat of gold in 1995 was 98 yuan.

When she got married Xue also carried a handkerchief that had been made for her by her patrilateral cross-cousin (father's sister's daughter). There was no price for this.

their parents' homes. A young Hui woman spent some of this money on making herself "look like a bride"—cosmopolitan, fashionable, modern.

Older women recognized and frequently remarked upon the economic resources that young brides possessed. Many women who had married in earlier periods complained bitterly about the poverty of their weddings. During the Cultural Revolution, I was told, a bride who brought a single pair of leather shoes as a dowry was considered exemplary; two pairs were exceptional and occasioned teasing about how many feet the bride had. As Xue's mother, Aifeng, put it, "Back then we were poor. Today, they have everything" (*Nashihou, hen qiong. Jintian tamen shenme dou you*).

The lavishness or paucity of weddings influenced the social

standing of the families involved. Wedding gowns played a central part in establishing a family's economic success and cosmopolitanism. How the bride's appearance affected the status of her natal and marital families is especially apparent in Yue's case: what Yue wore for her wedding was too important to be left to her own whims. The prospect that Yue might fail to conform to local standards mobilized her female relatives to pressure her and insist on a wedding that demonstrated their knowledge of contemporary fashions and their ability to afford them. For a bride's in-laws, the beauty and fashionableness of the groom's family's "new daughter-in-law" (*xin xifu*) signified their success on the marriage market. This indicated that the family's economic level and social status were high and made the groom's family look good.

Don't Wear That! The Mosque and the State

Whereas most residents of the quarter approved of wedding gowns, tacitly or otherwise, ahong censured them. Common complaints were that the gowns were "against Islam" (*fan Yisilanjiao*) and "not like Hui people" (*bu xiang Huimin*). Some religious specialists said that the gowns too closely resembled the bridal attire of Christians. Residents stated that a few ahong had spoken out against wedding gowns during the exhortation at collective worship services on Fridays. Mingxin explained the ahong's disapproval by saying, "They are afraid that the young people will run away (*pao*) [from Islam]."

Some members of the religious establishment saw wedding gowns as a symbol of Islamic decline. This attitude was part of a more general suspicion that some older ahong held about goods associated with the West. These men rejected Western-style commodities that had no association with Islam, such as wedding gowns or mass-produced factory food. They feared that young people who adopted such trappings of a non-Muslim lifestyle would not adhere to Islam.

Evidence suggests that their concern was somewhat misplaced. First, the accounts of older residents indicate that strict Islamic observance even before the advent of communism was most frequently the domain of older and elderly Hui. Most residents thought it natural that young people spent less time in the mosque than older ones: young people were "too busy" and needed to be "attending to business" (*gan shiye*). The expectation was that women with small children would stay at home to care for them and that husbands would earn money for the family. As people got older they "had more time" and could go pray in the mosque or study the Qur'an. The strong association Hui made between age and religious observance was most obviously manifest in the disapproval that residents expressed toward young people who made the pilgrimage. Most residents thought the pilgrimage was only "meaningful" (*you yisi*) for Muslims over 50. When young people went it was "just like tourism" (*xiang lüyou yiyang*). Pilgrims were expected to observe the five duties of a Muslim with utmost strictness for the rest of their lives. Most Hui believed that this was impossible if a person made the pilgrimage when he or she was too young.

Second, many aspects of Islam as it was practiced in the quarter primarily involved men. For example, males were required to attend collective worship services by Islamic law but women were not; consequently, many more men than women visited the mosque regularly. More men, especially as adults, studied the Qur'an than women, in part because only men could serve as ritual specialists. More than one woman with whom I discussed various Islamic practices described such things as "men's business" (*nanren de shi*). The mosque's role in the lives of women, particularly young women, was comparatively limited.

The willingness of young women to violate the dictates of modesty during Hui weddings and the complicity of older women in helping them to do so suggest that the ahong were correct to be concerned about women's Islamic observance. Rather than signifying a decline brought about by Westernization or modernization, however, women's penchant for wedding gowns reflected preexisting gender biases in the local practice of Islam. Formal Islamic observance, historically and in the mid-1990s, was largely the prerogative of men. Certainly, the young Hui woman of 1995 spent far more time window shopping than she did worshipping, but a gendered division of religious labor was long-standing in the quarter. Superficially, the gowns may have appeared "not like Hui people," but the underlying pattern of behavior, whereby women were less closely involved in Islamic practice than men, seems far from new.

Older religious specialists were not the only ones who disliked wedding gowns. Government officials, both Hui and Han, expressed discomfort with the conspicuous consumption that bridal fashions embodied. For example, 56-year-old Liangxun criticized the Hui weddings of the 1980s and 1990s as excessively expensive. Liangxun stated that although he welcomed the public return of "traditional Hui" marriage practices, which were either performed secretly or omitted during the 1960s and 1970s, he worried that the elaborate marriage preparations put too much strain on a family's resources. Liangxun believed that families competed to host the most luxurious celebration. He worried that some families lacked the income they needed to afford to spend large sums of money on bridal attire, marriage payments, and wedding banquets without going severely into debt.

Liangxun's remarks, which I heard echoed by local officials who were Han, expressed concern with the class differences and social inequalities that were emerging in 1990s China. Weddings and wedding gowns showcased the consumerism and increasing importance placed on personal wealth that characterized the PRC since the Deng reforms. Weddings entailed the expenditure of large sums on activities that some officials saw as ephemeral and "unproductive." Liangxun wanted residents to invest in economic production and expansion, rather than fritter money away on consumer practices that highlighted the growing inequality between rich and poor.

Xue's exercise of her consumer rights, even if it was unsuccessful, shows that the government was minimally involved in personal consumption. Even though the policies that caused this to happen had originated with government officials, state power had nevertheless diminished (see Davis 1999a). The increased incomes and access to consumer goods characteristic of the 1990s gave

Chinese citizens the tools to create and maintain social relationships outside of the government's purview. Wedding gowns demonstrate that Chinese citizens wanted things that existed outside of the government's capacity to provide. On one level, wedding gowns were literally outside of the state's domain: as far as I know, government enterprises did not produce or sell wedding gowns and thus could not regulate their consumption.[9] In Xi'an, at least, official control over wedding gown distribution was limited to licensing or refusing to license marriages.

As is true of all governments to some degree, the PRC government of the mid-1990s wanted to control the identity of the populace it governed. One way it did this was through establishing the terms with which people interpreted their experiences and understood themselves. Officials provided the categories, such as "Hui nationality" (*Huizu*) and "private entrepreneur" (*getihu*), and taught people to use them. After the market reforms, however, the CCP had to compete with an outside world increasingly able to influence China through tourism, the media, and commerce. Economic privatization and the accompanying decline of the work-unit system further decreased the government's control by giving individuals the opportunity and incentive to work for themselves.

Wedding gowns exemplified a generalized longing on the part of many residents for modernization. Their consumption demonstrates both the CCP's success at teaching Chinese citizens to believe in and pursue modernization and the limits of their ability to control this process. In the Muslim district, wearing wedding gowns allowed Hui to contravene the state's official evolutionary classification of their race as "backward." The Chinese government regarded almost all of the PRC's minority races as primitive and less advanced than the Han majority (see, e.g., McGranahan 1996; Harrell 1995b; Gladney 1991; and Swain 1990). In the service of their evolutionary ideology, officials promoted "nationality customs and habits" such as nationality costumes. Romanticized and fetishized images of minority women in colorful garb represented the minority races in official pictorials, state-sponsored tourism advertisements, and even government-approved theme parks (see, e.g., Swain 1990; McGranahan 1996). Through such representations, the state legitimated its classification of the minority races as premodern. When Xi'an Hui brides donned wedding gowns, they rejected this government label. Residents of the quarter wanted to see themselves and wanted to be seen as modern. By emulating the fashions of modernized, wealthy places, they counteracted their official classification and placed themselves at the developed end of the primitive-modern spectrum.

The Paradox of Wedding Gowns: Conformity and Agency

On one level, bridal attire was about conformity, a conformity that women enforced on other women. Yet on another level, wearing the long pink wedding gown and accompanying apparel was about agency. The wedding gowns reveal the agency of women in relation to the religious establishment. They show the agency of young women compared to that of their mothers and the economic conditions of the past. Finally, the gowns also illustrate the agency of the Hui race in relation to the government's evolutionary discourse and program of modernization.

By the mid-1990s, wedding gowns were virtually indispensable to Xi'an weddings. A significant feature of the gowns was that they created an opportunity for young Hui brides to wear "immodest" clothing. Most young women eagerly seized this chance and were strongly supported by their older female relatives in doing so, despite the reproach of the religious establishment. That young Hui women wore wedding gowns testified to their autonomy from the mosque. In some respects, wedding gowns made the differences in men's and women's religiosity public and visible.

Although local wedding attire was extremely standardized, women in the 1990s had a wide selection of clothes and fashions available to them. The mothers of the 1990s brides had not been able to purchase or rent such clothes; at that time there were none to be found, and the mother of a 1994 bride had married when the state paid close attention to the appearance of Chinese citizens (see Finnane 1996:120–3). During the reform period, women, including young Hui women, could wear makeup, high heels, and feminine clothing if they had the money to buy them. More and more young Hui women, and many other Chinese urbanites, had both the desire and the ability to follow such trends.

On a collective level, although wedding gowns demonstrated the quarter's ideological conformity to the state's vision of social development, they also allowed residents to overturn government stereotypes of the Hui as less able to modernize than the Han. The gowns were a way that residents grasped modernization for themselves, without the guiding force of the government. Wedding gowns symbolized the economic success and cosmopolitanism of the Xi'an Hui. The gowns showed that neither the state-assigned "race" nor the official level of "culture" of the Hui could prevent the quarter's residents from modernizing on their own terms.

Chapter Eight

CONSUMPTION AND MODERNIZATION

As the weeks drew nearer to Yan's wedding, several members of her family began to contribute to her dowry. First, Xue offered to sell her sister a number of objects that she had purchased in Beijing for her own dowry: some cloisonné ornaments, two crystal sugar and jelly bowls, a small silver-plated coffee set, and two miniature decorative swords. A few weeks later, Yan's mother bought a set of eight china bowls and chopsticks and gave them to Yan. Not long after this, Yan showed me a toiletry set that she had purchased for her dowry, which included matching toothbrushes, toothpastes, combs, brushes, washcloths, and cups, when her father stepped in to complain. He said disapprovingly that Yan was only buying "play things" (*wanr de dongxi*) rather than making important purchases. In short, Yan's family worried that Yan was not spending enough money or time on her dowry.

During the three or four days before her wedding ceremony, Yan put all the items that she had accumulated into her parents' ground-floor bedroom, which also served as a parlor. Washing machine, refrigerator, television, coat rack, lamps, glassware, clocks, ornamental flowers, a large framed poster of what appeared to be Niagara Falls, a bicycle—gradually the room began to fill. Everything needed to be in place by the first day of the wedding ceremony, when guests would come to feast, view the dowry, and help deliver it to the "new house" that the groom and his family had prepared. Many female friends, relatives, and neighbors dropped by bringing gifts, including comforters, towel sets, and even a couple of large stuffed animals. Yan and her mother put out Western-style cakes, "traditional Hui" pastries, seeds, nuts, and other foods for the visitors to eat; much of this food had also been gifts. Conversations during these visits were almost exclusively devoted to Yan's dowry: what she had purchased, how much she had paid, how the goods she had bought compared to the things that other women had had in their dowries.

Yan's dowry, like the other dowries I saw in the quarter, contained a wide range of goods. A good proportion of the things that she and other brides purchased were objects associated with "modernization." Some of these commodities saved labor and time, such as washing machines and vacuum cleaners. Others, for example, motor scooters, made transportation quicker and easier. Refrigerators facilitated storage and reduced spoilage. Air conditioners made homes more bearable during the hot Xi'an summers. Television and video recorders provided entertainment. Many of the "modern" goods that residents consumed made life more convenient, comfortable, and interesting.

The utilitarian features of the commodities that residents bought, rented, and used should not be ignored, yet it would be a mistake to reduce them to their use value. The products that Yan accumulated for her dowry, and all the other goods and fashions discussed in this study, possessed ideological significance, and their symbolic meanings strongly affected residents' consumption choices. Houses and apartments, mosques and Qur'an schools, traditional food and factory food, alcohol and wedding gowns all had their practical uses, but they also represented ideas. When residents of the quarter chose apartments over private homes or Arabic education over the local *jingtang* form, they were influenced by their desire to modernize more than by practical concerns. When they chose wedding gowns over tunics and trousers, Arabic mosque architecture over traditional Chinese architecture, and mass-produced factory food over traditional Hui cuisine, their consumption choices had no significant utilitarian advantages, but they did demonstrate that residents of the quarter were "modern." Through the commodities they consumed, residents showed that they wanted to modernize and were capable of modernizing themselves.

Consumption, Modernization, and the State

In many respects, the consumption activities described in this book were made possible by the changes in production, distribution, ownership, and resource generation that Deng Xiaoping's economic reforms produced. By the mid-1990s, the PRC government had relinquished its Mao-era role as central provider of goods. Official control over individual incomes had diminished, and the state was less capable of determining the commodities that Chinese citizens owned and used (Davis 1999a). Once, the possession of such items as cigarette lighters, flashlights, and pens had indexed a person's access to the state (which determined his or her social status), but by the late 1980s and 1990s, the links between party politics and consumption had attenuated (see Yan 1992). Government officials no longer monopolized conspicuous consumption; this was one obvious piece of evidence that relations between objects, people, and the state had changed. Liangxun, an official, had a residence that was fitted out with a huge television, stereo system, computer, and matching furniture set, but the homes of many of the quarter's private entrepreneurs rivaled Liangxun's in the quantity and quality of the consumer durables that they possessed. With greater disposable income and more goods available on the market, residents of the quarter displayed their economic achievements and expressed their personal taste through their consumption practices. They used consumption to modernize themselves, in the manner that they chose to modernize, rather than allow the government to dictate how modernization should occur or wait for the state to make them modern.

The consumption practices that I have described took place on a bedrock of development for which the PRC government had been largely, but not entirely, responsible. Many aspects of modernization in the Muslim district occurred under Mao. Perhaps the most obvious way that the state had "modernized" the quarter was infrastructural. Between the late 1950s and early 1960s, the government had paved roads, installed a limited number of water pipes and electricity wires, built public lavatories, and centralized waste disposal. Another form of "modernization" that affected the quarter was industrialization. Older men remembered how, in the early 1950s, the government had closed the district's private businesses and sent local men to work in state factories and work units. Women followed men to the factories in 1958, the year that residents remembered the government had instigated a massive campaign to "liberate women" (*jiefang funü*). The mode of liberation that the state adopted was to integrate women into productive (wage) labor: a number of residents described how party members had walked up and down the streets of the quarter calling for women to come out to work. Yet another domain that the CCP government "modernized" was education. Although the KMT (Kuomintang) or Nationalist government had opened two public schools in the Muslim district during the early 1940s, residents recalled that the CCP government had expanded and restructured the quarter's schools in the 1950s. PRC officials also instituted work unit programs to increase adult literacy at this time. Guangsheng, a meat seller in his 60s, remembered how people from his work unit had come by his house after dinner to take him to night school. "Adults were taught then just like children are today," he said. The changes in education were accompanied by a state buildup of the media; these two institutions were crucial tools in the government's ideological efforts to teach the Hui (and other Chinese citizens) to reform their culture and abandon their "feudal" habits.

When the CCP adopted Deng Xiaoping's "reform and opening" (*gaige kaifang*) economic policies in 1979, they did so in pursuit of modernization. Many of the policies that Mao had implemented were perceived to be hampering China's development. Officials dismantled many collectives and much of the work unit system and encouraged Chinese citizens to go into private business. Production controls were lifted and centralized decision making was largely abandoned, in the attempt to make industry and agriculture responsive to market demand. These changes diminished official control over some aspects of social life, but they did not mean that the party's role as guide to and purveyor of modernization had ended. Rather, the government promoted social policies and bureaucratic regulations and disseminated official propaganda that reaffirmed that modernization was happening under the government's direction.

As had been the case in China since the early twentieth century, the post-Mao government based its modernization program on a stage-sequence theory of unilinear evolution. This theory combined elements of Western social evolutionism with indigenous, Sinocentric ideas about racial difference, culture, and civilization. During the reform era, the government's affirmative action–style programs for minority nationalities, birth control campaigns, urban renewal projects, and village compacts explicitly manifested this ideology of progress. The evidence from the mid-1990s demonstrates the government's success at persuading residents of the quarter (and other Chinese citizens) to evaluate themselves according to this interpretive framework. Concepts such as "feudal," "traditional," "race," "culture," "modernization," and "civilization" were part of daily discourse in the Muslim district. They affected how residents perceived themselves, how they understood their experiences, how they viewed others, and how they behaved.

One arena in which the impact of the CCP's conceptual apparatus could be seen was consumption. When residents of the quarter described their consumption practices, they used categories that came from the state's model of social development. For example, when Xue called Hui women "feudal" for not wearing miniskirts, she characterized herself and her neighbors in terms of the official ideology. However, even though residents operated within the discourse of "modernization" and social evolution when they consumed goods and when they thought about consumption, they did so in ways that diverged from the government's position. Xi'an Hui applied the official developmental ideology so as to position themselves more favorably within an evolutionary framework.

The inability of government officials to control how ideas about social development and modernization were applied was particularly apparent in the realm of consumption practices. After implementing the reform policies, the state no longer dictated what the populace could consume and had a limited ability to influence the meanings that Chinese citizens assigned to commodities. The government continued to regulate some aspects of consumption in the quarter, such as when it implemented policies for qingzhen labeling. However, the official regulations did not determine the significance that Xi'an Hui attached to the goods that they consumed. In the case of qingzhen foods, qingzhen meant "Hui nationality" to the government, but to residents it meant "Muslim," "clean," "honest," "superior," and a host of other things. Housing and mosque reconstruction were also subject to official intervention, and the consumption practices related to housing and mosques in the quarter both exemplify the influence of state-sponsored ideas about modernization. However, in this domain, the government could neither control the architectural style that residents chose to adopt nor delimit the meanings they assigned to their built environment. Government officials were least effective in regulating consumption or affixing meaning when it came to clothing. Officials criticized wedding gowns as extravagant, bourgeois, and wasteful, but this did not prevent Xi'an Hui from wearing the gowns or viewing them as symbols of prosperity, cosmopolitanism, and modernization.

Hegemony and Counterhegemony

Residents of the quarter wanted and believed that they needed to modernize. They accepted as fact the notion of a unilinear history that proceeded in developmental stages from primitive to modern. Following the government's lead, residents acknowledged that they needed to gain "culture" and pursue secular education to modernize. They agreed that Hui and Han were two distinct "peoples." They accepted that they, because they were Hui, had "nationality customs and habits" and willingly spoke of their "traditions." On occasion, residents appeared to accept their relatively backward status by describing the quarter, its residents, and local practices as "feudal." These things clearly indicate that residents had internalized the developmental paradigm that the government espoused. Yet Xi'an Hui applied these ideas in ways that countered official understandings and reframed the government's position to their own best advantage. Islam and the Middle East were the two most important sources of legitimation that enabled residents to escape the government's characterization of the "Hui nationality" as "backward," "uncivilized," and developmentally retarded.

Islam provided an index of civilization that differed from the state's paradigm. The basis of Islamic civilization as Xi'an Hui understood it was purity. Considerations of purity affected what residents ate and drank, who they married, where they lived, how they cooked and washed, how they ran their businesses, and how they socialized. The Qur'an and the Hadith, as interpreted by the quarter's religious specialists, established the guidelines for purity and civility. They also provided a model of civilization through their descriptions of the Prophet's sayings and acts and their depiction of the social order that Muhammad created.

According to some residents, Islam also contained within it modernization. Several residents thought that modernization was first and foremost located within the Qur'an. Many Xi'an Hui spoke proudly of the "scientific" truths that the Qur'an contained. A number cited the correlation between the pork taboo and trichinosis as evidence of how "scientific" the Qur'an was. Others pointed to different kinds of "facts" that the Qur'an recorded. For example, one man stated that the Qur'an had within it information, such the number of bones in the foot and the number of blood veins in the body, that modern medicine had discovered to be accurate 1,000 years later. Another told me that the Qur'an stated there were nine levels of heaven and nine levels of earth and both of these things had been confirmed by modern astronomers and geologists. These residents believed that the "science" of the Qur'an proved Islam to be the "one true religion." At the same time, the "science" of the Qur'an demonstrated that those who adhered to it had a high level of advancement and a superior capacity to modernize.

In addition to commentary about the scientific truths that the Qur'an held, I also heard repeated several times the story of an astronaut who had converted to Islam. The details of this story varied, but its purpose was always the same: it was designed to prove the superiority and "modern" nature of Islam and of Muslims. Some said that the astronaut was a Russian and the events had taken place in 1989; others thought he was American or European and did not provide a date. The basic gist was that an astronaut was in space (some said orbiting the planet) when he heard some unfamiliar sounds. At the time he didn't recognize them, so he wrote them down and after he returned to Earth he searched for someone who could tell him what they were. Finally, he visited Saudi Arabia, where he learned that the sounds were the sounds of the Qur'an being recited. As a result, he and his whole family converted to Islam.

Whether this story or the "scientific" Qur'an have any factual basis is unimportant. Hui convictions about the Qur'an's "science," the astronaut's conversion to Islam, and the analogous stories that they told about Han professors who had become Muslims showed that they perceived themselves to be well equipped to modernize and more "modern" than other people. Through these stories and commentary on the Qur'an's "science," residents defined themselves and their religion as both modern and moral. Their belief in the intrinsic proclivity of Muslims for modernization was supported and reaffirmed by the prosperous and highly developed countries of the Middle East.

As sources of civilization and modernization, Islam and the

Middle East were exclusively available to the Hui (in Xi'an, at least). Xi'an Han were ignorant of the "one true religion" and entrenched in pollution. They knew nothing of the enlightened social model that Muhammad had conveyed to his followers. As non-Muslims, Han also lacked any connection to the Middle East as a site of modernization. By contrast, residents of the quarter believed that they possessed an intimate relationship with the Middle East. As Zenglie put it, "We [Hui] are a little Arab" (*women you yidianr Alaboren*). Residents of the quarter believed that they were purer and more civilized than Han and more closely related to places that were wealthier, more developed, and more modern than Xi'an or China. This understanding allowed residents to relocate themselves within the government's evolutionary ideology based on what they saw as their superior capacities for modernization. Islam and the Middle East gave residents the support they needed to evaluate themselves positively on a developmental scale.

In addition to ranking themselves above the Han because the Han did not meet Islamic criteria for purity and civility, residents sometimes co-opted the government's construction of "traditional China" and applied it to the Han nationality. "Traditional China," or the "old society" as most Chinese called it, was officially castigated as feudal, parochial, rural, poor, and underdeveloped. It was the flaws of "traditional China" that had enabled the foreign incursions of the late nineteenth century; it was "traditional Chinese culture" that required the reforming guidance of the CCP. When residents of the quarter criticized the Han race for engaging in uncivilized, unsanitary, and disruptive social behaviors, they equated the Han with the "Chinese culture" that had failed to modernize. In resident's eyes, Han people did not wash their hands after using the toilet or washed in water that was stagnant because they were too "backward" to know any better. When residents saw the Han as "ahead" of the Hui, as in housing facilities or secular education, they attributed this to official favoritism and anti-Hui prejudice rather than to a racially superior Han capacity to modernize.

Producing Modernization

The preceding discussion of Islam suggests that it would be a mistake to attribute the PRC government's inability to dictate the beliefs of its citizens to Deng's policies. Islam long predates the economic reforms. The data provided here indicate that during the 1990s Islam helped residents of the quarter to rework the government's developmental ideology in a manner more favorable to themselves. It may very well have served similar purposes before the Deng era. What was new about Islamic observance during the reform period was the freedom and economic well-being that residents possessed to engage in religious activity, the widespread presence of Arabic goods and fashions in the quarter, and the increased amount of information available about Islam and the Middle East.

In addition to encouraging consumerism, Deng's "reform and opening" policies expanded the channels through which images, stories, and ideas could reach the quarter. Media such as television programs, radio, and advertising brought knowledge of goods and people into the quarter. Although television, radio, and the newspapers continued to be government organs in the mid-1990s—with the exception of foreign television channels that could be received in China, such as Hong Kong's Star TV (this may have changed since Hong Kong's return to the mainland in July 1997)—the state allowed many more topics and programs to be offered (including American television shows such as *Hunter* and *Dallas*) than had been the case under Mao.[1] The numbers of travelers abroad (for example, Hui who made the pilgrimage), tourists, and foreign students all increased during the 1980s and 1990s; such persons were also sources of information about other societies and modernization. Deng's platform of privatization, marketization, and increased contact with the outside world enhanced the opportunities for multiple and competing ideas to find public expression.

The lifestyles that residents of the quarter saw depicted on foreign television programs, glimpsed through their contacts with tourists, and, for a few, witnessed during foreign travel, reinforced, if they did not create, an association between consumerism and modernization. The denizens of America, Europe, and the Middle East all demonstrated their propensity to consume. Media representations promoted the image of great wealth and advanced "material civilization" in such foreign places. The international tourists who visited the quarter spent what residents considered to be enormous sums buying souvenirs. This strengthened the association that residents made between modernization and purchasing power. Those Hui who had traveled abroad to Mecca, Cairo, Japan, and elsewhere confirmed the link between modernization and consumerism with their stories about the eight-lane highways, exotic and expensive foods, and 30-story high-rises they had seen.

The relationship that residents drew between modernization and consumption encouraged them to use consumer goods to resituate themselves within a narrative of progress and modernization. This process occurred on both personal and collective levels. Individuals demonstrated their modernization and cosmopolitanism through the clothes they wore, the vehicles they rode or drove, the foods they ate, and the methods they adopted for studying the Qur'an. Families showed their technological advancement and modernization through the goods with which they equipped their houses, the kinds of homes they built, and the foods they offered their guests. On a broader collective level, renovating the mosque in an Arabic style, providing running water for the neighborhood, and banning alcohol all demonstrated that the quarter was modernizing and becoming a "civilized society." Such messages were undoubtedly most powerful and meaningful to local residents. However, the image that Xi'an Hui consumption created also affected the Han inhabitants of Xi'an, if only by generating the stereotype that the Hui were "rich." Hui from other parts of China were also affected, as the large numbers of beggars who descended on the quarter during the month of Ramadan and for the Feast of Sacrifice attest. The steps that officials took to quench the antialcohol movement also indicate that the government recognized residents' efforts to modernize the quarter for themselves and was disturbed by the implications that such efforts had for the CCP's role as the guide to and purveyor of modernization.

Making Tradition an Asset

One unanticipated outcome of the CCP's policies during the Maoist era was to increase the value of tradition. The PRC government created nostalgia for tradition by attempting to suppress the traditional practices that the party classified as "feudal" and "superstitious." When Deng's economic reforms were implemented, the state then opened the space for the public expression of this nostalgia, often in ways that involved consumer practices. Nostalgia for tradition could be seen in the quarter in the reconstruction of traditional mosque architecture, the reopening of family restaurants that used recipes that were passed down in the family, and the consumption of traditional foods. Analogous phenomena could be seen in many other parts of China (see, e.g., Jing 1996:96–162; Ikels 1996:249–62).

The rights of "minority nationalities" to be non-Han were also reinstituted under Deng. The reform-era state created and upheld various practices as "nationality habits and customs" and preserved a number of cultural monuments with "nationality flavor." Through these protective acts, government officials defined "tradition" as the privileged domain of "minority nationalities." For example, in the quarter, officials designated the "traditionally built" Great Mosque as a national historic site and a monument of the Hui "nationality" (see Figure 11). The government made Barley Market Street the official "Hui food and drink street" where "nationality cuisine" was sold. Officials developed regulations that defined and protected qingzhen as a category of "nationality" food. Such acts differentiated the Hui from other urbanites by making them the ones who had "culture" in the sense of "customs and habits."

When it served their interests, residents capitalized on the "traditional" and "nationality" labels that the government provided.

They marketed the Great Mosque as a tourist spot and charged admission to visitors. They made a good living selling qingzhen "traditional Hui cuisine." They advertised their restaurants as having a "long and glorious history," using "traditional preparation techniques." They also used their "nationality" classification to garner special treatment from local officials such as tax concessions, exemptions from zoning requirements, and permissions to engage in mosque reconstruction and private building projects. Residents happily accepted the state's affirmative action–style policies for minority nationalities, which allowed Hui women to have two children and let Hui students attend college with lower entrance examination scores. In short, when Hui benefited from a "traditional" or "nationality" identification, they willingly adopted—and adapted—these labels.

Arabization, Consumption, and the State

Xi'an Hui gravitated toward the goods and fashions of the Islamic heartland because they brought residents closer to the sacred center and source of Islamic authenticity. In addition, Arabic architectural styles, Modern Standard Arabic and Qur'anic language cassettes, Middle Eastern video tapes, and Arabic clothing were also attractive because they embodied the prosperity, technological development, and modernization of the Middle East. Ironically enough, given the cachet of Arabization, Middle Eastern commodities had no more of a direct link to what was written in the Qur'an than did the goods and fashions that the Hui themselves produced. Despite this, residents generally accepted the credentials of an Arabicized Islam as superior to those of local practices. Ultimately, even those who sought to preserve the local heritage were forced to justify their actions in terms of the relationship between Hui traditions and the Islam of Muhammad's time, as was the case with those residents who supported traditional mosque architecture and *jingtang* Qur'anic education techniques.

Arabization also affected the relationship that existed between the residents of the quarter and the state. In the mid-1990s, government officials took all material expressions of Hui difference from Han as Hui "nationality customs and habits," regardless of whether they were "traditional Hui foods," historic Hui mosques, or Arabic architectural or educational fashions. In fact, the district government supported Arabization by using the Arabic architectural style on the gateway officials constructed for Barley Market Street. One factor behind the official support for Arabization and the state's policies that allowed Hui to engage in "normal religious activities" was the government's desire to turn Hui links to the Middle East to the PRC's economic and political advantage.

Although the state hoped to capitalize on the Hui to build ties with the Middle East, the strength of the quarter's attachment to the Arab world and to Islam also made local officials uneasy. An obvious expression of the government's discomfort was the proposal to limit the number of pilgrims to Mecca during 1997 (which Liangxun ultimately persuaded the other officials to abandon). The revitalization of Islamic practices, frequently related to Arabization, caused officials to monitor religious activities closely by, for example, conducting the extensive survey of the quarter's religious establishments during 1995. In general, consumption practices that related to Islam and the Middle East received far more government attention than did those related to non-Muslim forms of modernization. For example, although officials complained about the conspicuous consumption that wedding gowns represented, they made no efforts to influence marriage practices in the quarter aside from requiring all marrying couples to register with the state. When it came to qingzhen foods, the antialcohol movement, mosque construction, and Qur'anic education, however, government officials restricted local consumption practices by creating regulations about qingzhen, prohibiting the formation of nongovernment organizations, withholding state funds for restoring old or building new mosques, and developing official Qur'anic schools.

The CCP's response to the specifically Islamic forms of consumption that occurred in the quarter suggests that descriptions of the PRC government's withdrawal from consumer practices require refinement. Scholarly discussions of consumption in China during the reform era have tended to focus on the government's decreasing intervention in the lives of Chinese citizens (see, e.g., Davis 1992, 1999a; Gillette 1999; Kraus 1999). Consumption is primarily presented as exemplifying the increased agency of China's inhabitants and perhaps signifying the emergence of a public sphere. This approach builds upon the work of scholars outside of the China field who have shown how consumers manifest creativity and control in the process of buying and using commodities (see, e.g., de Certeau 1984; Miller 1995b; Mintz 1996; McCracken 1988).

This book supports the notion that consumption provides individuals and groups with opportunities to actively create self-images and influence how they are perceived—within contextual constraints. The evidence provided here indicates that the CCP government refrained from interfering in those types of consumption that furthered an officially defined and guided trajectory for modernization. Officials encouraged consumer activities that promoted the state's economic goals. However, they continued to monitor and regulate consumption practices, such as the Islamic examples described in this study, that showed signs of deviating from the official paradigm. In the quarter, residents deviated from the government's model of social development less in goals than in the means they used to achieve those goals, but this destabilized the party's control over modernization.

Islam and Arabization posed subtle threats to the Chinese government. In the case of the Xi'an Hui, there was no danger of an Islamic separatist movement, as some of the uprisings that occurred in Xinjiang during the Deng era could be described. The government's racial categorization of the Hui as "non-Chinese" aside, residents of the quarter were unambiguously Chinese and unambiguously part of China. Where Islam and Arabization caused trouble for the state was in their capacity to provide residents with an index of civilization, a vision of modernization, and the means for achieving civilization and modernization that differed from those the state provided and existed outside of the state's purview. Arabization and Islam enabled residents to combat the official classification of the Hui as "feudal" and developmentally "behind" the Han. "Arabic" goods and fashions were one means for residents to assert their own modernization while appealing to paradigms that the PRC government neither sponsored nor controlled. Because the CCP was unwilling to relinquish its role as the sole guide to modernization, the state continued to concern itself with Hui consumption. In the Muslim district of the mid-1990s, residents chose the goods they consumed and how they used them and determined the significance of this consumption. The state responded by intervening in or retreating from their consumption practices in pursuit of behaviors that conformed to the official vision of a CCP-led progress toward modernization and the place that the "Hui nationality" should properly occupy in China's developmental trajectory.

Appendix

FOOD DIARY 7–14 JUNE 1997

Peng, an eleven-year-old Hui boy, kept a food diary for one week at my request. During this week, Peng was in school (elementary school). Peng was asked to record the time of day he ate, the foods he ate, where the foods came from, and their price, if known. Although the record of intake is complete, for some entries Peng did not provide price or indicate from where the food was procured. A yuan, or Chinese dollar, was equal to about one-eighth of an American dollar. A mao is one-tenth of a yuan.

June 7, 1997

9 a.m.: Two fried cakes, one made from rice flour, the other from wheat. Purchased from a food stall operated by his father's maternal uncle's daughter. 5 mao per cake. One soda. Purchased from his paternal aunt, who ran a restaurant outside the entrance to his home. 3 yuan per can.

3 p.m.: One bowl of steamed noodles (*liang pi*) at his mother's father's restaurant. 2.5 yuan per bowl (free for Peng).

7 p.m.: Stir-fried vegetables and rice purchased from a restaurant on the street where his family lives. Eaten at home. 34 yuan total cost (for four persons).

June 8, 1997

7:00 a.m.: One package of instant noodles (*fangbianmian*), at home. 8 mao per package.

Noon: Red bean and rice porridge. At his mother's father's restaurant. No price.

Between 6 and 6:30 p.m.: Three pieces of chocolate; several pieces of a candy made from sugar, orange peel, and plum (*huahuadan*); one piece of pineapple candy; and several slices of watermelon. At home, from family cupboards. Price unknown.

7 p.m.: Noodles with egg and tomato. At home, prepared by his mother.

June 9, 1997

7 a.m.: Meat and vegetable steamed stuffed buns (*baozi*). Purchased from a food stall. 3.5 yuan total.

8 a.m.: One container of juice drink, at 5 mao per box, and chewing gum (*paopaotang*) at 3 mao per package, purchased from the convenience store at the entrance to the school. Total 8 mao.

12:30 p.m.: Three pieces of chocolate, six pieces of candy, at home from the family cupboard. No price. One ice cream bar (brand name *shiziwang*) from a convenience store on his street,[1] 1 yuan. Fried eggplant and squash, at his mother's father's home, prepared by his aunt. No price.

5 p.m.: Two packages of juice drink, purchased at the convenience store outside the school's entrance (this brand of juice drink comes in plastic bags), 1 yuan. Two packages of dried fruit (*wuhuaguo*), 4 mao. One bag of candy (*lilixing*), 5 mao. One ice cream bar (*baipanggao*), 1 yuan.

7 p.m.: Fried egg and rice. At home. Prepared by his mother.

June 10, 1997

8 a.m.: One bottle of soda, no price. One package of chips (*guoba*), 1 yuan. Purchased from store outside school gate.

12:30 p.m.: Sandwich (cooked beef inside a pan-baked, non-yeast local bread [*tuotuomo*]). Prepared by his father, at home. Three pieces of chocolate and some candy, from family cupboards, at home. One ice cream (*baipanggao*), purchased from store on the street, at school, 1 yuan.

5 p.m.: One ice cream bar, purchased from store on street, 1 yuan. One banana, no price.

7 p.m.: Fried eggplant and fried egg and tomato with local non-yeast bread (*tuotuomo*). Purchased from restaurant down the street. Total 11 yuan.

8:30 p.m.: One package of chips (*guoba*), 1.3 yuan.

June 11, 1997

7 a.m.: One bowl of meatball soup (*hulatang*) and one local bread (*tuotuomo*). Purchased from his father's brother's wife's food stall, 3 yuan.

12:30 p.m.: Eggplant and cucumber, prepared by his father. One piece of local non-yeast bread, 5 mao. One bottle of soda (*bing feng*), 1 yuan.

5 p.m.: Packaged puffed rice snack with toy. Purchased from local store, 1 yuan.

7 p.m.: Mixed vegetable stew (*shaguo*), with rice. Purchased from restaurant down the street, 5 yuan.

June 12, 1997

Noon: Steamed noodles, one bowl. From his mother's father's restaurant, 2.5 yuan (no charge to Peng). One local non-yeast bread, 5 mao.

2 p.m.: One ice cream bar (*zhanwangshen*). Purchased at convenience store outside school, eaten in school yard, 1 yuan.

4 p.m.: One ice cream bar (*bingwang*). Purchased at convenience store outside school, eaten in school yard, 1.5 yuan.

7 p.m.: Frozen popsicle. Purchased at local store, 1 yuan.

June 13, 1997

9 a.m.: Fried cakes made from rice flour. Purchased from street stall, eaten at home. 5 mao per cake.

9:30 a.m.: One ice cream bar (*baipanggao*), 1 yuan.

Noon: Fried meat and vegetables stuffed in local non-yeast

bread. Prepared by his father. One bowl of rice porridge. Eaten at home.

Afternoon: One bottle of soda, 1 yuan.

7:30 p.m.: Cucumber, squash, and cured meat. Prepared by his father.

8 p.m.: One bottle of soda, 1 yuan.

June 14, 1997

11 a.m.: One fried rice cake, 5 mao. Purchased on street and eaten at home. Some melon. One bottle of soda, 1 yuan. Eaten at home.

1 p.m.: One bowl of steamed noodles from his mother's father's restaurant. 2.5 yuan (no cost to Peng). One bowl of mung bean porridge, prepared by Peng's father. One bottle of soda, 3.5 yuan.

6 p.m.: One bowl of noodles fried with egg and tomato. Prepared by Peng's father. One bottle of soda.

CHARACTER LIST

ahong 阿訇
aiguo aijiao 愛國愛教
Alabo de 阿拉伯的
Alaboyu jiaocai 阿拉伯語教材
Allahu Akbar 安拉呼呵克白

Baipanggao 白胖高
ban niang 半娘
banlang 半朗
banshichu 辦事處
Beijingren zai Niuyue 北京人在紐約
bi xie 避邪
biaozhun 標準
bijiao 比較
Bingfeng 冰峰
Bingwang 冰王
Bosi 波斯
bu ran yue qing, bu wei yue zhen 不染曰清不偽曰真
bu shou xinyong 不守信用
bu xiang Huimin 不象回民
bu xiaojing 不孝敬
bu xiguan 不習慣
bu zhongshi wenhua 不重視文化

cai xing qi lai le 才興起來了
cengci di 層次低
chahuahui 茶話會
chaiqian 拆遷
chaoji shichang 超級市場
chaoying ganmei 超英赶美
chen yi huan yi 稱一還一
chi bu bao 吃不飽
chi bu dao yikuar 吃不到一塊兒
chi shen luo ti 赤身裸體
chi shenme bu shenme 吃什麼補什麼
chuan jiao 傳教
chuantong caozuo 傳統操作
chuantong Huimin shipin 傳統回民食品
chuantong jianzhu 傳統建築
cu 粗

da kuan 大款
da rou 大肉
dafensan xiaojizhong 大分散小集中
Damaishi jie 大麥市街
dangdi wenhua 當地文化
Dapiyuan 大皮院
dashi 大事
dongtou 東頭
duikang 對抗

fan ke 蕃客
fan Yisilanjiao 反伊斯蘭教
fan yizabu 翻義扎布
fang 坊
fangbianmian 方便面
fangshang 坊上
fangshang yinian siji dou you gaifang 坊上一年四季都有蓋房
fayin 發音
fei zhu 肥豬
feifa 非法

feifa zuzhi 非法組織
fengjian 封建
fengjian mixin 封建迷信
fengsu xiguan 風俗習慣
fenhongse 粉紅色
fenjie 分解
fenzheng niuyang rou 粉蒸牛羊肉
fojiao diao 佛教調

gaige kaifang 改革開放
gaitou 蓋頭
gan shiye 干事業
ganjing 干淨
gaodian 糕點
Gedimu 格迪目
getihu 個體户
gong, nong, bing 工農兵
gongdian jianzhu 宮殿建築
gua yangtou mai gourou 挂羊頭賣狗肉
guoba 鍋巴

Haixing haiwai gongsi 海星海外公司
halamu (haram) 哈拉目
Hanyu de awen 漢語的阿文
hazhi (hajji) 哈知
hen you qiantu 很有前途
Hu Dengzhou 胡登洲
Hu taishi baba 胡太師爸爸
huahuadan 花花彈
huajuanr 花卷兒
huashengsu 花生酥
Huifang jinxie shipin jiagongchang 回坊禁協食品加工廠
Huijiao 回教
Huili 回歷
Huimin 回民
Huimin shanyu shengyi, bu shanyu wenhua 回民善于生意, 不善于文化
Huimin yinshi jie 回民飲食街
Huiminfang 回民坊
Huizu 回族
hula tang 糊辣湯
hunsha 婚紗

Ikhwan (Chinese Yihewani) 伊赫瓦尼

jianshe wenming shehui 建設文明社會
jianshi 簡史
jiaomen bijiao haode 教門比較好的
jiefang funü 解放婦女
jingshen wenming 精神文明
jingtang jiaoyu 經堂教育
jinjiu xiehui 禁酒協會
jiucheng gaizao 舊城改造

kaifang yishi 開放意識
kang 炕
kexue xiandaihua 科學現代化
kouqi 口氣

la niuyang rou 腊牛羊肉
lao banfa 老辦法
Lao Ma Jia 老馬家
Laogaidi 老格迪
laorenjia 老人家
liangpi 涼皮
lilixing 粒粒星
lishi youjiu 歷史悠久
liuxing 流行
lixiangren 離鄉人
lou fang 樓房
loufang bi pingfang hao 樓房比平房好

lü dougao 綠豆糕
luohou 落後

mada de hen 麻大的很
manyue 滿月
mei sha 沒啥
meirimei 美日每
minggui shipin 名貴食品
minzu 民族
minzu diqu 民族地區
minzu jieri 民族節日
mullah (Chinese manla) 滿拉
mumin 穆民
mumin zhi guang 穆民之光
Musilin shangpin 穆斯林商品

naoshi 鬧事
nian yixia jing 念一匣經
nian yizabu 念義扎布
nianjing bu chi, chifan bu nianjing 念經不吃, 吃飯不念經
nietie 乜貼
Ningxia 寧夏

paopaotang 泡泡糖
ping jing li jiao 憑經立教

qifa 啓發
qingzhen 清真
Qingzhen Dasi 清真大寺
qingzhenjiao 清真教
qingzhensi 清真寺
qingzhenyan 清真言

raoshu 饒恕
rouchuan 肉串
rouse 肉色

Santai 三抬
sewabu 色瓦布

Shaanxi 陝西
shaguo 沙鍋
shangye 商業
shanliang 善良
shaoshu minzu diqu 少數民族地區
sheng de 聖的
Shiziwang 獅子王
shoujiu 守舊
shuipen 水盆
shurao 恕饒
siguanhui 寺管會
siheyuan 四合院
simiao jianzhu 寺廟建築
sixiang gongzuo 思想工作
Sunnaiti 孫奈體
suzhi 素質

tiangan dizhi 天干地支
tianke (zakat) 天課
tuo tuo mo 飥飥饃

wanr de dongxi 玩儿的東西
wenhua luohou 文化落後
wenming cun 文明村
wenming danwei 文明單位
wenming jingshen 文明精神
woersi 臥爾思
women Huimin bijiao fengjian de 我們回民比較封建的
women you yidianr Alaboren 我們有一點兒阿拉伯人
wuhuaguo 無花果
wuzhi wenming 物質文明

Xi yu 西域
Xi'an techan 西安特產
xiandaihua 現代化
xiangxia 鄉下
xianjin 先進

xiao 孝
xiao shengyi 小生意
xiaochi 小吃
xiaojing 孝敬
Xiaopiyuan 小皮院
xin xifu 新媳婦
xingcheng 形成
xitou 西頭
xiuti 羞體
Xiyangshi 西羊市
xizhuang 西裝

yangrou paomo 羊肉泡饃
Yili 伊歷
Yingli 營里
Yisilanjiao 伊斯蘭教
you wenhua 有文化
yougao 油糕
youmei 優美
yousheng 優生
youtiao 油條
youxiang 油香
yuanwen 原文
yuletang 娛樂堂
yuqi 語氣

zhan ling fei 占領費
Zhangwangshen 丈王神
zhengge chengshi dou guihua le 整個城市都規劃了
zhengshi zongjiao huodong 正式宗教活動
zhongceng 中層
zhongdian 重點
Zhongshan zhuang 中山裝
zhu nao 豬腦
zhu rou 豬肉
zhuma (juma) 主麻
zongjiao gaige 宗教改革
zongjiao sixiang 宗教思想

NOTES

Chapter One

1. The relevant work by Morgan is *Ancient Society* ([1877] 1978). See Layton 1997:1–26 and Greenfield 1996:3–8 for general discussions of Western ideas about social development. See Dikötter 1992:97–125 for the impact of these ideas in early twentieth-century China.

2. See Li (1971:75–107) for a fairly comprehensive list of the Chinese terms for these new concepts; see also Cohen 1994b.

3. Aubin suggests that the Yuan dynasty is the earliest period for which a Muslim presence in China can be conclusively proven (1991), but Lipman provides sound evidence of Muslims dating from the Tang and Song dynasties (Lipman 1997:24–31).

4. For fuller, more nuanced ethnographic accounts of the Maoist era, see Huang (1989), Jing (1996), and Ruf (1998). Lieberthal (1995:83–120) provides a general chronology from a political science perspective.

Chapter Two

1. Several families in the quarter privately owned at least one taxi that a family member drove for employment. One family owned five. Parking in the quarter was extremely limited, so several of the mosques that had large courtyards rented parking space to Hui taxi owners during the night. See Chapter 3 for a more detailed discussion of the quarter's mosques.

2. See Huang (1989:35–6) and Ruf (1998:65, 84–9) for ethnographic accounts of the CCP's attack on Chinese popular religion during the 1950s. See Ikels (1996:249–62) for a description of the revival and reconstitution of Chinese popular religion during the reform era.

3. During 1995, private individuals founded two "Islamic universities" in the quarter. These were not recognized by the government as educational institutions. The curriculum consisted of Qur'anic instruction, Chinese, Islamic history, and politics. Chapter 3 provides more information about religious education.

4. Fewer Xi'an middle school students entered high school than in

the city of Guangdong. In 1992, 78 percent of Guangdong middle school students entered high school (Ikels 1996:148). In Xi'an, the 1992 figure was 59 percent.

5. Xi'an Hui I knew claimed that the Hui living in these areas were "outsiders" (*wailai de*) from Henan or the southern part of Shaanxi. Their categorization suggested that all Hui living in the quarter were Xi'an natives, but this was not accurate. Some Hui in the quarter traced their roots to Jiangsu (Nanjing), Henan, Gansu, and southern Shaanxi provinces, and I met several Hui who were first-generation immigrants from these places.

6. Any changes to the property required the consent of all shareholders, which in most cases was a group of brothers. Although women were legally entitled to an equal share of their parents' property, I knew of none who claimed it. No compensation, other than the continuation of close relations between siblings, was made.

7. For a detailed explanation of the architecture of Chinese houses, see Knapp 1990.

8. Although agnates (relatives whose kinship is traced through males) usually shared houses, there were exceptions. For example, I knew one family in which two brothers had married two sisters in the 1950s. These brothers owned a half-empty courtyard complex, since they were their father's only sons and their parents were dead. The sisters who these men married came from a large family, so they invited some of their siblings to live in the brothers' residence. This situation lasted until the 1970s, when the sisters' children reached marrying age and so became old enough to need houses of their own.

9. *Laorenjia*, a respectful form of address for the elderly, in the quarter referred to "those whose religious knowledge and observance were good" (*jiaomen bijiao hao de*). Xi'an Hui used the term exclusively for men. Many thanks to Jonathan Lipman for pointing out the Mandarin equivalent of the dialectal term that I knew.

10. According to Gladney (1991:419), *yizabu* is a transliteration from Arabic. It comes from the verb *ijab*, meaning "to make a contract" (Jonathan Lipman, personal communication).

11. Lanying's father's noodle business earned enough to pay Lanying a salary of 400 yuan per month for the nine months of the year it was open, plus an annual bonus of 5,000 yuan. Her younger sister and her sister-in-law, both of whom also worked in the enterprise, received the same amount. In addition to covering business and household expenses for Lanying's father and mother, the store's earnings had also paid for the reconstruction of the family home and the weddings of Lanying's four younger brothers. High levels of profitability were com-

mon for the quarter's food businesses in the mid-1990s. For example, during 1995 Mingjie's small restaurant on Barley Market Street grossed 15,000 yuan per month. By contrast, the salary that a basic work unit employee received in Xi'an was 250–300 yuan per month.

12. Religious specialists determine the dates of these feasts according to their observance of the new moon. In both 1994 and 1995, different mosques saw the new moon on different days, which meant that some parts of the quarter celebrated the feasts earlier than others. The lack of a fixed date for these holidays was an annual source of irritation to the local government, in part because it made it difficult to decide when to extend official holiday greetings to the quarter and when to air news of these "nationality" holidays on television.

13. Most mosques engaged in some form of business as a result of the government's demands that religious institutions be self-supporting. See Chapter 3 for a more detailed discussion of the quarter's mosques.

Chapter Three

1. An exhortation, or *woersi* in Chinese (transliterated from the Arabic *wa'z*), was generally given once each day. On Fridays, the exhortation occurred at the worship time known as *zhuma*, the high point of the Islamic ritual week, which was just after midday (and properly speaking was followed by the ordinary midday worship). Most men in the community attended *zhuma* at the mosque, as did a few women. On other days, the exhortation took place just after sunset.

2. *Ahong* is the Chinese transliteration of the Persian term *akhund*, which means teacher. All male religious specialists in the quarter were called ahong. At minimum, an ahong could recite the entire Qur'an in Arabic. For the most part the term was reserved for men whose primary occupation was the study and transmission of Qur'anic knowledge. These men gave exhortations at collective worship, witnessed weddings, and prayed and recited the Qur'an at Hui rituals. Each mosque had at least one ahong.

3. The Ka'aba is a large black stone building, one of Mecca's holiest sites. Muslims who make the pilgrimage must circumambulate the Ka'aba seven times. Some say that the Ka'aba is where Abraham prepared to sacrifice his first-born son, in accordance with God's commands; after ascertaining Abraham's absolute obedience, God provided him with a black-headed ram to use as a substitute. Before Islam, the Ka'aba was a sacred site for the tribes of the Arabian peninsula.

4. It is important to note that Islamic reform was not a unified

movement in the Middle East or elsewhere. I limit my discussion of reformist groups to the two that affected the Xi'an Muslim district.

5. Lipman notes that Ma Wanfu himself temporarily resided in Shaanxi (1997:208).

6. Women need not worship during *zhuma*, although they can if they wish.

7. Xi'an Hui commemorated the Hui Uprising on the seventeenth day of the fifth lunar month of the Chinese calendar. Members of the Ikhwan mosques did not collectively remember lunar 5/17 or the Prophet's Birthday because such practices were not advocated in the Qur'an or Hadith. For more information on the Hui Uprising, see Chu 1966, Lipman 1997:117–38, and Ma 1993. Gillette 1997. addresses the mid-1990s commemorations of this event in Xi'an.

8. The Qur'anic injunction against idols has been interpreted with varying degrees of severity throughout Islamic history, as even a cursory glance at any Islamic art history text will reveal.

9. For other examples and more information about the worldwide trend toward a "pan-Islamic" style of mosque architecture that is based on Arab models, see Haidar 1996; Khan 1990; Grabar 1983; MMJ 1991; and Slyomovics 1996.

10. As did the silver bracelets that some Hui gave their children to wear. Giving children silver bracelets to wear and dressing them in red garb were common Han customs, done to "avoid evil" (*bi xie*). Some Hui adopted these practices. They explained that the bracelets or the color red were supposed to protect the wearer, "but we Hui don't believe in that."

11. Unlike Han, Xi'an Hui used the term "baba" to mean "grandfather," not "father" (which they pronounced "da").

12. Rather than having her fees paid by the state. The government paid for students who received high marks on the college entrance exams to attend school. Before the 1980s, only full-scholarship pupils could continue their education. However, by the 1990s many universities accepted students whose marks had not been high enough to enter college through the standard means but who could pay school fees in order to generate extra income. See Ikels 1996:168–70.

Chapter Four

1. See the selections "Dietary rules," "Halal," and "Purification" in Esposito 1995 and Khallaf 1949 for further information on the Muslim diet. Qur'anic citations are taken from Ali's 1984 English translation.

2. Some residents used a Chinese transliteration of the Arabic word

haram (Chinese *halamu*) to refer to unlawful (*feifa*) foods.

3. The residents that I spoke with about this custom did not know why they used the term "hai" instead of "pig." I would like to thank James Millward for explaining this usage.

4. Tapper (1994) probes the importance of water to Muslims in the Middle East. He suggests that cleaning the body with water and the ban on alcohol are practices that set off and define Muslims (1994:227).

5. Although a variety of Hui men used the term *haram* in conversations with me, only religious specialists or Qur'anic students ever used the word *halal*, the Arabic term for "lawful." The word *qingzhen*, with its much broader connotations, was used almost exclusively instead of the term *halal* in local conversation.

6. As previously noted, a few Han families also lived in the quarter. Their number was decreasing as local Hui bought out Han houses. I saw two cases of Hui purchasing houses previously owned by Han during 1994 and 1995. The few Han I spoke with who resided in the Muslim district thought that living there was vastly inferior to living elsewhere in Xi'an.

7. Broomhall, writing in 1910, stated that Hui made Han who wanted to become Muslims eat baking soda to purify their mouths as part of the conversion process (Broomhall [1910] 1966:229).

8. Given that Han Chinese also believe in the incorporative power of eating, the symbolic significance of Han eating practices and "traditional cuisine" in the post-Mao PRC deserves further research.

9. As previously noted, Ikhwan adherents (about 20 percent of the quarter's residents) tended to replace oral recitation of the Qur'an with an exhortation by an ahong and refrained from commemorating those events not written in the Qur'an (e.g., the Prophet's Birthday and the communal remembrance of the Hui Uprising).

10. The public prayer and obeisance were "communal" because, as described in Chapter 3, in addition to the relatives and friends mourning the dead, representatives from each of the quarter's ten mosques also attended these services.

11. Many thanks to Jonathan Lipman for providing the Mandarin equivalent (*laorenjia*) for the dialectal term I learned.

12. When I returned to the quarter in 1998, residents told me this practice had been abandoned because "no one likes to eat them." A kind of wrapped steamed bread (*huajuanr*) had been substituted instead. I was surprised to hear this, because during 1994 and 1995 several residents had commented about how tasty *youxiang* were. Some informants suggested that families did not want to go to the trouble of making *youxiang*.

Chapter Five

1. A fen is 1/100 of a yuan.

2. As of June 1998, no Hui families ran Western-style fast-food joints, so none of my informants had ever eaten hamburgers, hot dogs, pizza, or American-style fried chicken.

3. The word *gao* in Chinese is usually translated "cake," but these foods do not resemble Western oven-baked cakes in the slightest. They were made of seeds, nuts, sugar, and oil compressed into squares.

4. A mao is one-tenth of a yuan.

5. The annual mourning for what is known as the "Hui Uprising" (*Huimin qiyi*) takes place in the quarter on the seventeenth day of the fifth lunar month of the Chinese calendar. See Gillette 1997 and Ma 1993 for further information on residents' views of this late nineteenth-century massacre. The Prophet's Birthday occurs on the twelfth day of the third lunar month of the Islamic calendar, but it was always celebrated in January in the quarter.

Chapter Six

1. Many thanks to Jonathan Lipman for encouraging me to think about reputation as a valuable good.

2. At the time of the rally, the Yingli Mosque was experiencing serious infighting. The congregation included both Small Study Street residents and Hui from elsewhere in the quarter. Members had severe differences of opinion about the Yingli Mosque's ahong. A few months before the rally, the conflict had erupted in fistfighting, and the local government had to intervene. Not surprisingly, the allegiances of the congregation's members broke down upon residential lines: the Small Study Street Yingli Mosque adherents formed one faction, the others (mostly from Dapiyuan Street) another. When the antialcohol rally was held, the Yingli Mosque was officially closed by the government. The poster's unusual inscription resulted from these events.

Chapter Seven

1. See Finnane 1996 for a historical examination of women's attire in China, focusing specifically on the *qipao*.

2. What I saw in Xi'an was quite similar to the Han weddings Whyte describes (1993).

3. What I describe here as "low-cut" was not low by contemporary American fashion industry standards, but was quite low relative to the

usual neckline worn by Hui women, including young women. The neckline of the wedding dresses is relevant to the following discussion of modesty.

4. "Maid of honor" and "bridesmaid" are the terms that I have applied to the young women who played a significant role at Xue's wedding. They helped the bride dress, accompanied her on her journey to the groom's home, and stayed with her during the evening's public ritual activities. At other weddings, only one woman attended the bride. Once I heard such women referred to as "half brides" (*ban niang*), but most Hui did not use a formal term for women in these roles.

5. Margery Wolf describes a similar custom for rural Taiwan in 1959. See Wolf 1972:138–9.

6. When I first met Xue in February 1994, she worked at a department store. Later she succumbed to pressure from her father and fiancé and quit, going to work in her family's eatery.

7. One of the two wore a deep pink Western-style suit with a calf-length skirt. The other donned a red silk tunic and thin floor-length skirt elaborately embroidered with a dragon and phoenix, an ensemble her fellow guests called "traditional." In both cases, the bride's accoutrements and the general effect she produced closely resembled that of her bride peers. Three of the nine brides discussed here wore dragon and phoenix gowns for at least one of their formal wedding portraits (usually a bride had several portraits taken, mostly alone but a few accompanied by her groom). In my reading, dragon and phoenix bridal costumes were a modernized version of the qipao. They embodied a claim to be modern in a distinctly Chinese way by referring to the "traditional" qipao while maintaining the glamour of the Western-inspired fashions.

8. One exception to this rule was Jingxian, the principal of the Hui Middle School. Jingxian frequently wore skirts and dresses to school. However, her education at a military college in Harbin and professional work experience made her exceptional in the quarter.

9. Information on the production of wedding gowns is extremely scanty. Informants told one anthropologist working in Nanjing that the gowns available in China came from Taiwan and Hong Kong; when dress styles changed, the older gowns were shipped to the PRC (Lida Junghans, personal communication).

Chapter Eight

1. Media coverage of national and international events was still restricted. One example of government censorship at work in the quar-

ter was the case of a Hui entrepreneur who was beaten to death by low-level government officials; this incident was never reported publicly.

Appendix

1. Peng referred to the ice cream bar solely by its brand name. Many of the snack foods Peng recorded were written in this way; Peng explained what they were to me when we went over the food diary.

BIBLIOGRAPHY

Abu-Lughod, Lila. 1986. *Veiled sentiments: Honor and poetry in a Bedouin society*. Berkeley: University of California Press.

Agence France-Presse. 1997. Couples look west for latest wedding styles. *South China Morning Post* Dec. 6, 1997.

Agnew, Jean-Christophe. 1993. Coming up for air: Consumer culture in historical perspective. In *Consumption and the world of goods*, edited by John Brewer and Roy Porter. London: Routledge, 19–39.

Ahern, Emily. 1981. The Thai Ti Kong Festival. In *The anthropology of Taiwanese society*. Stanford: Stanford University Press, 397–425.

Ali, Ahmed, trans. 1984. *Al-Quran: A contemporary translation*. Karachi, Pakistan: Akrash Publishing.

Anagnost, Ann. 1992. Socialist ethics and the legal system. In *Popular protest and political culture in modern China*, edited by Jeffrey Wasserstrom and Elizabeth Perry. Boulder, Colo.: Westview Press, 177–205.

———. 1997a. Constructions of civility in the age of flexible accumulation. In *National past-times: Narrative, representation and power in modern China*. Durham, N.C.: Duke University Press, 75–97.

———. 1997b. Chilli pepper politics. In *National past-times: Narrative, representation and power in modern China*. Durham, N.C.: Duke University Press, 138–60.

Appadurai, Arjun. 1986. Introduction: Commodities and the politics of value. In *The social life of things*. Cambridge: Cambridge University Press, 3–63.

———. 1996. *Modernity at large*. Minneapolis: University of Minnesota Press.

Aubin, Francoise. 1991. A glimpse of Chinese Islam. *Journal of the Institute of Muslim Minority Affairs* 12(2): 335–45.

Bai Jianbo, ed. 1992. *Qingzhen shipin zhinan* (Guide to Qingzhen foods). Xi'an: Shaanxi Science and Technology Publishers.

Bai Shouyi. 1951. *Huihui minzu de xingcheng. Guangming Ribao,* Feb. 17, 1951.

Baker, Hugh. 1979. *Chinese family and kinship*. London: Macmillan.

Balazs, Etienne. 1964. China as a permanently bureaucratic society. *Chinese civilization and bureaucracy*. New Haven, Conn.: Yale University Press, 13–27.

Barber, Benjamin R. 1995. *Jihad vs. McWorld*. New York: Times Books.

Barth, Fredrik. 1969. Introduction. In *Ethnic groups and boundaries*. Boston: Little, Brown and Company, 9–38.

Belk, Russell. 1995. Studies in the new consumer behavior. In *Acknowledging consumption*, edited by Daniel Miller. London: Routledge, 58–95.

Bell, Daniel. 1976. *The cultural contradictions of capitalism*. New York: Basic Books.

Bellah, Robert, Richard Madsen, William W. Sullivan, Ann Swidler, and Steven M. Tipton. 1985. *Habits of the heart*. New York: Harper and Row.

Berman, Marshall. 1988. All that is solid melts into air: Marx, modernism and modernization. In *All that is solid melts into air: The experience of modernity*. New York: Penguin Books, 87–129.

Bernal, Victoria. 1994. Gender, culture and capitalism: Women and the remaking of Islamic "tradition" in a Sudanese village. *Comparative Studies in Society and History* 36(1): 36–67.

Bianco, Lucian. 1971. *The origins of the Chinese revolution*. Translated by Muriel Bell. Stanford: Stanford University Press.

Boddy, Janice. 1989. *Wombs and alien spirits: Women, men, and the* zar *cult in northern Sudan*. Madison: University of Wisconsin Press.

Bourdieu, Pierre. 1984. *Distinction: A social critique of the judgment of taste*. Translated by Richard Nice. Cambridge: Harvard University Press.

———. 1990. Social space and symbolic power. In *In other words: Essays towards a reflexive sociology*, translated by Matthew Adamson. Stanford: Stanford University Press, 123–39.

Brenner, Suzanne. 1996. Reconstructing self and society: Javanese Muslim women and "the veil." *American Ethnologist* 23(4): 673–97.

Bringa, Tone. 1995. *Being Muslim the Bosnian way*. Princeton, N.J.: Princeton University Press.

Broomhall, Marshall. [1910] 1966. *Islam in China: A neglected problem*. New York: Paragon.

Brubaker, Rogers. 1996. *Nationalism reframed: Nationhood and the national question in the new Europe*. Cambridge: Cambridge University Press.

Brugger, Bill, and Stephen Reglar. 1994. *Politics, economy and society in contemporary China*. Stanford: Stanford University Press.

Buitelaar, Marjo. 1993. *Fasting and feasting in Morocco: Women's participation in Ramadan*. Oxford: Berg Publishers.

Campo, Juan. 1995. Dietary rules. In *The Oxford encyclopedia of the modern Islamic world*, edited by John Esposito. Oxford: Oxford University Press, 375–7.

Caplan, Lionel. 1995. Certain knowledge: The encounter of global fundamentalism and local Christianity in urban south India. In *The pursuit of certainty: Religious and cultural formations*, edited by Wendy James. London: Routledge, 92–111.

Caplan, Pat. 1992. Feasts, fasts, famine: Food for thought. *Berg occasional papers in anthropology* 2. Oxford: Berg Publishers.

Chan, Anita, Richard Madsen, and Jonathan Unger. 1984. *Chen village*. Berkeley: University of California Press.

Chase, Holly. 1994. The *Meyhane* or McDonald's? Changes in eating habits and the evolution of fast food in Istanbul. In *Culinary cultures of the Middle East*, edited by Sami Zubaida and Richard Tapper. London: I. B. Taurus, 73–85.

Chatterjee, Partha. 1993. *The nation and its fragments: Colonial and postcolonial histories*. Princeton, N.J.: Princeton University Press.

Chee, Berna. 2000. Eating snacks and biting pressure: Only children in Beijing. In *Feeding China's little emperors: Food, children and social change*, edited by Jun Jing. Stanford: Stanford University Press.

Cheng Wanli. 1991. *Chinese traditional architecture*. Hong Kong: Wanli Bookstore.

Chu Wen-djang. 1966. *The Moslem rebellion in northwest China 1862–1878*. The Hague: Mouton.

Cohen, Myron. 1994a. Being Chinese: The peripheralization of traditional identity. In *The living tree: The changing meaning of being Chinese today*, edited by Tu Wei-ming. Stanford: Stanford University Press, 88–108.

———. 1994b. Cultural and political inventions in modern China: The case of the Chinese "peasant." In *China in transformation*, edited by Tu Wei-ming, Cambridge: Harvard University Press, 151–70.

Cohen, Paul. 1984. Moving beyond "tradition and modernity." In *Discovering history in China*. New York: Columbia University Press, 57–96.

Cooper, Eugene. 1986. Chinese table manners: You are *how* you eat. *Human Organization* 45(2): 179–84.

Crossley, Pamela. 1987. *Manshou yuanliu kao* and the formalization of the Manchu heritage. *Journal of Asian Studies* 46(4): 761–90.

Dannin, Robert. 1996. Island in a sea of ignorance: Dimensions of the prison mosque. In *Making Muslim space in North America and Europe*, edited by Barbara Daly Metcalf. Berkeley: University of California Press, 131–46.

Davis, Deborah. 1989. My mother's house. In *Unofficial China*, edited by Perry Link, Richard Madsen, and Paul Pickowicz. Boulder, Colo.: Westview Press, 88–100.

———. 1992. Job mobility in post-Mao China. *China Quarterly* 132: 1062–85.

———. 1999a. Introduction. In *The consumer revolution in urban China*. Berkeley: University of California Press.

———, ed. 1999b. *The consumer revolution in urban China*. Berkeley: University of California Press.

de Certeau, Michel. 1984. *The practice of everyday life*. Berkeley: University of California Press.

Diener, Paul, and Eugene Robkin. 1978. Ecology, evolution, and the search for cultural origins: The question of Islamic pig prohibition. *Current Anthropology* 19(3): 493–540.

Dikötter, Frank. 1992. *The discourse of race in modern China*. Stanford: Stanford University Press.

Dillon, Michael. 1996. *China's Muslims*. Hong Kong: Oxford University Press.

Douglas, Mary. [1966] 1994. *Purity and danger: An analysis of the concepts of pollution and taboo*. London: Routledge and Kegan Paul.

———. 1971. Deciphering a meal. In *Myth, symbol and ritual*, edited by Clifford Geertz. New York: Norton.

Douglas, Mary, and Baron Isherwood. 1980. *The world of goods: Towards an anthropology of consumption*. New York: Penguin Books.

Drakulic, Slavenka. 1987. *How we survived Communism and even laughed*. London: Hutchinson.

Dreyer, June. 1976. *China's forty millions*. Cambridge: Harvard University Press.

Duara, Presenjit. 1995. *Rescuing history from the nation*. Chicago: University of Chicago Press.

Eberhard, Wolfram. 1982. *China's minorities: Yesterday and today*. Belmont, Calif.: Wadsworth Publishing Company.

Eickelman, Dale. 1992. Mass higher education and the religious imagination in contemporary Arab societies. *American Ethnologist* 19(4): 643–55.

Eickelman, Dale, and James Piscatori. 1990. Social theory in the study of Muslim societies. In *Muslim travellers: Pilgrimage, migration, and the religious imagination*. Berkeley: University of California Press, 3–25.

Elvin, Mark. 1994. The inner world of 1830. In *The living tree: The changing meaning of being Chinese today*, edited by Tu Wei-ming. Stanford: Stanford University Press, 35–62.

Engels, Friedrich. [1883] 1972. *The origin of family, private property, and the state.* New York: Penguin Books.

Esposito, John. 1988. *Islam: The straight path.* Oxford: Oxford University Press.

———, ed. 1995. *The Oxford encyclopedia of the modern Islamic world.* Oxford: Oxford University Press.

Faison, Seth. 1996. It's a lucky day in May, and here come the brides. *New York Times* May 22.

FBIS (Foreign Broadcast Information Service). 1990. Washington, D.C., June–September.

Feng Zenglie. 1994. *Huizu yanjiu zai renshi jize qianyi* (A few reconsiderations for research into the Hui nationality). *Xibeiminzuyanjiu* (Northwest Nationality Research) 15(2): 33–44, 88.

Finnane, Antonia. 1996. What should Chinese women wear? A national problem. *Modern China* 22(2): 99–131.

Fitzgerald, John. 1996. *Awakening China: Politics, culture and class in the Nationalist revolution.* Stanford: Stanford University Press.

Frazer, James George, Sir. [1922] 1952. *The golden bough: A study in magic and religion.* Abridged edition. New York: Macmillan.

Friedman, Jonathan. 1990. Being in the world: Globalization and localization. In *Global culture*, edited by Mike Featherstone. London: Sage, 311–28.

Gillette, Maris. 1997. Contemporary Chinese Muslims (Hui) remember ethnic conflict: Stories of the late 19th century "Hui Uprising" from Xi'an. Paper presented at the Association for Asian Studies meeting, March, Chicago.

———. 1998. Exchange and the role of the state in Hui mortuary rituals. Paper presented at the Association for Asian Studies meeting, March, Washington, D.C.

———. 1999. What's in a dress? Brides in the Hui quarter of Xi'an. In *The consumer revolution in urban China*, edited by Deborah Davis. Berkeley: University of California Press, 80-106.

Gilley, Bruce. 1995. Islamic teaching comes under fire: Tianjin acts to stifle the influence of mullahs by banning unofficial language and religion classes. *Eastern Express* July 22.

Gladney, Dru. 1987. Muslim tombs and ethnic folklore: Charters for Hui identity. *Journal of Asian Studies* 46(3): 495–532.

———. 1990. The ethnogenesis of the Uighur. *Central Asian Survey* 9(1): 1–28.

———. 1991. *Muslim Chinese: Ethnic nationalism in the People's Republic.* Cambridge: Council on East Asian Studies, Harvard University.

———. 1992. The Hui, Islam, and the state: A Sufi community in

China's northwest corner. In *Muslims in Central Asia*, edited by Jo-Ann Gross. Durham, N.C.: Duke University Press.

———. 1998a. Getting rich is not so glorious: Contrasting perspectives on prosperity among Muslims and Han in China. In *Market cultures: Society and morality in the new Asian capitalisms*, edited by Robert Hefner. Boulder, Colo.: Westview Press, 104–25.

———. 1998b. Clashed civilisations? Muslims and Chinese identities in the PRC. In *Making majorities*. Stanford: Stanford University Press, 106–31.

Gold, Thomas. 1993. Popular culture in greater China. *China Quarterly* 136: 907–25.

Goldstein-Gidoni, Ofra. 1997. *Packaged Japaneseness: Weddings, business and brides*. Honolulu: University of Hawaii Press.

Goody, Jack. 1982. *Cooking, cuisine and class*. Cambridge: Cambridge University Press.

Gould, Mark. 1999. Race and theory: Culture, poverty, and adaptation to discrimination in Wilson and Ogbu. *Sociological Theory* 17(2): 171–200.

Grabar, Oleg. 1983. Symbols and signs in Islamic architecture. In *Architecture and community: Building in the Islamic world today*. New York: Aperture, 25–32.

———. 1987. *The formation of Islamic art*. New Haven, Conn.: Yale University Press.

Greenfield, Liah. 1996. Nationalism and modernity. *Social Research* 63(1): 3–40.

Guldan, Georgia. 2000. Infant and child feeding transition in China and Hong Kong: Is it a healthy development? In *Feeding China's little emperors: Food, children and social change*, edited by Jun Jing. Stanford: Stanford University Press.

Guo Yuhua. 2000. Children's food, cultural transmission, and social change in Beijing. In *Feeding China's little emperors: Food, children and social change*, edited by Jun Jing. Stanford: Stanford University Press.

Habermas, Jurgen. 1989. The public sphere. In *Jurgen Habermas on society and politics: A reader*, edited by Steven Seidman. Boston: Beacon Press, 231–6.

———. 1992. On morality, law, civil disobedience and modernity. In *Autonomy and solidarity: Interviews with Jurgen Habermas*, edited by Peter Dews. London: Verso.

Haidar, Gulzar. 1996. Muslim space and the practice of architecture: A personal odyssey. In *Making Muslim space in North America and Europe*, edited by Barbara Daly Metcalf. Berkeley: University of California Press, 31–45.

Han Zhongping and Liu Yingjie. 1987. *Xi'an shi Huimin binyiguan* (The funeral parlor of the Hui people of Xi'an). In *Xi'an wenshi ziliao: Xi'an Huizu shiliao zhuanjuan*. Vol. 12. Xi'an: Lianhu District Friendship Printing Factory.

Harrell, Stevan. 1982. *Ploughshare village*. Seattle: University of Washington Press.

———. 1989. Ethnicity and kin terms among two kinds of Yi. *New Asia Academic Bulletin* 8: 179–99.

———. 1990. Ethnicity, local interests, and the state: Yi communities in southwest China. *Comparative Studies in Society and History* 32(3): 515–48.

———, ed. 1995a. *Cultural encounters on China's ethnic frontiers*. Seattle: University of Washington Press.

———. 1995b. Introduction: Civilizing projects and the reaction to them. In *Cultural encounters on China's ethnic frontiers*. Seattle: University of Washington Press, 3–36.

———. 1995c. The history of the history of the Yi. In *Cultural encounters on China's ethnic frontiers*. Seattle: University of Washington Press, 63–91.

———. 1996a. Introduction. In *Negotiating ethnicities in China and Taiwan*, edited by Melissa J. Brown. Berkeley: Institute of East Asian Studies, University of California at Berkeley, 1–18.

———. 1996b. The nationalities question and the Prmi prblem. In *Negotiating ethnicities in China and Taiwan*, edited by Melissa J. Brown. Berkeley: Institute of East Asian Studies, University of California at Berkeley, 274–96.

Hart, Laurie Kain. 1999. Culture, civilization, and demarcation at the northwest borders of Greece. *American Ethnologist* 26(1): 196–220.

Hendry, Joy. 1993. *Wrapping culture*. Oxford: Clarendon Press.

Herzfeld, Michael. 1991. *A place in history*. Princeton, N.J.: Princeton University Press.

Horvatich, Patricia. 1994. Ways of knowing Islam. *American Ethnologist* 21(4): 811–26.

Howell, Jude. 1993. *China opens its door: The politics of economic transition*. Boulder, Colo.: Lynne Reinner Publishers.

Hu Zhenhua, ed. 1993. *Zhongguo Huizu* (China's Hui). Yinchuan, China: Ningxia People's Publishing House.

Hu Zhenhua and Zhao Hongqing. 1994. *Zhongguo Huizu gaikuang* (The general situation of China's Hui). In *Zhongguo Huizu* (China's Hui), edited by Hu Zhenhua. Yinchuan, China: Ningxia People's Publishing House, 1–10.

Huang Shu-min. 1989. *The spiral road*. Boulder, Colo.: Westview Press.

Humphreys, Caroline. 1995. Creating a culture of disillusionment: Consumption in Moscow, a chronicle of changing times. In *Worlds apart: Modernity through the prism of the local*, edited by Daniel Miller. London: Routledge, 43–68.

HZJS (*Hui jianshi*). 1978. Yinchuan, China: Ningxia Renmin Chubanshe.

Ikels, Charlotte. 1993. Settling accounts: The intergenerational contract in an age of reform. In *Chinese families in the post-Mao era*, edited by Deborah Davis and Stevan Harrell. Berkeley: University of California Press, 306–33.

———. 1996. *The return of the god of wealth*. Stanford: Stanford University Press.

Ivy, Marilyn. 1995. *Discourses of the vanishing*. Chicago: University of Chicago Press.

Jankowiak, William. 1993. *Sex, death, and hierarchy in a Chinese city*. New York: Columbia University Press.

Jin Binggao. 1984. *Shilun Makesizhuyi minzu dingyi de chansheng jiqi yingxiang* (Discussion of the production and effect of the Marxist definition of nationality). *Zhongyang minzu xueyuan xuebao* (Central Minorities Institute newsletter) 3: 64–7.

Jing, Jun. 1996. *The temple of memories*. Stanford: Stanford University Press.

———, ed. 2000. *Feeding China's little emperors: Food, children and social change*. Stanford: Stanford University Press.

Khallaf, Abdul. 1949. Animals slaughtered by non-Muslims and their consumption by Muslims. *Islamic Review* 37(9): 31–5.

Khan, Hasan-Uddin. 1990. The architecture of the mosque, an overview and design directions. In *Expressions of Islam in buildings*. Cambridge: Aga Khan, 109–27.

Knapp, Ronald. 1990. *The Chinese house*. Oxford: Oxford University Press.

Kraus, Richard. 1999. Public monuments and private pleasures in the parks of Nanjing: A tango in the ruins of the Ming Emperor's palace. In *The consumer revolution in urban China*, edited by Deborah Davis. Berkeley: University of California Press.

Kuban, Dogan. 1990. Comments. In *Expressions of Islam in buildings*. Cambridge: Aga Khan, 128–34.

Lai Cunli. 1992. *Zhongguo Huizu shehui jingji* (The society and economy of the Hui people). Yinchuan, China: Ningxia People's Publishing Company.

Lambek, Michael. 1990. Certain knowledge, contestable authority: Power and practice on the Islamic periphery. *American Ethnologist* 17(1): 23–40.

———. 1995. Choking on the Qur'an: And other consuming parables from the western Indian Ocean. In *The pursuit of certainty*, edited by Wendy James. London: Routledge, 258–81.

Lao Yang, Zhao Liwen, and Luo Wenke. 1993. *Xi'an minfang da chaiqian* (The big destruction and removal of the Xi'an people's houses). *Shaanxi Huibao* (Shaanxi pictorial) 5: 16–9.

Layton, Robert. 1997. *An introduction to theory in anthropology*. Cambridge: Cambridge University Press.

Li Fanwen and Yu Zhengui, eds. 1988. *Collected research materials on the Hui rebellion of the Northwest* [in Chinese]. Yinchuan, China: Ningxia People's Publishing Company.

Li Yu-ning. 1971. *The introduction of socialism into China*. New York: Columbia University Press.

Lieberthal, Kenneth. 1995. *Governing China: From revolution through reform*. New York: W. W. Norton and Company.

Link, Perry. 1992. *Evening chats in Beijing: Probing China's predicament*. New York: W. W. Norton and Company.

Lipman, Jonathan. 1984. Patchwork society, network society: A study of Sino-Muslim communities. In Vol. 2 of *Islam in Asia*, edited by Raphael Israeli and Anthony Johns. Jerusalem: Hebrew University Press, 246–74.

———. 1987. Hui-Hui: An ethnohistory of the Chinese-speaking Muslims. *Journal of South Asian and Middle Eastern Studies* 11(1 and 2): 112–30.

———. 1997. *Familiar strangers: A Muslim history in China*. Seattle: University of Washington Press.

Litzinger, Ralph. 1995. Making histories: Contending conceptions of the Yao past. In *Cultural encounters on China's ethnic frontiers*, edited by Stevan Harrell. Seattle: University of Washington Press, 117–39.

Liu Zhiping. 1985. *Zhongguo Isilanjiao jianzhu* (Islamic architecture of China). Urumqi, China: Xinjiang People's Publisher.

Lozada, Eriberto. 2000. Warring chickens: Kentucky Fried Chicken and the emergence of a children's culture in Beijing. In *Feeding China's little emperors: Food, children and social change*, edited by Jun Jing. Stanford: Stanford University Press.

Lu Hanlong. 1999. *"Datong shehui" li de "xiaokang" fazhan mubiao* ("Comfort" as the goal of development in an "ideal society"). In *The consumer revolution in urban China*, edited by Deborah Davis. Berkeley: University of California Press.

Lu Yang. [1966] 1969. How should the wedding be arranged? *Chinese Sociology and Anthropology* 1(3): 32–6.

Ma Changshou, ed. 1993. *Tongzhi nianjian Shaanxi Huimin qiyi lishi diaocha jilu* (Records of the historical investigation into the Shaanxi

Hui righteous uprising of the Tongzhi Period). Xi'an: Shaanxi People's Publishing House.

Ma Tianfang. 1971. *Huimin wei shenme buchi zhurou?* (Why do Muslims not eat pork?). Taiwan: n.p.

Macaulay, Thomas Babington. [1835] 1971. On education for India. In *Imperialism*, edited by Philip Curtin. New York: Walker and Company, 178–91.

MacInnis, Donald. 1989. *Religion in China today: Policy and practice*. New York: Orbis Books.

Macleod, Arlene. 1991. *Accomodating protest: Working women, the new veiling, and change in Cairo*. New York: Columbia University Press.

Madsen, Richard. 1993. The public sphere, civil society and moral community: A research agenda for contemporary China studies. *Modern China* 19(2): 183–98.

Marx, Karl. [1848] 1988. *The communist manifesto*. New York: W. W. Norton and Company.

———. [1858] 1989. *Precapitalist economic formations*, edited by Eric J. Hobsbawm. New York: International Publishers.

McCracken, Grant. 1988. *Culture and consumption: New approaches to the symbolic character of consumer goods and activities*. Bloomington: Indiana University Press.

McGranahan, Carole. 1996. Miss Tibet, or Tibet misrepresented? The trope of woman-as-nation in the struggle for Tibet. In *Beauty queens on the global stage*, edited by Colleen Cohen, Richard Wilk, and Beverly Stoeltje. New York: Routledge, 161–84.

McKhann, Charles. 1995. The Naxi and the nationalities question. In *Cultural encounters on China's ethnic frontiers*. Seattle: University of Washington Press, 39–62.

Metcalf, Barbara Daly, ed. 1996. *Making Muslim space in North America and Europe*. Berkeley: University of California Press.

Miller, Daniel. 1987. *Material culture and mass consumption*. Oxford: Basil Blackwell.

———. 1992. The young and the restless in Trinidad: A case of the local and the global in mass consumption. In *Consuming technologies: Media and information in domestic space*, edited by Roger Silverstone and Eric Hirsch. London: Routledge, 163–82.

———. 1994. *Modernity: An ethnographic approach*. Oxford: Berg Publishers.

———. 1995a. Consumption as the vanguard of history: A polemic by way of an introduction. In *Acknowledging consumption: A review of new studies*. London: Routledge, 1–57.

———. 1995b. Consumption studies as the transformation of anthropology. In *Acknowledging consumption: A review of new studies.* London: Routledge, 264–95.

Miller, Robert F., ed. 1992. *The developments of civil society in communist systems.* Sydney: Allen and Unwin.

Mintz, Sidney. [1985] 1986. *Sweetness and power: The place of sugar in modern history.* New York: Penguin Books.

———. 1996. *Tasting food, tasting freedom.* Boston: Beacon Press.

MMJ. 1991. *Yisilanjiao wenhua mianmianjian* (An introduction to the culture of Islam). Beijing: Qilusushe.

Moore, Wilbert. 1965. *The impact of industry.* Englewood Cliffs, N.J.: Prentice Hall.

Morgan, Lewis Henry. [1877] 1978. *Ancient society.* Palo Alto: New York Labor News.

Murphy, Christopher. 1986. Piety and honor: The meaning of Muslim feasts in old Delhi. In *Food, society, and culture*, edited by R. S. Khare and M. S. A. Rao. Durham, N.C.: Carolina Academic Press, 85–119.

Nagata, Judith. 1984. *The reflowering of Malaysian Islam: Modern religious radicals and their roots.* Vancouver: University of British Columbia Press.

Nanji, Azim. 1995. Halal. In *The Oxford encyclopedia of the modern Islamic world*, edited by John Esposito. Oxford: Oxford University Press, 93–4.

Orlove, Benjamin, and Henry Rutz. 1989. Thinking about consumption: A social economy approach. In *The social economy of consumption.* Lanham, Md.: University Press of America, 1–57.

Pigg, Stacy Leigh. 1992. Inventing social categories through place: Social representations and development in Nepal. *Comparative Studies in Society and History* 34(3): 491–513.

Pillsbury, Barbara. 1975. Pig and policy: Maintenance of boundaries between Han and Muslim Chinese. In *Minorities: A text with readings in intergroup relations*, edited by B. Eugene Griessman. Hinsdale, Ill.: Dryden Press, 136–45.

———. 1978. Being female in a Muslim minority in China. In *Women in the Muslim world*, edited by Lois Beck and Nikki Keddie. Cambridge: Harvard University Press, 651–73.

Qiu Shu Lin, ed. 1992. *Zhongguo huizu dacidian.* Jiangsu: Jiangsu Ancient Relics Publishers.

Rankin, Mary. 1993. Some observations on a Chinese public sphere. *Modern China* 19(2): 158–82.

Reinhart, A. Kevin. 1990. Impurity/no danger. *History of Religions* 30(1): 1–24.

Robertson, Jennifer. 1995. Mon Japon: The revue theatre as a technology of Japanese imperialism. *American Ethnologist* 22(4): 970–96.

Rofel, Lisa. 1994. Liberation nostalgia and a yearning for modernity. In *Engendering China*, edited by Christina Gilmartin, Gail Hershatter, Lisa Rofel, and Tyrene White. Cambridge: Harvard University Press, 226–49.

Rowe, William. 1993. The problem of "civil society" in late imperial China. *Modern China* 19(2): 139–57.

Ruf, Gregory. 1998. *Cadres and kin: Making a socialist village in west China, 1921–1991*. Stanford: Stanford University Press.

Schama, Simon. 1987. *The embarrassment of riches*. New York: Alfred A. Knopf.

Schein, Louisa. 1990. Gender and internal orientalism in China. Paper presented at the American Anthropological Association meeting, December.

Schwarcz, Vera. 1995. No solace from Lethe: History, memory, and cultural identity in twentieth-century China. In *The living tree*, edited by Tu Wei-ming. Stanford: Stanford University Press, 64–87.

Schwartz, Benjamin. 1994. Culture, modernity, and nationalism—further reflections. In *China in transformation*, edited by Tu Wei-ming. Cambridge: Harvard University Press, 233–53.

Seregeldin, Ismail. 1990. Contemporary expressions of Islam in buildings: The religious and the secular. In *Expressions of Islam in buildings*. Cambridge: Aga Khan, 11–22.

Siu, Helen. 1993. Reconstituting dowry and brideprice in South China. In *Chinese families in the post-Mao era*, edited by Deborah Davis and Stevan Harrell. Berkeley: University of California Press, 165–88.

Slyomovics, Susan. 1996. The Muslim world day parade and "storefront" mosques, New York City. In *Making Muslim space in North America and Europe*, edited by Barbara Metcalf. Berkeley: University of California Press, 204–16.

Spence, Jonathan. 1981. *The Gate of Heavenly Peace: The Chinese and their revolution, 1895–1980*. New York: Viking Press.

Stafford, Charles. 1995. *The roads of Chinese childhood: Learning and identification in Angang*. Cambridge: Cambridge University Press.

Swain, Margaret. 1990. Commoditizing ethnicity in Southwest China. *Cultural Survival Quarterly* 14(1): 26–9.

Tapper, Richard. 1994. Blood, wine and water: Social and symbolic aspects of drinks and drinking in the Islamic Middle East. In *Culinary cultures of the Middle East*, edited by Sami Zubaida and Richard Tapper. London: I. B. Taurus, 215–31.

Tapper, Richard, and Nancy Tapper. 1986. "Eat this, it'll do you a power of good": Food and commensality among Durrani Pashtuns. *American Ethnologist* 13(1): 62–79.

Taylor, Charles. 1995. Two theories of modernity. *Hastings Center Report* 25(2): 24–33.

Tayob, Abdulkader. 1995. Purification. *The Oxford encyclopedia of the modern Islamic world*, edited by John Esposito. Oxford: Oxford University Press, 370–2.

Thompson, E. P. 1967. Time, work discipline, and industrial capitalism. *Past and Present* 38: 56–97.

Thompson, Stuart E. 1988. Death, food, and fertility. In *Death ritual in late imperial and modern China*, edited by James L. Watson and Evelyn S. Rawski. Berkeley: University of California Press, 71–108.

Ting, Dawood C. M. 1958. Islamic culture in China. In *Islam—The straight path*, edited by Kenneth Morgan. New York: Ronald Press Company, 344–74.

Upton, Janet L. 1996. Home on the grasslands? Tradition, modernity, and the negotiation of identity by Tibetan intellectuals in the PRC. In *Negotiating ethnicities in China and Taiwan*, edited by Melissa J. Brown. Berkeley: Institute of East Asian Studies, University of California at Berkeley, 98–124.

Veblen, Thorstein. [1899] 1953. *The theory of the leisure class*. New York: Mentor Books.

Wakeman, Frederick. 1993. The civil society and public sphere debate: Western reflections on Chinese political culture. *Modern China* 19(2): 108–38.

Walder, Andrew. 1989. Social change in post-revolutionary China. *Annual Review of Sociology* 15: 405–24.

Warren, G. G. [1920–1921] 1940. *Investigations on Chinese Moslems*. Reprinted from the *New China Review*, n.p.

Wasserstrom, Jeffrey, and Liu Xinyong. 1995. Student associations and mass movements. In *Urban spaces: Autonomy and community in contemporary China*, edited by Deborah Davis, Richard Kraus, Barry Naughton, and Elizabeth Perry. New York: Cambridge University Press, 362–93.

Watson, James L. 1982. Of flesh and bones: The management of death pollution in Cantonese society. In *Death and the regeneration of life*, edited by Maurice Bloch and Jonathan Parry. Cambridge: Cambridge University Press, 155–86.

———. 1987. From the common pot: Feasting with equals in Chinese society. *Anthropos* 82: 389–401.

———. 1988. The structure of Chinese funerary rites: Elementary forms, ritual sequence, and the primacy of performance. In *Death rit-*

ual in late imperial China, edited by J. Watson and E. Rawski. Berkeley: University of California Press, 3–19.

———. 1991a. Feeding the revolution: Public canteens in Maoist China. The great leap forward and the CCP's attack on the family. Inaugural lecture, Harvard University.

———. 1991b. The renegotiation of Chinese cultural identity in the post-Mao era. In *Perspectives on modern China: Four anniversaries*, edited by Kenneth Lieberthal, Joyce Kallgren, Roderick MacFarauhar, and Frederic Wakeman Jr. Armonk, N.Y.: M. E. Sharpe, 364–86.

———. 1993. Rites or beliefs? The construction of a unified culture in late imperial China. In *China's quest for national identity*, edited by Lowell Dittmer and Samuel Kim. Ithaca: Cornell University Press, 80–103.

———, ed. 1997a. *Golden arches east: McDonald's in East Asia*. Stanford: Stanford University Press.

———. 1997b. Introduction: Transnationalism, localization, and fast foods in East Asia. In *Golden arches east: McDonald's in East Asia*. Stanford: Stanford University Press, 1–38.

Watson, Rubie S. 1981. Class differences and affinal relations in south China. *Man* 16: 593–615.

———. 1986. The named and the nameless: Gender and person in Chinese society. *American Ethnologist* 13(4): 619–31.

———. 1995. Palaces, museums, and squares: Chinese national spaces. *Museum Anthropology* 19(2): 7–19.

Watts, Michael. 1996. Islamic modernities? Citizenship, civil society and Islamism in a Nigerian city. *Public Culture* 8(2): 251–89.

Weber, Eugen. 1976. *Peasants into Frenchmen: The modernization of rural France*. Stanford: Stanford University Press.

Whyte, Martin King. 1993. Wedding behavior and family strategies in Chengdu. In *Chinese families in the post-Mao era*, edited by Deborah Davis and Stevan Harrell. Berkeley: University of California Press, 189–216.

Wilk, Richard. 1994. Consumer goods as dialogue about development: Colonial time and television time in Belize. In *Consumption and identity*, edited by Jonathan Friedman. Switzerland: Harwood Academic Publishers, 97–118.

Willis, Susan. 1991. *A primer for daily life*. London: Routledge.

Wolf, Arthur. 1970. Chinese kinship and mourning dress. In *Family and kinship in Chinese society*, edited by Maurice Freedman. Stanford: Stanford University Press, 189–207.

Wolf, Margery. 1972. *Women and the family in rural Taiwan*. Stanford: Stanford University Press.

Wu, David. 1994. The construction of Chinese and non-Chinese identities. In *The living tree: The changing meaning of being Chinese today*, edited by Tu Wei-ming. Stanford: Stanford University Press, 148–67.

Wu Zhongshao. 1992. Execute well nationalities and religious work, serve the goals of economic development and stability [in Chinese]. Government papers of the Lianhu District Nationalities and Religious Affairs Office, Jan.–Dec., 99–116.

Xi'an Statistical Bureau, ed. 1988. *Xi'an shi shehui jingji tongji nianjian* (Xi'an social and economic statistical yearbook). Xi'an: Xi'an Statistical Bureau.

———, ed. 1996. *Xi'an tongji nianjian* (Statistical yearbook of Xi'an). Beijing: China Statistical Publishing House.

Xiang Yang. 1983. *Guide to tourism in Xi'an* (*Xi'an lüyou zhinan*). Beijing: China Tourism Publishers.

Yan Yunxiang. 1992. The impact of rural reform on economic and social stratification in a Chinese village. *The Australian Journal of Chinese Affairs* 27: 1–23.

———. 1996. *The flow of gifts: Reciprocity and social networks in a Chinese village*. Stanford: Stanford University Press.

———. 1997. McDonald's in Beijing: The localization of Americana. In *Golden arches east: McDonald's in East Asia,* edited by James L. Watson. Stanford: Stanford University Press, 39–76.

Yang Ch'ing-ch'u. 1981. Born of the same roots. Translated by Thomas Gold. In *Born of the same roots*, edited by Vivian Hsu. Bloomington: Indiana University Press, 228–36.

Yu Zhengui. 1992. Research on the Hui people and Islam in Ningxia. *Asian Research Trends* 2: 227–32.

Zhang Zhigang. 1966. The new daughter-in-law breaks away from old practices. *Survey of Chinese Mainland Magazines* 515 (March 14).

INDEX